This book is dedicated to:

My wife Emily
because this book was made during our engagement
and
it was completed just before our wedding
let us have a marriage oozing
with love and endurance
no matter what curve balls life throws at us

Take A Picture of The Book Cover and Share it!

#EndureTheBook

Twitter

Facebook

Instagram

Pinterest

Let Your Friends and Followers Know What You're Reading!

Acknowledgements

First off thank you for buying this book and helping to bring my dream of becoming an author to life.

I have to thank my parents for always pushing me to follow my dreams no matter how difficult they may seem. My parents have given me so much and I could never pay them back for even half of it.

I also want to thank all of the athletes who took the time to share their stories with others. It is your stories that are going to go on to change lives.

Last but not least, thank you to everyone who has always believed in me.

Table of Contents

THE STORIES OF THE JOURNEY   67

APPLYING THIS BOOK TO YOUR LIFE   91

ATHLETES' STORIES   114

ENDURE

AN ATHLETE'S GUIDE TO FAITH, HOPE & SUCCESS

Introduction

We rejoice in our sufferings, knowing that suffering produces endurance, and endurance produces character, and character produces hope and hope does not put us to shame, because God's love has been poured into our hearts through the Holy Spirit who has been given to us.
–Romans 5:3–4 (English Standard Version)

Day in and day out, we do all the little things: We change our diets, sleep more, grind harder, train longer, and still come up short of our goals. How does that make sense? Isn't it supposed to be easier than that? Why work toward something if we're not guaranteed to get the result we want when we want it?

As athletes, we dedicate much of our lives to improving our skills to reach the next level. All it takes is one unjust moment, one tough loss, or a serious injury, and the world we know falls apart. There has to be more to the story. There must be a better way to hold on.

It's not easy to work at anything knowing there's no guarantee of the desired result, but it's this lack of a guarantee that actually builds great character. To know we risked it all but have nothing to show for it says a lot. The world will never praise us for this, but God knows our hearts and what we've been through.

The truth is, the majority of us will quit as soon as anything gets hard. This happens because we lose sight of the reason we've been chasing our dream in the first place. On the flip side though, we can chase that dream so hard that we do it for all the wrong reasons. What started as giving glory to God and others becomes about praising our own name. How do we find the balance?

Endurance is not for the faint of heart. It's for those of us who are willing to put our trust in God for strength to go on. Endurance is for those of us who can decrease ourselves to see a much bigger picture. We're willing to get burned walking through the fire because we see God's plan on the other side of it.

Remember the day when you first became an athlete? In those early years, we were innocent, and we did it simply for the passion in our hearts. As we grow older, it gets more complicated because money comes into play in some form. This brings different pressures, and we lose sight of everything that brought us to the sport in the first place. We become blinded, and we begin to run a different race and chase the wrong crowns.

After you read this book, on those days when quitting seems like the most viable option, you'll push through. That's not to say that life won't knock you down sometimes. But, when life does knock you down, you'll be able to laugh because your perspective will be different.

I've Got a Story to Tell

I wanted a perfect ending. Now I've learned, the hard way, that some poems don't rhyme, and some stories don't have a clear beginning, middle, and end. Life is about not knowing, having to change, taking the moment and making the best of it, without knowing what's going to happen next.
–Gilda Radner

This book is composed of different stories, all with the purpose of showcasing endurance at its finest. Regardless of the source, each story has a unique message designed to make us think. All of us will get something different from each story, but the fact is that we'll get something. That something is called hope.

Where This Book Came From

You are the light of the world. A city set on a hill cannot be hidden. Nor do people light a lamp and put it under a basket, but on a stand, and it gives light to all in the house.
–Matthew 5:14–15

I decided to write this book because I feel everyone has a story to tell and these stories often go untold. We all go through situations that we can help others with, but instead of spreading our light, we put it under a basket. What good is any light that is covered? We all possess greatness inside us. We all have the ability to push and motivate others; we just need the chance to do so. I wanted to give as many athletes as I could a chance to light another candle. That is the magic of the fire inside us—giving it to others doesn't reduce our own flame.

I've been an athlete for almost eighteen years now. That means years of stories, lessons, injuries, setbacks, and failures I've endured. That's also eighteen years of meeting other athletes who have their own stories to tell.

It's one of the worst feelings in the world when we see someone doing something wrong and, instead of helping him or her, we stay quiet. We know that we could've made a difference in people's lives, but we chose to do nothing. I want more people to choose to put their stories out there. We shouldn't hide our failures but embrace them, so we can all learn from them.

Why This Book Isn't Just About Sports

If you faint in the day of adversity your strength is small.
–Proverbs 24:10

For while bodily training is of some value, godliness is of value in every way, as it holds promise for the present life and also for the life to come.
–1 Timothy 4:8

If you're expecting a bunch of stories about athletes who endured and went on to become pro athletes, you're wrong. It would be easy to fill this book with the typical stories we hear of athletes like Tom Brady, who was barely drafted and is known for his poor National Football League (NFL) combine performance. Yet, he endured to win multiple Super Bowl championships and is considered to be one of the best quarterbacks ever to play the game. There are many cool stories like his, but I want to show you how inspiration can come from anyone. It can come from a celebrity, but it can also come from a janitor struggling to make ends meet.

This book is for athletes, but it's not about winning. This book is for athletes, but any person can apply the concepts. This book is for athletes, but it's filled with stories of life, because being an athlete is all about life and purpose.

There's no such thing as an athlete who's just an athlete, yet some act that way. We should be able to take that part of our lives away and know we still have more to offer the world. Many of us are given great athletic gifts. We should use them to the best of our abilities, but there's more to it than that. Sometimes, when depression kicks in because our athletic career isn't going as well as planned, it's because being an athlete has become everything we are. Our identity, passion, self-worth, self-respect, confidence, and gifts have all become wrapped up in winning and statistics.

The ability to endure isn't just valuable for an athlete; it's vital for life itself. Our bodies will eventually fail us; then, we have to depend on our minds. Our minds will eventually fail us, but our spirits can endure forever. Being an athlete just happens to be an optimal time to develop our willpower to hold on.

If we get injured and quit because we think it's too much to handle, how long will it be before we quit our marriage because it's too hard? If a tough loss makes us turn our backs, how will we stand when we lose our job? There's no difference between life and athletics. It's all one big, interconnected web, but most of us only realize this once we're finished with athletics. Then, we look back on our career, finally seeing how much it poured into us.

Understand How This Book Is Meant To Be Read

To make the stories easier to navigate, this book is broken into five parts: The stages to success, biblical stories of endurance and faith, stories of the journey, application to sports and beyond, and the athletes' stories. Some of the stories' morals will cross over, but each story brings a unique perspective.

Reflect on the Bible Verses

What has been is what will be, and what has been done is what will be done, and there is nothing new under the sun.
–Ecclesiastes 1:9

I strongly believe in this verse and the fact that there's nothing new that people can bring to the table. It's all been done before. Our hard times now are no different than the hard times that people faced when the Bible was being written. This is one of the most wonderful parts about the Bible. We might read the stories, thinking things like that don't happen anymore. We might feel as if the things we're going through now are much different; for example, because technology changes. This feeling is both true and false. It's true because the times now are different from those of biblical times. It's also false because, when we look at the roots of biblical stories, they relate to what we're going through today.

Get Comfortable in the Word

This is the perfect time to dig deep into our Bibles. One of the reasons I pursued the idea for this book was because it would give me a chance to get to know God's word even better. If I chose to include the word of God in the book, it meant I had to know it myself. I'm not perfect, nor do I claim to know everything about the Bible. I just had faith that God would guide me through the process.

As you move through this book, go to your Bible and read the verses pointed out in the text. Many times, we take a Bible verse out of context because we don't read the entire chapter or book. Reading the verses in this book represents the gun to start the race, not the tape at the finish line.

I encourage and challenge you to dig into God's word.

Speak It Into Existence

Words are powerful, and often we speak the negative ones. That changes now! Some of the stories in this book end with positive words to be spoken out loud. This is about consistency. Eventually, you'll begin to believe the words more and more, and before you know it, you'll become exactly what you've spoken. This practice shows why we must also keep negative words out of our mouths — we could eventually become them.

Think of this like all of the training we've done. If we just looked at training plans and read articles, we'd never make changes or take steps toward our athletic goals. Eventually, we have to get off our butts and put in the work. The same is to be said for our endurance. If we want to be better at it, we have to work. The first step of the work is to speak positive words into our lives.

One of the most difficult things everyone has to learn is that for your entire life you must keep fighting and adjusting if you hope to survive. No matter who you are or what your position is you must keep fighting for whatever it is you desire.
–George Allen

PART 1

The Nine Stages to Success

About The Nine Stages

Success seems to be connected with action. Successful people keep moving. They make mistakes, but they don't quit.
–Conrad Hilton

Each story in this book takes place at one of nine stages on the journey to success. The better you understand these stages, the easier it'll be to fight through the hard times in your life.

I created these stages after noticing a pattern in my life and the lives of many others. The journey to success is one that never ends, and it goes through stages that look similar across people and dreams. This is not a book about how to be successful, but that's often the goal when we meet a crossroad and want to quit. If we weren't trying to succeed at something, then we wouldn't have a reason to quit.

Once we understand what the journey to a successful moment looks like, it's easier to find our way there. Notice I said "successful moment" – success is a journey to a moment. That moment often comes and goes rather quickly, and then we begin a new journey. An athlete may have a goal to get a National Collegiate Athletic Association (NCAA) Division I scholarship. Once signed, the letter of intent is considered to be success on that day.

On the signing day, we take pictures and receive congratulatory texts and calls – then the moment is gone! We eventually enroll in school and set our sights on new goals. If success were an actual destination, then signing that letter of intent would be the end of the story. It wouldn't matter what happened after signing with a school. This doesn't mean we shouldn't be thankful in that moment. It just means we have to wrap our heads around the way life always changes.

The better we can recognize the stage we're in, the easier it'll be to push forward because we'll realize we're getting closer to the final step. When we begin working toward something, we often underestimate how hard it'll be to arrive at that place. It's not always that we think it'll be easy; it's more that we just don't expect it to be as hard as it ends up being. It's human nature to avoid pain.

When we're young and we touch a stove, our brain automatically calculates that touching a stove is bad because it causes pain. Just like any successful moment, we also have painful moments. The painful ones come and pass just like the successful ones, but we get stuck in thinking that neither of them will pass.

We are optimistic in thinking success lasts forever and pessimistic in thinking pain will never go away. Pain never lasts! The stages to success show why we should always look to turn the corner — the only way to find successful moments.

Focus on the journey, not the destination. Joy is found not in finishing an activity but in doing it.
–Greg Anderson

Stage 1: The Dream Stage

An idea comes to us, and it becomes all we think about. We can picture what life would be like to accomplish this idea. We all personally know a big dreamer, the person who has the greatest ideas in the word but often has an excuse not to go after them.

The dream stage is an ugly place to be. No one gets credit for having awesome dreams. It's what we're able to do with them that counts. God doesn't want us to just sit on our dreams; he wants us to work at them.

How many times have we heard about a successful company that is being sued by random people who say the company's ideas were theirs? Intellectual property lawsuits are always interesting because there's always a person who had a concept and a person who worked on that concept.

A dream isn't much more than a thought. It's a premise that lives inside our heads. We sleep, and it wakes, but eventually we wake, and it goes to sleep. That's the irony of dreams: You can't get closer to making them reality by sleeping or pondering them.

This is not to discredit the importance of this stage because we have to start somewhere. The idea is when we first think of what we want. It's when we first begin to taste what life will be like with it. We can't ever forget about this stage because it's the glue for many of the later stages. When we forget this stage, it can cause the subsequent stages to fall apart.

The dangerous thing is that dreaming is only the first stage. We can convince ourselves that dreaming is the stage right before success, but it's far from it. Everyone has to start somewhere, but we have to know we can't get our feet stuck in the first stage. Getting stuck here is like having a brand new Bentley that we can't drive forward. The car will only stay wherever they drop it off to us. We'd probably choose a very busy location, so as many people as possible could see the car.

We could spend hours a day in the car, and we'd feel great for a while as people walked by and complimented us, but eventually it would wear off. People would soon no longer compliment us because they'd realize the car doesn't move; we just sit there all the time. We'd eventually realize that moving nowhere yet looking nice is a horrible place to be. It would be better to have a beat-up car that just barely makes it across town than it would be to have that Bentley.

Stage 2: The Analyzing Period

During this stage, we begin to think about the actual work it'll require to bring our dream to life. Believe it or not, sometimes we quit right here. We find out what we want is not actually that easy to attain. The last thing we want for our life is to spend it flipping between stages 1 and 2.

We dream it and get excited, we analyze what it'll take, and we change our minds. We repeat this process over and over, never moving anywhere. For example, I decided I wanted to write this book years ago, but I kept finding reasons not to. I told myself everything from not having enough money to not knowing if I could write well enough.

Most of our time is spent thinking during this stage. Thinking can be dangerous because we constantly have to battle those negative thoughts that creep into our heads. Once all of the thinking is done, we naturally flow into a planning stage.

The key to the analyzing period is to break our monstrous dreams down into the smallest possible steps. When we begin working toward our goals, we need to see progress as quickly as possible. If our steps are too large, it'll seem as if we're not going anywhere.

We often quit when we feel as if we're not making any sort of progress. We can't let ourselves fall for this trap. In 2012 when the Olympics were upon us, I knew it was a possibility I could make the team. That was the goal, but I didn't think about it all the time. I had small tasks I knew I needed to handle throughout the year.

Here's an example:

Goal: Make Olympic team.

Stepping stone: Stay healthy.

Everyday steps:
- Get frequent massages from my wonderful girlfriend (now my wife).
- Foam roll every day.
- Stretch every day.
- Treat every injury like it could be a season ender, no matter how minor.
- Do injury prevention exercises in the weight room once a week.

Stepping stone: Approach every workout as if it were my last.

Everyday steps
- Leave morning weight workouts with no energy for class.
- Leave track workouts with no energy for the next day.
- Do not complain.
- Make no excuses.
- Visualize having a good practice before each practice.
- Focus on the process, not the result.

The dream is clear, but working toward something so big is tough unless we see progress. I knew staying healthy was important, and my baby steps made sure that happened. I could see progress because I was healthy and able to train. As long as I could train, I was able to focus my energy on making sure that, when that season was over, I had nothing left to give. I could rest well knowing that every day was full of small accomplishments.

Therefore do not be anxious about tomorrow, for tomorrow will be anxious for itself. Sufficient for the day is its own trouble.

–Matthew 6:34

Day by day, it seems like nothing changes, but when we look back over a year, everything has changed! It's because God made us to live day by day, sufficient for the day. That means we cover inches with each day, and by the end of a year, we'll have traveled quite some distance.

Stage 3: The First Step

Blessed are they who see beautiful things in humble places where others see nothing.
–Camille Pissarro

The plan is now in place, and we're ready to take the first step. Everything that exists today once was nothing until someone took action. Every master and expert once knew nothing, but they chose to change that.

Starting anything can be tough because it always requires us to change. We're resistant to change as humans. We often will do anything we can to keep things the way they currently are. What is it that you've wanted to change but you've been afraid to take the first step on?

It's vital that we push ourselves to take this step. Many times, when we make a time commitment, it binds us to finishing what we started. It's why so many of us stay in bad relationships long after we know we should've left. It's because we look at how far we've come instead of how far we have to go.

When I began writing this book, I started with a blank Word document. I committed to getting one thousand words down. I stopped for about a month after that because my commitment wasn't strong enough. When I brought myself back to the writing, I committed to getting twenty thousand words down. I did this because I knew that I'd never write twenty thousand words and not finish what I started. That's too much time and effort to waste.

When we get stuck at a point where we can't start, it's usually not due to a lack of knowing what to do. We went through the analyzing stage, so we already have a good idea of what needs to be done. Our being stuck is almost always associated with a fear of failure.

The result of that fear is that we constantly make excuses for why we can't do something. We talk ourselves out of it to make ourselves believe that not going after what we want logically makes more sense.

We subconsciously make this story in our heads that by not taking that step, we can avoid failure. The truth is, if we don't try, we've already failed. No amount of money, accolades, or safety can replace how it makes us feel doing what we've always wanted to do.

Taking the first step means becoming someone we're not. The result of that step is a form of growth and empowerment. The person we were will not recognize the person we become after taking the step. It causes us to walk to places we never thought we could go, and we start learning things we never thought we could. A simple step pushes us to become a brand new person from the inside out. The first step is the first real accomplishment in the journey.

Stage 4: The Work Period

It's now time to go to work and build on our dream. The fun about dreaming is all over now. It's time to do things we don't want to do and make the sacrifices we don't want to make. The work period is designed to wash out the fakers. Fake people never last when it's time to work.

This is where we are put to the test. Are we made of steel, or are we just glass with a coat of steel paint over it? Stage 4 is designed to show which people really want what they say they want. We can easily convince ourselves we're giving 100 percent. Then, we're thrown into a situation that makes us push harder than ever because we have no choice.

It's like running on a treadmill when we're dead tired. Then, someone comes and builds a fire pit behind us. If we fall off, we die! I'll bet we'd all find more energy to turn up that run a few levels. The only way to survive the work period stage is to constantly ask, "Am I giving everything I have?"

We can't let the work period make us quit, because if we quit, it's a reflection of our work ethic. This is the perfect time to learn the true meaning of effort. If we resist that lesson, we'll always give up because the work is too much to handle. This is when we'll see the gap between who we are and the person our dreams require us to be.

It bothers me to even think about it, because I have quit at this stage too. I quit, realizing I'd have to become something greater, and I wasn't up to the challenge. When I look back and have to say that, it's such a disappointment.

To make a dream a reality, we may have to get up at five o'clock in the morning and lift weights for an hour. The person we are might say, "I'm not a morning person." Our dreams might need us to change our diets and cut out all processed foods, but the person we are now might say, "But, I love those foods too much!" All the required changes are possible; it's just that we have to get our laziness out of our way. We have to hug change instead of push it away.

We can't be one of those people who show up to the work period and then vanish, never to be heard from again. How many athletes did we know as we grew up who had all the talent in the world, but when it came time to work, they'd never do it? Eventually, their talent ran out, and everyone else was able to catch up because of a stronger work ethic.

I remember when I first started Cover Ground—a blog dedicated to helping athletes succeed. The work period almost took me out for good. Writing just one article a month was such a challenge for me. It required me to change my habits. It meant I needed to spend more time reading and writing and less time watching TV and playing video games. That's a tough change for anyone to make, but I had to do it if I was going to get through this stage. Now, I don't even think about TV. The Ian who watches TV could never be the Ian who writes a book. It's that simple.

The work period is not about the rest of the world. This stage is about proving to ourselves we actually have a work ethic, showing ourselves we can commit a large amount of time and effort toward something with no guarantees. For others looking in on us from the outside, we should almost seem a bit obsessive if we're going to succeed.

People who excel in this stage always go on to find plenty of successful moments. If we can learn how to work as hard as possible at anything we touch, it's a trait that sticks with us forever. Hard workers are hard workers, and that's the end of that story. It's like getting a high school diploma; once we get it, we never give it back.

We can't return to being lazy and letting opportunities pass us by. When the cell phone market was growing, companies came out with rollover minutes. This meant any minutes we didn't use one month would be added to our next month's total. In the same way, if we fail at one thing, the lessons and work ethic are simply rolled over into whatever we touch next.

Stage 5: The Tired Period

Be wary, this is the stage that eats up hard workers who have no patience. It's horrible. In the previous stage, we were just patting ourselves on our backs for working hard, but now the doubts creep in.

In this stage, we look back on the preceding years of our lives, only to realize we'd done everything we possibly could. We gave it all up for our dreams, but we're not where we thought we'd be by this time. We figure we're just not cut out for it, and we want to throw in the towel.

The tired period is a stage even the most persistent struggle through. We think it'll take one year of training to have a breakout year, only to find our time will not come for another twelve years. We think running a business for three years will get us to where we want to be. However, we eventually find out we may have to run the business for ten years to reach our goal.

That's tough to swallow! If we thought we'd be at a certain point in three years but it takes an additional seven, think about how we'd feel during year five or six. We'd have doubts creeping in from every corner of our minds. We'd eventually become tired of all the hard work. Sometimes, working hard and keeping our eye on the prize just gets tough.

We'd slowly begin to drift to the easy path, but this path doesn't lead us to where we want to be. It leads us to a crowded area full of people who don't have what it takes to push through the tired period. When we end up here, we look back at all the work we did, and we're disappointed we gave up. All that work we did was actually getting us closer, but we became fixated on how hard it was. We lost sight of the dream.

Stage 6: The Second Wind

At this point, we're dead tired, but by the grace of God, we dig deep and give it another go. We almost have to be insane to succeed at most things because all reason says we should've already quit. However, we choose to keep digging for the gold because we've come too far to stop.

We've already invested the money in the mining equipment, we paid for labor, we risked getting trapped in the mine, we put in long hours every day, and we've got dirt in our fingernails and rocks in our hair. We've already invested a lot of work and time.

The definition of a second wind is a new strength or energy to continue something that's an effort. Success is getting closer, and we've already spent enough time moping and feeling sorry for ourselves. This isn't a stage to quit; it's the stage when we recommit to our dream. Deep down inside, we know we have more to give.

We've already given so much; we may as well get some gold from it. We become more zoned in than ever. It's coming to that last quarter or period, the last part of the race, and the finish line is drawing near. We feel the competition creeping up on us. The only way to hold them off is to dig deeper.

Why should they take what we have worked so hard for? We dig so deep that we find strength we didn't know we had. We start losing our sight because we push so hard our bodies want to shut down. The second wind represents 110 percent of what we have.

Stage 7: The Breaking Stage

When our vision returns, we see we're still short of our goal. We kicked it into overdrive, but we still don't see the result we're looking for. The problem with so many talks about success is they brainwash us into believing that, if we work hard, we'll succeed right away. But, that's a lie because, most of the time, we'll work hard and still be disappointed.

In this stage, some form of hopelessness will kick in, and our self-esteem will drop a few levels. We'll feel as if we're a huge failure. We'll feel sick to our stomachs and empty inside. No words will make us feel better because we've had enough of our dreams and life altogether.

We get broken in half, and it feels like our pathetic lives just aren't fair. When we quit at this stage, there's no chance we can forget we gave up. It'll stick with us for life as a huge moment when we gave up instead of that moment when we pushed through. When we have the mindset that pain can last forever, the only option that makes sense is to quit. We need to cling to the powerful idea that pain will pass if we just hold on.

When we climb a long rope, the worst part is that it hurts our hands. We want to let go so badly, and we forget that letting go will just be an exchange for a different pain. We either let our hands burn or break a leg when we hit the floor. We don't think about hitting the floor when we have our hands around the rope; we just think about our hands. If we can grip that rope tightly, our hands will burn, but that ledge we're climbing to reach is right there. The pain in our hands will never hurt more than the pain of dropping and hitting that floor.

While I was in college, my brother and I started our own clothing line, Parilexx. But, I quit on it before I finished college. It's the most painful lesson I've ever taught myself. We'd had moments when we'd done extremely well. One of those moments was followed by a huge mistake I made.

I ordered a shirt I thought would be huge because I loved it, but I didn't check to see if our customers would feel the same way. It broke me because I was so ashamed of myself, and I wasted a lot of our profits. I lost all faith in my ability to run a business. I felt like the biggest failure in the world. I'd invested so much in it, just like that gold mine. I would've been better off if I'd just kept at it, but things didn't come as quickly as I wanted. I took my mistake to heart, and what goes to the heart goes to the rest of the body. When I let go, the free fall was relieving—until I hit the floor.

After some time, I regretted letting it go, and that was a huge inspiration for this book. The number of people who told me I shouldn't have quit showed me they saw something I never saw at the time. I realized each struggle had actually taught me an important business lesson. I just needed to change, not quit. We often confuse those two words.

The good news is, when we drop from that high and hit the floor, the next time we climb a rope, we'll never let go. We'll work on our grip, we'll work on our technique or do whatever it takes, but when we decide to grab that rope again, we'll be ready to finish what we start. Don't let go!

Stage 8: The Endurance Point

The endurance point is a lot like love. Love is not a feeling; it's a choice we make every day. We're seeing divorce rates skyrocket because our society's lost on the idea of love. Love is not about our own happiness; it's about choosing to make the one we love happy, no matter what.

If two people approach marriage with that mindset, divorce won't come their way no matter how hard things may be. We may have a spouse who pisses us off every day, but we choose to love her or him. We may have a spouse who doesn't look as good as she or he used to, but we choose to love her or him, regardless. If we can't understand that choice, we'll never stay in love. Likewise, if we don't understand that endurance is a choice, we'll never find success.

The endurance stage is about choosing to keep going through all the down times and depression. We don't give up on what we want, because we want it that badly. If we think we've quit at this stage before, we've never really made it to the endurance point. We don't quit here; we either go on to succeed or we die. We make the ultimate choice that, no matter what, we'll keep hanging on. The only way we're coming down from that rope before we reach the top is if we die while holding on.

At this point, we've already hit many low points in the work period, the tired period, the second wind, and the breaking stage. We've been through it all and have proven we have something few people do.

People who become rich don't give their money to people easily. It's not that they don't like to give; they simply understand what it took to get where they are. The process and the journey made them into something great. It'd be a shame to allow others to skip their own journey by giving them everything.

By the time we work through all the different stages of success, we'll have given ourselves something more valuable than any dollar figure could. We'll realize it's never about actually becoming successful; it's about how the journey changes us. The process will change every fiber of who we are because we have to give up so much up. We often have to sacrifice fun, sleep, money, time, friendships, and family, and the list could go on and on. We realize we have come too far to lose hope.

Endurance is what this book is about. My goal is for you to smile as you go through each stage because you already know what the journey looks like. Your success is inevitable because, once you know you're in the endurance stage, you'll know the next step is success.

They say success is always around the corner. The problem is we've turned so many corners and not seen the beautiful face of success. We stop believing it even exists. Endurance is the final corner. It may be the toughest one to get around, but when we do, we move on as champions.

For you have need of endurance, so that when you have done the will of God you may receive what is promised.
–Hebrews 10:36

Stage 9: The Successful Moment

You're now at a successful moment because you endured. Through it all, you learned so much about yourself. Everyone has a different definition of what success is. You'll need to have a good idea of what you expect success to be for yourself. Otherwise, you'll run after things until other people consider you a success.

It's vital to remain humble during this stage because the moment won't last. Nothing lasts forever, and once it ends, the entire process starts over, struggles included.

You now have the blueprint to success. After all, once you've walked through the stages, there's no reason you can't do it again. You may have plenty of successful moments in your lifetime, but only if you can hold on.

When I chased after money, I never had enough. When I got my life on purpose and focused on giving of myself and everything that arrived into my life, then I was prosperous.
–Wayne Dyer

My son, do not forget my teaching, but let your heart keep my commandments, for length of days and years of life and peace they will add to you. Let not steadfast love and faithfulness forsake you; bind them around your neck; write them on the tablet of your heart. So you will find favor and good success in the sight of God and man.
–Proverbs 3:1–4

PART 2

Biblical Stories of Endurance and Faith

About The Biblical Stories

Because all faith and endurance comes from God, there's no way I could write a book about the topic without going through different stories in the Bible. The Bible is full of examples of people who stayed the course when things got tough.

In this section, I'll touch on many of these stories' key points, but I won't go through the entire story. By doing this, I hope to inspire you to pick up your Bible and read the stories in their entirety. My book is not meant to replace the Bible; in fact, I hope you'll want to spend more time reading the Bible.

The Story of Job

The book of Job is a great example of Old Testament biblical endurance. In times of defeat, this is a great story to read because not many of us can say we've experienced what Job was put through. To understand the story's background, you have to know a bit about Job.

Job is

- Blameless
- Upright
- Fearful of God
- Able to turn away from evil
- A family man
- Very wealthy

Satan has a goal to show God that Job only praises him because of how much God has blessed him with. Satan wants to prove that, if things in Job's life take a turn for the worse, Job's attitude and faith in God will do the same. God allows Satan to put Job to the test. Job loses all of his children in one day.

Think about how you'd act and what you'd say if this happened to you. Now, put this in the context of your life and what you're trying to endure. In comparison, doing this makes our problems seem much smaller. It's not easy to say, but realizing others experience challenges worse than ours helps us endure our own tough times.

What we're going through may be difficult, but we can use Job as an example of how to respond to problems. It's not that Job isn't hurting because of his loss. His pain is great, but he chooses not to lose sight of the fact that his God is greater. The key part of the story early on is in Job's response.

Then Job arose and tore his robe and shaved his head and fell on the ground and worshiped. And he said "Naked I came from my mother's womb, and naked shall I return. The Lord gave, and the Lord has taken away; blessed be the name of the Lord." In all this Job did not sin or charge God with wrong.
–Job 1:21

The man is stripped of much of his family in one day, and he still gives God praise. Some of us will lose a pencil in class and lose faith that God is out there. When God grows in our lives, our endurance grows because the issues causing us to give up shrink. We have to compare our problems to the size of our God instead of only looking at the size of our problems.

Job continues to praise God because he understands God has the right to allow good and bad in our lives. Job understands his children are a gift from God. They're not something he has control over. It's like when someone invites us over and offers us a free meal. We have no right to complain because we're being given a gift.

God owns every single thing we have, so we can't worry when things are lost, broken, or stolen. In my time at Iowa State, I managed to lose five iPods. Every time I lose things, I just say, "Hey, it belonged to God anyway, so there's no point in fussing." It changes our mindset when we realize we don't own anything because God owns it all.

To the contrary, if your enemy is hungry, feed him; if he is thirsty, give him something to drink; for by doing so you will heap burning coals on his head. Do not be overcome by evil, but overcome evil with good.
–Romans 12:20–21

This verse from Romans is counterintuitive to human nature and the way the world handles situations. The world says if someone slaps us, we slap back. The Bible says if someone slaps us, we show the other cheek. Then, we are to go home and pray for that person. That's tough to do!

The story of Job challenges us in a very similar way. The world tells us that, when things don't go our way, we pout, we ask God why, and we complain to others because we want our way. How easy is that to do? Behavior like this is not rare, but doing what God calls us to do is a true challenge.

The next time things don't go your way, try to respond in the way that Job does and praise God for what you have. Try to live in a manner counterintuitive to what the world tells us to do.

Stage: Breaking

Speak it into existence: If things go my way, I will thank God for the blessing. If things don't go my way, I will thank God for the lesson and the eventual blessing.

The Story of Joseph

This is a great story for those of us who sense we're far from our God-given purpose. It's a great example of how bad things that happen to us are all part of God's glorious plan. The actual story is quite long, but the summarized main points are easy to understand.

The story takes place in Genesis, chapters 37–45.

Early story:

- Joseph is a seventeen-year-old boy and the youngest of many brothers.
- His brothers become very jealous of him because their father makes him a colorful robe, and they feel their father loves Joseph more.
- Joseph has two different dreams, and both of them are symbolic of his brothers' bowing down to him.
- This makes his father show him more attention and increases his brothers' jealousy.

Joseph's brothers:

- Joseph's brothers conspire to kill him; they say a wild animal has eaten him.
- His brother Reuben spares his life, suggesting that killing him is a bad idea.
- The brothers take Joseph's coat and throw him into a pit.
- They see some Ishmaelite's on their way to Egypt passing by.
- They sell Joseph into slavery in exchange for twenty shekels of silver.
- The brothers dip Joseph's robe in blood and tell their father an animal has eaten him.

Joseph in Egypt:

- Joseph is purchased by Potiphar, who's an officer of the Pharaoh.
- God is still with Joseph, and even as a slave, Joseph succeeds.
- Potiphar puts Joseph in charge of his house and everything he owns.
- Potiphar's wife becomes very interested in Joseph and asks him to lie with her, but Joseph refuses.
- One day, as Joseph's working and no one else is home, Potiphar's wife grabs a piece of his garment and demands he lie with her.
- Joseph runs, tearing a piece of his garment.
- After Joseph flees, Potiphar's wife yells to the guards that he has tried to sleep with her.

Another fall:

- Potiphar is now upset and sends Joseph to prison.
- God is still with Joseph; Joseph is given favor in prison.
- The guards pay no attention to what Joseph is in charge of.
- In prison with Joseph are a cupbearer and a baker.
- One night, they each have dreams.
- In the morning, they look sad, so Joseph asks them why.
- They tell Joseph they've had dreams, but there's no one to interpret them.
- Joseph tells them he has a gift from God to interpret dreams.
- He asks them, when they get out of prison, to tell the Pharaoh about his gift; they agree.

- For the cupbearer, the interpretation is that in three days he'll return to work for the Pharaoh as his cupbearer.
- When the baker sees the cupbearer has a favorable interpretation, he asks to have his dream interpreted.
- The baker's interpretation is that, in three days, the Pharaoh will cut the baker's head off and feed his body to the birds.
- In three days, both interpretations come true, but the cupbearer doesn't remember to tell the Pharaoh about Joseph.

The rise:

- After Joseph has been in prison for two years, the Pharaoh has a dream no one can interpret; it reminds the cupbearer of Joseph.
- The Pharaoh has Joseph brought to him and asks him if he can interpret.
- Joseph replies, "It is not in me; God will give Pharaoh a favorable answer." (Genesis 41:16)
- The Pharaoh tells Joseph his dreams.
- Joseph says that God has shown the Pharaoh what he's going to do.
- There'll be seven years of great harvest throughout the land.
- These years will be followed by seven years of famine.
- Joseph tells the Pharaoh this is coming soon and that the Pharaoh needs to appoint someone to oversee the following plan: The plan is to save one-fifth of each field and to consume that food during the famine.
- The Pharaoh is so pleased with Joseph's plan, he appoints Joseph over his house and all his people.
- Only the Pharaoh has more rule than Joseph now does.
- Joseph is given fine linen, a ring, and a gold chain, and he rides in the Pharaoh's second chariot.

- Joseph is thirty years old at this time, which means he has endured thirteen years after being sold by his brothers.

The true test:

- Joseph's brothers venture to Egypt for grain because the famine is severe.
- All of Joseph's brothers go to see him, expect for Benjamin, the younger brother he's never met.
- Joseph is in charge of selling the grain.
- His brothers come and bow before Joseph, asking for grain, but he treats them as if he doesn't know them.
- His brothers don't recognize Joseph.
- Joseph becomes angry and calls his brothers spies to see the barren land.
- He put them all in prison for three days.
- On the third day, he makes one brother stay in prison while the rest go home with grain. Joseph tells them they must return with Benjamin.
- Joseph is unaware of Benjamin, so he thinks he'll catch them in a lie.
- When the brothers get home, their father is distressed because he could potentially lose another son.
- The brothers travel back to Egypt.
- When Joseph sees they've returned with Benjamin, he brings them into his house and dines with them.
- Many times, Joseph leaves his brothers' sight because his emotions are too much to handle.
- Joseph puts his brothers to the final test.
- He tells his stewards to fill their sacks with food for the trip home.
- He then tells them to sneak his silver cup into Benjamin's sack.

- Just after the brothers leave, Joseph's stewards chase after them, asking why they would repay good with evil.
- The stewards tell the brothers a silver cup is missing and whoever is found with it will die.
- The brothers deny doing anything wrong.
- The brothers are searched; the stewards eventually get to Benjamin and find the cup in his sack.
- They go back to Joseph's house, where Joseph's prepared to punish Benjamin.
- The eldest brother pleads to Joseph and comes clean about what they've done to one of their brothers.
- He pleads that their father has endured much pain, but he can't handle the loss of another son.
- The eldest brother tells Joseph it would be better if Joseph lets Benjamin go and holds him for punishment instead.

Joseph's reveal:

- Joseph can't hold in his emotions any longer, and he starts to weep.
- He finally tells his brothers who he really is.
- He says, "I am your brother Joseph, whom you sold into Egypt. And now do not be distressed or angry for God sent me before you to preserve life." (Genesis 45:5)
- Joseph tells his brothers to tell their father he is alive and to get him and their families and come and live in Egypt with him.
- Joseph forgives them.

Joseph and his father knew Joseph had a great purpose from a young age, and this story shows God's plan on a grand scale. Joseph and his father knew he was destined to do something special. But, just because God has big plans for us, that doesn't mean those plans will work on our own itinerary.

God let a boy be sold into slavery so that same boy could rise up and rule over many. It shows us how, even in some of our darkest moments, God is still with us. We may not feel like he is, and we may feel more lost than ever, but all we have to do is whisper to him for strength. There must have been times when Joseph doubted if he'd ever get out of prison.

He had to endure all those problems in life, knowing it was his own family who'd put him in that situation. It's horrible enough to be sold into slavery, but to have it done by your own family members is unfathomable. I have one older brother, and I grew up adoring him. I can't imagine his selling me like some old DVDs.

Joseph still forgave his brothers in the end. He could've easily had his revenge against his brothers, but he didn't. He loved them in the same way he did when he was a child. When we get caught up in how unfair life can be, we need to think about Joseph's story. Nothing that happened to him was fair. He tried to do the right things, but it seemed his life only got worse.

All the bad things that happen to us will lead to something we can only understand in the end when we look backward. If it weren't for Joseph's being sold as a slave, all of Egypt and the surrounding areas would've starved during the famine. That includes Joseph and his family.

We can probably look back on some tough moments in our lives and now understand clearly why we had to go through what we did. If we can't understand yet, then we must be patient for that time. That pain of yesterday becomes the fiber of our flesh tomorrow. Much of what we know how to do, and much of the reason we know how to help others, is because of what we've been through. Do you think the story would've ended the same way if Joseph hadn't had to struggle?

Let's pretend the story were different. Let's say that, when Joseph was a boy, a man from Egypt came to his home playing a trumpet to name him as the next ruler of Egypt. At this point though, he hadn't endured anything in life. He just went from being a boy who received special treatment from his father to being a ruler of Egypt.

He wouldn't rule with the same sovereign heart because he wouldn't understand others who struggled. He wouldn't have had one humble bone in his body. Maybe his gift of interpreting dreams would've become something he hogged for his own benefit. Certainly, we know the story would've been much different. We don't respond the same way to life when we're given something as we do when we have to fight for it. The endurance gives us a soft heart for others, but it also gives us thankfulness and the drive to make the most of every opportunity we have.

The challenge of applying this story to our own lives is that we can't see where we'll end up. Even if we could, would we have faith that God will actually get us there? We see that Joseph became a ruler, so we expect and hope that our hard times will lead to a great success.

At the same time, we don't want to go through pain like Joseph's. We want the happy ending that he had, but we don't want any of the pain. But, it never works that way. The greater the purpose, the greater the pain will be. When we have a great purpose, we have to struggle because it prepares us to handle what we'll face in the future. God sees us for what we can become. He sees the finished sculpture within us.

We might be lazy, for example, but for greatness, God needs more diligence from us. He pulls out his chisel and starts chipping away—and it hurts. For some of us, this process seems like a never-ending one because we aren't willing to let him remove the ugly parts of our sculpture. We have jagged edges, and the corners aren't smooth yet. God wants to fix these things, but we want to stay the same. Instead of letting the chipped pieces fall, we catch them and try to glue them back on. This only makes our sculpture even worse. We'll never be what we're supposed to be until we allow that sculpture to be complete.

Stages: Tired period to successful moment.

To one who has faith, no explanation is necessary. To one without faith, no explanation is possible.
–St. Thomas Aquinas

Speak it into existence: When I submit to God's plan, it will start with a struggle and end with a purpose.

David and Goliath

This story is well known, but so many people miss the amount of courage and faith the story is packed with. It's often seen as just a story for the underdog. It represents much more than that. This is one of the easiest stories we, as athletes, can apply to our lives on a daily basis. Even if we're considered to be the favorite, we can put ourselves in Goliath's shoes and learn from his mistakes.

The story takes place in 1 Samuel, chapter 17.

The story:

- The Philistines and Israelites have been in battle for a while, and the Philistines have killed many of the Israelites.
- There's a valley, sided by two mountains, in which both sides stand.
- From the Philistines comes a champion name Goliath.
- He's a giant who has expensive armor and weapons.
- He shouts to the Israelites to choose someone to represent them and fight him.
- If Goliath is killed, the Philistines will become servants to the Israelites; if the Israelite fighter loses, then the Israelites will become servants to the Philistines.
- Israel is terrified to hear this.
- For forty days straight, evening and night, Goliath says the same thing, looking for a challenger.
- David has just been anointed to be the next king of Israel.
- Currently, his job is simply to take care of the sheep.
- One day, David leaves the sheep and goes to the battlefield; he hears what Goliath has proposed.
- He wonders who Goliath thinks he is to defy the army of God in such a way.

- Many Israelites are upset with David for saying such a thing because they're terrified.
- The old king, Saul, tells David he can't fight Goliath because he's too weak and has no battle skills.
- David explains that, when a lion or bear threatens to take one of his lambs, he goes after the animal and kills it.
- He says, "The Lord who delivered me from the paw of the lion and who delivered me from the paw of the bear will deliver me from the hand of this Philistine." (1 Samuel 17:37)
- Saul says to David, "Go, and the Lord be with you!" (1 Samuel 17:37)
- Saul helps prepare David for battle with armor and a sword, but David chooses not to use them because he's never used either before.
- He puts five stones in his pouch and has his sling in his hand.
- Goliath sees that his opponent is young and taunts him.
- David replies, "You come to me with a sword and a spear and with a javelin, but I come to you in the name of the Lord of hosts, the God of the armies of Israel, whom you have defied. This day the Lord will deliver you into my hand, and I will strike you down and cut off your head. And I will give the dead bodies of the host of the Philistines this day to the birds of the air and to the wild beast of the earth, that all the earth may know that there is a God in Israel, and that all this assembly may know that the Lord saves not with sword and spear. For the Battle is the Lord's, and he will give you into our hand." (1 Samuel 17:45-47)
- Goliath draws near to David; David reaches into his sling, grabs a rock, puts it into his sling, and shoots it straight into Goliath's forehead.
- Goliath dies.

The first thing we need to take in about this story is the true source of David's power. Everyone is scared of Goliath because of his size and his physical strength. Many people may look at this story and say God just gave David a lucky shot. We may hear this story but not see any realism in it. We feel we'd be slaughtered if we ever went up against a giant. There are a few details to this story that we often miss. David was not as much of an underdog as it may have seemed. David stepped out like a true champion for God. He had faith that no matter what happened, God would give him victory in the end. He didn't know how, and he didn't really care.

We might miss the fact David was skilled with a weapon that could hit someone from a distance. He didn't use his physical strength to kill Goliath. The whole time though, the Philistines assumed the fight would be battle with swords and fists. David never planned to do that. He knew his strengths and stuck to them. It'd be like the strongest human in the world today deciding to fight a skilled sniper. Would the sniper throw a punch? No way! The sniper would crouch down, aim, and shoot the strong man in the head from as far away as he could. This is the faith we must have. Even if we can't see our advantage, we must trust God to know it and to open our eyes to it when he's ready.

This situation was a matter of life and death. It was a fight for the freedom of many people. Although much was on the line, we never read the story and get the sense that David is scared. He steps out to battle as if victory is already his because he has that much faith! Why do we worry about money, losses, failure, and so many others things that we lose faith over? Many of our situations aren't even life and death. If David could step out to face Goliath with unwavering faith, we can too.

If any of you lacks wisdom, let him ask God, who gives generously to all without reproach, and it will be given to him. But let him ask in faith, with no doubting, for the one who doubts is like a wave of the sea that is driven and tossed by the wind. For that person must not suppose that he will receive anything from the Lord; he is a double-minded man, unstable in all his ways.
–James 1:5–8

When David stepped out to fight Goliath, he didn't do it as a double-minded man. When we reach any tough situation, we have to remember how David stepped into this fight.

Stage: Endurance point/Successful moment.

When you have come to the edge of all light that you know and are about to drop off into the darkness of the unknown, faith is knowing one of two things will happen: There will be something solid to stand on or you will be taught to fly.
–Patrick Overton

Speak it into existence: I can't control the size of my problem, but I can always control the size of my faith.

Samson and Delilah

I've known the details of this story since I was young, but I had never analyzed what happens. As a child, I thought this story was all about Delilah. I used to get mad at her for getting my man Samson caught up. I now know that, although she's a big part of the story, Delilah isn't the most important part. The end of the story provides the true lesson we can use when everything in our life has fallen apart.

I watched a series on the History Channel titled *The Bible* during my last year of college, and the Samson and Delilah story caught my attention. The story's end captivated me. I felt everyone should watch it.

The story: This story takes place in the book of Judges, which is before the David and Goliath story. The David and Goliath story tells how the Israelites finally came out from under the hand of the Philistines. This story sets the stage for the fall of the Philistines.

And the people of Israel again did what was evil in the sight of the Lord, so the Lord gave them into the hand of the Philistines for forty years.
–Judges 13:1

And the angel of the Lord appeared to the woman and said to her, "Behold, you are barren and have not borne children, but you shall conceive and bear a son. Therefore be careful and drink no wine or strong drink, and eat nothing unclean, for behold, you shall conceive and bear a son. No razor shall come upon his head, for the child shall be a Nazirite to God from the womb and he shall begin to save Israel from the hand of the Philistines."
– Judges 13:3–5

Summary of events:

- Samson decides he wants to marry a Philistine woman.
- His parents advise him multiple times this is a bad idea for numerous reasons.
- Samson doesn't listen to his parents.
- As Samson is going to see the Philistine woman, a lion approaches; Samson tears the lion to pieces with his hands because the Lord is with him.
- Samson eats the lion's body and gives some to his parents but doesn't tell them where it came from.
- Samson marries the Philistine woman.
- Samson makes a riddle among the Philistines and says, if any of them can figure it out in seven days, he'll give them gifts; if not, they'll have to give him gifts.
- After three days, the Philistines can't figure out the answer to the riddle.
- They go to Samson's wife and tell her she needs to entice Samson to tell them the answer, or they'll burn down her family's house.
- She pleads to Samson to tell her the answer.
- On the last day, he tells her the answer to the riddle, and she tells her people.
- They come to Samson and tell him the answer, but Samson knows it's only because they have gotten to his wife.
- The spirit of the Lord comes over Samson; he strikes down thirty Philistine men.

Samson's anger:

- A misunderstanding between Samson and his father-in-law bothers Samson; Samson sets out to anger the Philistines.
- He sets fire to torches and lets foxes go into their grain and olive orchards.

- The Philistines are upset with Samson.
- For revenge, they burn his wife and her father to death.
- Samson isn't happy about this and sets out to avenge his wife's death.
- Samson's people ask if they can tie Samson up and give him to the Philistines because they're still rulers over them.
- Samson agrees as long as they don't attack him themselves.
- Once Samson is in the hands of the Philistines, the Spirit of the Lord comes over him, and he frees himself.
- Samson goes on to strike down one thousand men.

Delilah's entrance:

- Samson falls in love with Delilah.
- The Philistines approach her and encourage her to seduce Samson and find out where his strength comes from.
- In return, she'll receive 1,100 pieces of silver.
- Samson tells Delilah three different lies; she gives this information to the Philistines.
- After each lie, the Philistines attack Samson to see if they can take his strength.
- Delilah pleads to Samson that he doesn't love her because he keeps lying to her.
- Finally, he tells her he can't cut his hair because that's where his strength lies.
- At night, she calls another man while Samson is sleeping and has the man cut off seven locks from Samson's head.
- She then torments Samson and tells him the Philistines are coming.
- He thinks he'll be able to shake himself free from the Philistines, as he's always be able to do.

- But, the Lord was his strength, and God is no longer with Samson.
- The Philistines capture Samson and dig his eyes out, blinding him.
- They shackle him and throw him into prison.

Samson's death:

- The Philistines bring Samson out to entertain the Philistines.
- They put him in between two pillars.
- About three thousand Philistines are present.
- Samson prays to God to strengthen him just this one last time.
- Samson grabs both pillars and pulls them down.
- The building crashes down, killing Samson and all of the Philistines.

Some of the lessons in the Samson and Delilah story are obvious, but some are tricky. We can miss how we can apply them to our own lives. This story is an excellent reflection of what we often look like in the mirror. The story is much more extreme, as many people are killed, but it applies nonetheless. All we have to do is switch up some of the details, and we have our own lives.

For example, switch Delilah with a bad relationship of yours, in which you did things that took you farther away from the person you're called to be. Take Samson's hair and trade it for the work ethic that you're blessed with. We have a work ethic and work hard for things, but we often forget who gave us that work ethic. We also forget God can take it away at any time. The story fits into our lives perfectly; we just have to open our eyes.

Delilah is the scapegoat

When I first heard this story in elementary school, I asked why Delilah would do that to Samson. The truth is, Delilah isn't the problem in this story; Samson is. It's a harsh reality many of us have faced in life time and time again. We search out the easy source to blame because it makes us feel better when we look in the mirror.

The misguided read this story and do what I did when I was young—blame Delilah. The wise know the real issue is that Samson needed a change of heart and direction. I'm not saying what Delilah did was right, but it would've never happened if Samson hadn't put himself in that position. Delilah was really just the tipping point for Samson's downfall.

We should always be searching for the Delilah in our lives. Delilah could come in the form of a person or thing we're blaming our problems on. Samson's eyes were opened in prison. He then realized he'd caused his own destruction. If Samson had never had a change of heart, the Philistines would've killed him, and he would've died still blaming Delilah.

He would've died never understanding where he went wrong. On an even larger scale though, he would've died without fulfilling his purpose. That's such a shame, and many of us are still in this place today. The beauty of the Gospel is that it's never too late to have a change of heart.

We also have to watch for the Delilah's in our lives in the sense of reaching that tipping point. When we choose the wrong things so many times, we're in a position in which just the weight of one feather could land, and we'd fall. And, great that fall would be. It's never too late to turn around and go in the right direction. I can say from personal experience that, if we stand around and wait for that feather to drop, it will hurt.

When we finally buckle under all the weight on our shoulders, that crap will come down on top of us. The problems don't just go away because we fall; one by one, we have to deal with each item on us until we can climb back onto our feet. The question is, do we want to deal with it now on our feet, or do we want to deal with it when we're crushed on our backs under debris that is topped with a feather? We always have the choice, but God puts the consequences on us.

Blind before his eyes were dug out

Pride is the reason Samson was blind in his life and we may be in our lives. Samson literally had his eyes dug out, but he was blind long before that moment. When he had two good eyes, he couldn't see a thing. It's the same reason why we're supposed to train like number two. Number two is always hungry and humble compared to number one. When we're number two, we can't boast or brag, because we're not number one. The great athletes keep the mindset that they're always underdogs, no matter how many championships they win.

Humility is the one thing we no longer have once we think we do. Samson had a special purpose, but he lost sight of that and ran around doing whatever he wanted. Samson was born a Nasserite, which means "set aside for God." His mom was told this from birth, and Samson knew this.

Over time though, he forgot and began to run around thinking he gave himself strength. God allowed it for a while, staying with him. When Samson ate the body of the dead lion, it was something he wasn't supposed to do, just like cutting his hair. He thought he could do whatever he wanted. Eventually, God had to walk away and show Samson what life would look like without God. Samson had so much pride that, when his hair was cut, he still believed his strength would pull him through another tough situation. God wasn't with him though.

Pride is dangerous. We see it in life all the time. We make decisions based solely on our pride. We especially see this in our relationships with a significant other. We all know those moments when we're mad about something small and refuse to call or text the other person until she or he says something. We may be burning inside, but we won't call or text first. Why?

Pride is the reason this happens. Our ego wants to be padded by having the other person come running back to us. I spent my teenage years doing dumb stuff like this. One reason I knew I was ready to get married was because I wouldn't let moments like this happen. I was able to throw my pride out the window, reconcile the situation, and talk. Pride doesn't lead us to good places; it leads us to evil ones.

We'll often see athletes who won't quit a workout, knowing full well they've injured themselves.

All pride!

Athletes who win and praise themselves but lose and blame others.

All pride!

This list can go on and on. When does your pride tend to flare up? Just remember this story and say "All pride!" to yourself. You'll walk blinded if you don't.

The haughty looks of man shall be brought low, and the lofty pride of men shall be humbled, and the Lord alone shall be exalted in that day.
–Isaiah 2:11

Humble pie

Pride goes before destruction, and a haughty spirit before a fall.
–Proverbs 16:18

Humble pie is the only pie no one wants to eat but everyone loves to serve. Samson had nowhere left to go but to fall. He knew his strength was in his hair, yet he still told Delilah. How else could he come to realize he was no longer giving the glory to God? God had to walk away. Then, Samson was no longer able to glorify himself. He was blind, shackled, and surrounded by his enemy. That is a low place to be and a place we've all been at some point.

We need to remember this story when we want to puff out our chests. It's a constant battle to keep our thoughts and motives in check. We often use anything good to glorify our own name. Even in writing this book, I reminded myself this is not about Ian Warner – it's about God and others. It can't be about me because the second I make it about me, I'm going to be blinded.

As soon as our mindset becomes "look at me," we must prepare to get slapped in the head because it's coming our way. We can do charity work to help the poorest kids in the world, but if we only do it so we can put a picture on Instagram and people can say, "Wow, what an awesome person!" prepare to get slapped. It's not that other people's choosing to praise us makes us wrong; it just requires us to use "call forwarding." All the praise comes to us, but we must automatically redirect it to God.

In that dark place

For I, the Lord your God, hold your right hand; it is I who say to you, "fear not. I am the one who helps you."
–Isaiah 41:13

There comes a point when we realize we haven't been doing what we're supposed to do. For Samson, this moment came after losing his eyes and being in prison. He looked back and saw the dark place to which he'd traveled. When we're blinded, we also tend to lose all hope.

We get upset with God for taking us to such a horrible place. The truth of the situation is that, step by step, we fought his will and inched toward our own desires. Samson's parents told him about marrying the Philistine woman. But, he didn't listen, and that situation ended poorly. With Delilah, he yet again became blind because of his lust for a woman. Both women brought him to dark places. A lot of us can relate to how Samson must have felt. He lost his first wife, Delilah betrayed him, and he was blinded and in prison and had no strength.

We might be injured, brokenhearted, betrayed, and destroyed in every way a person could possibly be. That tunnel might be stretching out by a few miles per second, and that light at the end of the tunnel may seem farther away. These are the moments that separate the faithful from the faithless. It's never too late to get right with God and get our lives back on track.

I'd rather know I fulfilled my purpose before I died than live my whole life lost and confused, wondering why I'm here. I'd rather die and fulfill my purpose than live a life never taking responsibility for my own actions. We have to stand up and say, "God, I lost my eyes, but because of you, I can see more clearly than ever now. I thank you for that." Just like Samson, ask God for strength one more time.

We'll do what we're supposed to do

We should be thankful we're not told our purpose when we're born. If we put ourselves in Samson's position, it's easy to understand how he got there. It'd be tough to know we have a great purpose and not let our pride creep in. Samson and his great purpose seemed to be lost when he was in jail. How could he save the Israelites from the hand of the Philistines in his position?

Sometimes we get stuck thinking we know how things are going to play out, but we find things happen in a totally different way. If we knew our purpose at birth, we'd expect our story to be as simple as possible. For example, if our purpose were to become a billionaire and then give it all away, it'd go something like this.

Around age eight, we'd come up with some crazy invention while playing with our friends at recess. This invention would make us rich by the time we were ten, and by age eighteen, we'd be married and spend our days counting our billions. Sounds simple, but that may not be God's plan.

Maybe God's plan is that we won't be billionaires until age eighty-five. We'd be challenged to stay the course until that time. Or, maybe we'll do a few stints in prison for crimes we didn't commit, our family will hate us, our best friend will die in our arms, and we'll spend most of our lives homeless with no money. What if that were God's plan? Would we have what it takes to play it out until the fourth quarter?

We'll do what we're supposed to do. We'll have a purpose and, while running from it may delay it, we'll fulfill it. I had the idea for this book coming out of high school. I sprinted as fast as I could from it for six years of my life. Yet, you're reading this book. I don't know if this book is my purpose, but if I died right after publishing it, I'd be a happy man because I fulfilled the task I was called to do.

We have to walk the path. No matter how tough it is, we have to keep walking forward. The eighty-five-year-old billionaire can't quit because, if it weren't for him and his purpose, many others couldn't fulfill their purpose. When we only think about ourselves, it's easy to get lost in selfish ambition.

When we think about how we can change others, things get interesting. That billionaire who gives away his money will allow others the opportunity to also do something great, and that chain continues on and on. We'll do what we're called to do. It may not happen the way or when we would like, but eventually it'll happen. It just depends on our getting in line with what God wants.

Stage: Breaking, endurance, and successful moment.

But if you have bitter jealousy and selfish ambition in your hearts, do not boast and be false to the truth. This is not the wisdom that comes down from above, but is earthly, unspiritual, and demonic. For where jealousy and selfish ambition exist, there will be disorder and every vile practice.
–James 3:14–16

It is wise to direct your anger towards problems — not people: to focus your energy on answers — not excuses.
–William Arthur Ward

Speak it into existence: I will work to remove pride from my life, so I am not blinded. Lord, I pray that you give me strength so that I can honor you every day.

Saul to Paul

This is a story of a much different type of endurance compared to that in the rest of stories. We often think of endurance as being the story that starts badly and ends well. What about when we live a life free of persecution but walk into a life full of persecution and are thankful for it?

It can be awful when we look back at the person we once were and can't even recognize the character and values of that person. We think endurance usually comes in the form of a story character we feel really bad for, but that character doesn't give up and comes through in the end. With Paul, we don't feel sorry for him in the beginning, but by the end, we feel bad for him.

Paul's name was actually Saul before he accepted Christ into his life. This is the reason why many people don't realize that Paul had been persecuting Christians for much of his life. In chapter 13 of the book of Acts, Saul officially begins going by the name of Paul, which is what he is more commonly known as.

Paul is considered to be one of the most well known people in the Bible. He wrote the books of Romans, 1 Corinthians, 2 Corinthians, Galatians, Ephesians, Philippians, Colossians, 1 Thessalonians, 2 Thessalonians, 1 Timothy, 2 Timothy, Titus, and Philemon. That is a total of thirteen books of the New Testament. Like some of you may have, I assumed someone who wrote that many books was probably a pretty awesome person. I figured he or she wouldn't be perfect like Jesus but would be pretty close to it. This thinking actually makes no sense at all; I'm just trying to show you where my head was.

It's all a flawed way of thinking because we often equate bad and good with our own social standards. Therefore, if someone takes care of his or her kids, works a good job, and goes to church, we say that is a good person. If we ask a population of people if they are good, most of the answers will be yes. That's because we can think of someone who has done things we consider to be worse than what we've done. This makes us feel better about ourselves. But, that's garbage!

God only sees two types of people: the perfect people without even one sin and the people who've sinned and need to believe in Christ as their Lord and savior. That's it! There's no sort of or a magic number, so if we've sinned even once, we no longer meet God's standard for perfection.

Paul was the poster boy for what we'd call a bad person. If he were around in today's society, he'd be in prison for life. He was going from church to church persecuting those who followed Christ. Some of these people were killed, and others were thrown in prison. Paul was on a mission to take every believer down.

The story: As Paul traveled to another town one day, these events took place.

Now as he went on his way, he approached Damascus, and suddenly a light from heaven shone around him. And falling to the ground he heard a voice saying to him, "Saul, Saul, why are you persecuting me?" And he said, "Who are you, Lord?" and he said, "I am Jesus, whom you are persecuting. But rise and enter the city, and you will be told what you are to do." The men who were traveling with him stood speechless, hearing the voice but seeing no one. Saul rose from the ground, and although his eyes were opened, he saw nothing. So they led him by the hand and brought him into Damascus. And for three days he was without sight, and neither ate nor drank.
–Acts 9:3–9

Now there was a disciple at Damascus named Ananias. The Lord said to him in a vision, "Ananias." And he said, "Here I am, Lord." And the Lord said to him, "Rise and go to the street called Straight, and at the house of Judas look for a man of Tarsus named Saul, for behold, he is praying, and he has seen in a vision a man named Ananias come in and lay his hands on him so that he might regain his sight." But Ananias answered, "Lord, I have heard from many about this man, how much evil he has done to your saints at Jerusalem. And here he has authority from the chief priests to bind all who call on your name." But the Lord said to him, "Go, for he is a chosen instrument of mine to carry my name before the Gentiles and kings and the children of Israel. For I will show him how much he must suffer for the sake of my name."
–Acts 9:10-16

So Ananias departed and entered the house. And laying his hands on him he said, "Brother Saul, the Lord Jesus who appeared to you on the road by which you came has sent me so that you may regain your sight and be filled with the Holy Spirit." And immediately something like scales fell from his eyes, and he regained his sight. Then he rose and was baptized; and taking food, he was strengthened.
–Acts 9:17–19

From this point, Paul preaches about Jesus Christ. People still see him as the person he used to be—the man who persecuted Christians. These same people plot to kill Paul, so he runs away. The plot to kill Paul in Damascus was just the tip of the iceberg. God had chosen him to write much of the New Testament, but it wasn't going to come without its trials. All of these events occur within the book of Acts, which is before Paul ever wrote one book.

Paul's trials:

- They try to kill him in Damascus (mentioned above).
- They try to kill him in Jerusalem.

- In Antioch of Pisidia, the Jews persecute him as he teaches, and he's not allowed to return.
- In Iconium, he's almost stoned.
- In Lystra, the people of Antioch have already told them to stone him.
- In Philippi, Paul is beaten and thrown into prison.
- In Thessalonica, they attempt to seize him.
- In Macedonia, they plot against him.
- In Caesarea, Paul is taken under guard to be testified against.

Paul's lessons for us:

1. God can use anyone.

We convince ourselves that God only uses people whom we personally see as being "good people," but that's false. God can use anyone he wants, and he has the power to pick the most unlikely person. He proves that by taking a man who hated Christians and turning him into a man who spreads the word of God. Paul shows us why we have no reason to lose hope in others or ourselves. Even if we've done things others see as unthinkable, God still has enough grace to forgive and use us to glorify his kingdom.

2. His life was easier when he was doing the wrong thing.

When you think about it, doing wrong is pretty easy. Being righteous and always making a conscious effort to turn your back to sin are much harder to do. The problem is, we feel beat down when we think we're doing everything right, yet we're still being persecuted. We must remember Paul and his story. He had a great purpose, but that purpose wasn't going to come without trials.

It's another counterintuitive moment in our faith. Why would we want to do something good if we know it will just invite more bad things into our lives? The answer to that will always be Jesus. What he did was all good, and he suffered. When we set out to live like him, and preach the gospel, life's going to hurt. This hurt is a blessing though. All the pain we go through will build us up; the more we go through, the greater the purpose for which we're being built. Rejoice in each and every suffering you go through.

Stage: The first step.

For all have sinned and fall short of the glory of God, and are justified by his grace as a gift, through the redemption that is in Christ Jesus.
–Romans 3:23–24

Blessed are they who see beautiful things in humble places where others see nothing.
–Camille Pissarro

Speak it into existence: My past is my past, but today is an opportunity to create a new future.

The Life of Jesus Christ

Jesus died on the cross so that we could have an everlasting life. He was the only one to walk this planet and not sin once, yet he died like a common criminal. Look at Jesus and his life, and you'll see the ultimate story of endurance. He is the root of all endurance. If Jesus suffered to the point of death and he did nothing wrong, then why shouldn't we suffer like him when we've done much wrong?

The Bible calls us to be like Jesus. The only way to do that is to be tested, and tested often. This means that things won't always go our way because, clearly, things didn't always go Jesus' way. He didn't want to be beaten, spit on, and hung on the cross, but he humbled himself to God's glorious plan. How many of us would walk the path that he did? In reality, instead of walking his path, we decide our plans are easier and better.

His point of endurance was being on that cross, and he pushed through it to death because that was the plan. Then, he rose from the dead and proved to everyone he was who he said he was. Eternal life in heaven was proved to all. His name is praised the highest because he deserved nothing that happened to him. His name is exalted because he endured the ultimate suffering.

When we walk the path that God wants, just like Jesus, our name will eventually be exalted. Even though we know this, we must endure simply for God's glory, not for ours. Jesus didn't walk the path so that his name would be above all names; he walked the path because he was a humble servant.

Do nothing from selfish ambition or conceit, but in humility count others more significant than yourselves. Let each of you look not only to his own interests, but also to the interests of others. Have this mind among yourselves, which is yours in Christ Jesus, who though he was in the form of God, did not count equality with God a thing to be grasped, but emptied himself, by taking the form of a servant, being born in the likeness of men. And being found in human form, he humbled himself by becoming obedient to the point of death, even death on a cross. Therefore God has highly exalted him and bestowed on him the name that is above every name, so that at the name of Jesus every knee should bow, in heaven and on earth and under the earth, and every tongue confess that Jesus Christ is Lord, to the glory of God the father.
–Philippians 2:3–11

We aren't Jesus Christ, but the Bible demands us to live a life like his, which means we must endure like him. When it'd be much easier to throw in the towel and walk away, remember Jesus Christ and what he went through for you. Imagine if God had decided he no longer wanted his son to suffer. Imagine if Jesus had chosen, like every single one of us has done in our lives, to disobey God. What would that have meant for us?

It would mean we'd be liable for all of our sins, and we'd have no savior. We'd always be disconnected from God. God's standard is perfection, and because we don't have that, the only way to him is through Jesus. That's his gift to us all.

Jesus said to him, "I am the way, and the truth, and the life. No one comes to the Father except through me."
–John 14:6

Life is never about us, and this story is the best example of that. It can be tough to wrap our heads around that when we quit before we're supposed to. We make it all about us and not about our greater purpose to serve God and others. Jesus suffered for us. Whom are you willing to suffer for?

This means you have to push through your trials, so you'll have an impact on others' lives. Athletes want to be around winners for a reason. Winning is a culture; it floats around in the air and spreads like an air freshener. Losers want to be around winners, so that beautiful smell in the air can rub off on them. The same can also be said for the disease of losing and quitting.

Abide in me, and I in you. As the branch cannot bear fruit by itself, unless it abides in the vine, neither can you, unless you abide in me. I am the vine; you are the branches. Whoever abides in me and I in him, he it is that bears much fruit, for apart from me you can do nothing. If anyone does not abide in me he is thrown away like a branch and withers; and the branches are gathered, thrown into the fire, and burned. If you abide in me, and my words abide in you, ask whatever you wish, and it will be done for you.
–John 15:4–7

Choosing not to abide in God's plan can make us feel distant to our own lives. Waking up every day becomes a struggle because we know the time we're awake will consist of things we know we shouldn't be doing. When we humble ourselves and abide in the plan, we'll eventually receive what we need, but not always what we want. If we're asking for something only so we can fulfill our sinful desires, then it won't be given to us. Often, that's why the things we ask for aren't given to us.

We may want to succeed at something so badly. We plead to God to give it to us, and we believe fully in our hearts that he can and will. If we still want to succeed just to feed our own pride, then we haven't yet reached a place where we're humbling ourselves and abiding in the plan.

The endurance we show produces character, and it sets the stage for a great story. Jesus had everything, but his story wouldn't be the greatest story told if we weren't able to relate

64

to him. He was human and came with everything we come with today, except the sin.

Life is so unfair

For the kingdom of heaven is like a master of a house who went out early in the morning to hire laborers for his vineyard. After agreeing with the laborers for a denarius a day, he sent them into his vineyard. And going out about the third hour he saw others standing idle in the marketplace, and to them he said, "You go into the vineyard too, and whatever is right I will give you." So they went. Going out again about the sixth hour and the ninth hour, he did the same. And about the eleventh hour he went out and found others standing. And he said to them, "Why do you stand here idle all day?" They said to him, "Because no one has hired us." He said to them, "You go into the vineyard too." And when evening came, the owner of the vineyard said to his foreman, "Call the laborers and pay them their wages, beginning with the last, up to the first."

And when those hired about the eleventh hour came, each of them received a denarius. Now when those hired first came, they thought they would receive more, but each of them also received a denarius. And on receiving it they grumbled at the master of the house, saying, "These last worked only one hour, and you have made them equal to us who have borne the burden of the day and the scorching heat." But he replied to one of them, "Friend, I am doing you no wrong. Did you not agree with me for a denarius? Take what belongs to you and go. I choose to give to this last worker as I give to you. Am I not allowed to do what I choose with what belongs to me? Or do you begrudge my generosity?" So the last will be first, and the first last.
–Matthew 20:1–16

I love this parable because it explains the feeling of unfairness we often have throughout our lives. It's that feeling we get when we work so hard for something, but another person does less work yet does better than we do. It happens in sports, in school, and in the work force; it's all around us. It feels like such an injustice, but that's exactly how God works when it comes to his kingdom.

Some of us came to believe in Jesus when we were four years old and never lost sight of the Gospel. Others of us believed in the Gospel at a young age but walked away from it. Still others of us won't believe in Jesus until our last day alive. God doesn't treat any of us differently. We're all received in the same way because there's no amount of work we can do to get into heaven. There are only two ways to get to heaven: Be perfect or believe that Jesus Christ is your Lord and Savior.

When we look at life from that perspective, it actually makes enduring much easier. Sometimes we quit because we're not getting a result that we see other people getting, which we also want. It kills us to see others who may never put in the years of work that we have, yet they get the same results or even better.

Think about how Jesus put things: "The last will be the first, and the first will be the last." (Matthew 20:16) When we see things like this, we remember that life itself is a gift. We remember that having money, being a good athlete, and getting good grades don't put us in any higher standing with God. It's not about how much work we do but about how much faith we show. The only way we can showcase our faith is by being tested often.

Yet we know that a person is not justified by works of the law but through faith in Jesus Christ, so we also have believed in Christ Jesus, in order to be justified by faith in Christ and not by works of the law, because by works of the law no one will be justified.
–Galatians 2:16

Once we believe, we set up the rest of our lives to follow his word. That means that, regardless of what success others are having or work they're doing, it's up to us to give our all. You have a gift from God, so use it to honor him until you've exhausted that gift.

Stage: Endurance point.

If there is no struggle, there is no progress.
-Frederick Douglass

For to this you have been called, because Christ also suffered for you, leaving you an example, so that you might follow in his steps.
-1 Peter 2:21

Speak it into existence: To live a life like Jesus', I have to suffer like he did.

PART 3

Stories of the Journey

633,600 Inches

No temptation has overtaken you that is not common to man. God is faithful, and he will not let you be tempted beyond your ability, but with the temptation he will also provide the way of escape, that you may be able to endure it.
-1 Corinthians 10:13

Life is clearly full of choices both big and small. The small ones by themselves usually don't play a big role in changing our lives. But, when we take these small choices and add them up, they become a big deal, just like a colony of ants — useless alone but a force in numbers. The small choices we think are no big deal are the reason some constantly move forward while others stay the same or get worse.

For example, you can see how this works when you make the small choice not to go out on weekends. When a weekend comes, this small choice seems not to be a big deal, but it can have repercussions on your entire life. By staying in, you could spend more time doing homework, rest your body for training harder, and make it easier to stay away from sin. If you look at that small choice to stay in as one weekend, it has the potential not to be a big deal. However, when you look at it spread across fifty-two weeks, it's a completely different story.

When I was writing this book, I could've gotten away with not writing for one day. That one small choice, to miss a day of writing two thousand words, wasn't that big a deal. That choice replicated for weeks and months, though, has much different repercussions. It took me waking up daily and saying, "I choose to write something down today." Whether I wanted to or not, I did it.

It took going to bed later than an athlete ever should and waking early every morning. Even when I was tired, I had to think about why I was doing this. I just thought about how many opportunities God has blessed me with. I thought about my parents and everything they've given me in my life. I thought about how broke I was and how I was getting married soon. All of that was enough to get my feet on the floor. I also thought about upsetting the devil because he didn't want me to wake up. He wanted me to lie down and stay cozy in my bed. He wanted my room to feel extra cold, so I wouldn't dare step out into that cold air. He knew I was getting ready to spread the word of God. When we live a life for God, we must be prepared for the devil to be in our way often. He wants to stop us and bring God's work within us to a halt.

We're often hit with these small choices, and we make the wrong ones. We look for the easiest route. Every time we do it, we forget why we started in the first place. It wasn't ever for us or so that others would chant our name. We took that first step, so others, when they see us get up every morning and slave away, will know we're doing it for God—not for money, our friends, or even to call ourselves a success.

Some people just need someone to lead them to the word of God. They need to actually witness God in another person's everyday life. They need to see us not while we're "sometime living" or "feel like living," but when we're nonstop in pursuit of Christ. They see our hearts are made of something different. The things that faze them never faze us. The things they worry about, we smile about. The days they can't get up; we've been up for hours and have breakfast waiting for them. When angry, they spew hate while we project love.

During the times they're broken down and in the dark, we walk into their lives glowing brightly, so they can see clearly again. Life is about moments. Don't for a second think it's the big moments that make or break us. The big moments become easy choices when we live our lives every day making the right ones.

A journey of a thousand miles begins with a single step.
–Lao-Tzu

We need pain to grow, but this comes with knowing we need to change our thinking. That change in thinking means we see life in inches. We want to get to a place that's 10 miles (633,600 inches) away from where we are now. We know that every choice we make in our lives will either get us an inch closer or an inch farther from whatever we pursue.

At that moment, we stop inching backward. If we want to be a great athlete, why inch backward and convince ourselves we're young and should do whatever we want? Won't it be fun when we reach our destination? That's what makes the difference! When we understand the difference, we climb mountains and see others looking up at us upset and confused because they can't understand how we beat them there.

We get beat because we get out inched. Our goal can be great, but it can't be accomplished if our mindset is not also great. Anyone can say, "In a year, I want to be here." But, when we look at our lives, we see backward inches everywhere.

When I was working on this book, I'd go to bed upset. I'd keep looking at the clock, trying to squeeze out as many words as possible, because I didn't want to sleep. I couldn't write in my sleep. I couldn't gain inches in my sleep. I was pissed off because, when I looked back on my life, I had filled my college years with excuses. I'd wasted my time doing things that don't matter to me today. I had to live in a way that ensured I backed up everything I said with my character. Someone could have a camera on me all day, and I'd have nothing to worry about.

When that alarm goes off in the morning, we should fly out of bed with a smile. We should wonder why the heck our alarm took so long to go off. The blessing to have another day on this planet, doing things we love to do, will make our first step one that drops us to our knees. Nothing but praises will go up because we realize we can't do anything without him.

The work we can put in that amazes others—God put that in us.

The way we can attract people because they sense something special about us—God put that specialness in us.

The ability to turn away from those negative inches—God put that willpower in us.

What a gift! The only option for us from this point on is to dedicate to him every single inch we gain.

Half Time

Be sober-minded; be watchful. Your adversary the devil prowls around like a roaring lion, seeking someone to devour. Resist him, firm in your faith, knowing that the same kinds of suffering are being experienced by your brotherhood throughout the world.
-1 Peter 5:8-9

Eventually, we will be 316,800 inches into our journey. The halfway point is one of the worst places we can ever be, so we must move swiftly. The halfway point makes us question everything we've done on the journey so far. The devil goes to work at the halfway point because he wants us to stop. He doesn't like what we're becoming. He hates that we're starting to understand our purpose.

When we are halfway, we still have a chance to go back. It's far but not far enough that turning around isn't an option. The problem with turning around halfway, though, is we forget we'll have the same distance to travel, whether we go forward or backward.

We forget the success we've had to that point. The pain we think about hurts our mind. It sucks to know there'll be even more in the last 316,800 inches. But, we can't turn around! As easy as it would be, it wouldn't be rewarding in the end. You may feel safe on the journey back because you'll pass by familiar territory, but you'll be so upset when you arrive back to where you started.

Push past halfway—just one more inch past. You'll then be at 316,801 inches, which means you're now farther from where you started. Once you see you're closer to the destination than to where you started, it'll be easier to keep going. We all have things we feel we should've accomplished by now. The only thing that has stopped us from getting there is ourselves.

So we can confidently say, "The Lord is my helper; I will not fear; what can man do to me?"
–Hebrews 13:6

Stage: The tired period.

Ultimately we know deeply that the other side of every fear is freedom.
–Marilyn Ferguson

Speak it into existence: When the fears and doubts begin to creep into my head, I will put my trust in God and continue to walk forward.

The Center of Her Life

Much can be learned from relationship scenarios we see around us. One that always sticks out to me is the relationship in which the girl gives up everything for a guy who wouldn't do the same for her. All of us have either been part of this scenario or know someone who's been in a relationship like this.

The girl was raised in a home where people taught her what makes superb character. She then goes off to school and forgets it all. Her heart desires to love and be loved, but she makes the mistake of expecting someone to love her in the same way God does. This can't be done because God's love lasts forever and is perfect.

She searches for a man among boys, hoping that, just once, love can be found in the wrong place. All her girlfriends call her crazy, of course, until it's their turn to get lost in the mix. All her guy friends lurk in the back, either waiting for their turn or wondering how she can be fooled so easily. Some guys even take the time to explain the game to her, but she doesn't listen.

She throws away everything her character was built on to satisfy her heart's lusts. With that, God goes away. She pushes God out because she isn't able to listen to and please God. The pressures of living a life that will make her new boy happy are enough in themselves. When God does cross her mind, it makes her feel guilty, so it becomes easier not to think about it.

Deep down, she remains empty. The pain only deepens as the guy she gave it all up for leaves her for his next fix. His next fix will satisfy his desires for a while, but then he'll have to move on again. She now has nothing: no God, no man, no love, just pain.

She tries to cover up the pain. Maybe if she parties hard enough, the pain will go. Maybe if she drinks a lot, she won't think about him anymore. What if she acts like him and moves on to someone else? Will that new guy fill the gap? Maybe he'd be able to give her the love she yearns for.

Nothing works and each time she returns to the same dark place. No matter how many times her friends tell her she's wrong, no matter how many mistakes she makes, she needs to see for herself that what she's been missing all along is God.

The void that God fills can't be filled by anyone else. His love is too much for anyone of this world to replace. When she grounds herself on the word of God again, she begins to change from the inside. When she no longer needs a man for love, she finds the one who loves her for the right reason. She sees the joy she's searched so hard for comes from getting herself in line with God. Once she does this, she can see clearly the importance of finding a man whom God has already straightened out.

How many times do we see this scenario play out in our lives? I have seen this scenario play out, and I've also been the cause of this scenario. The center of your world can actually become another person. The world will teach us this is a good thing. But, God was meant to be the center of everything we do. When we try to replace him with something else, it will bring only temporary happiness.

Money is only satisfying until the second we get it; then we need more.

People can satisfy us, but everyone dies eventually.

Winning as an athlete can make us happy until we lose or our career ends.

Then what?

Athletes' relation to this woman

Keep your life free from love of money, and be content with what you have, for he has said, "I will never leave you nor forsake you."
–Hebrews 13:5

If being an athlete is the center of our world, we'll eventually hurt. Even if we go on to be the greatest athlete ever, eventually our body will fail us, and we'll be left with an empty space. The objective can't be to just win or succeed or make all those dreams and desires come true. There needs to be more. All those things will eventually not be enough.

Other people can see these issues in us, but we struggle to see them ourselves. All of us can think of a person who's giving everything up to be in a relationship or someone who's built his or her entire life around being an athlete. We can point out these people, but it can be so hard to see this in ourselves in moments when we've sunk are teeth too far into our pursuits. This is building our lives on a foundation of sand. It's possible, but it's not steady, nor will the building stand long.

To live for the eternal reward, we need to let go of the now. We need to release all the things we think we need, or want, to be happy or successful. We have to change our hearts and focus on the things that last forever. Jesus and his disciples were always struggling to get others to focus on the unseen, not the seen.

Once we've changed our sights, we must figure out how we can truly glorify God. It needs to be more than just winning; working hard to win is not that pleasing to God. He gives us favor and allows us to do those things, but the real take-away for Christian athletes is to endure through it all. Athletics provides us with plenty of opportunities to struggle and to learn to trust in God for the strength to hold on. When we understand we're athletes to show endurance, we live for a new and much greater reason. Remember the first verse in this book.

Not only that, but we rejoice in our sufferings, knowing that suffering produces endurance, and endurance produces character, and character produces hope and hope does not put us to shame, because God's love has been poured into our hearts through the Holy Spirit who has been given to us.
–Romans 5:3–5

That's what it's really about. Through this process, we might win some, and we might make a lot of money. But, the important part is we do it all knowing the beginning and end of everything we do are for God.

Stage: Breaking.

What oxygen is to the lungs, such is hope to the meaning of life.
–Emil Brunner

Speak it into existence: No matter how hard it may be, I must refocus and keep God at the center of everything I do in my life.

The Boy of Blame to the Man of Dreams

There was once a thirty-year-old man for whom God had great plans. This man always dabbled with helping others but never to the extent to which he was called. He spent his days watching too much TV and Netflix. On his couch is where he was the most comfortable, but he couldn't see how that was holding him back.

His neighbor and good friend was a wise man. His neighbor became disappointed with the man over time because he could see the man wasn't striving to fulfill his purpose. His neighbor knew that pain would be the only way the man would ever change his ways. His neighbor was a skilled electrician, but he also was passionate about cars, so he thought of a master plan.

The neighbor went over to the man's house and discreetly ruined the man's TV. The man was really upset because he really loved his TV, but he had no idea his neighbor had done it. Because he couldn't watch TV, the man then spent his time on Netflix. The man didn't change. His neighbor was still disgruntled, and a week later, went back and did the same thing to the man's computer. The man was in a world of hurt because his TV and his computer had blown out within a week of each other. The man still had no idea his neighbor was doing this.

The man hated his job and getting up every morning to go to a place he hated. He hated his job because it was far from his purpose. He naturally had no passion for his work; he only did it for the money. Money was his God. No matter how much he had, he always wanted more, so he could buy more. He now had no TV and no Netflix, but the pain still wasn't enough for him. He went to Best Buy and spent the remaining $4,000 in his bank account on a new TV and a computer. The man barely had money to get a carton of milk if he needed it. He thought he was happy though because he had his TV back. His life was miserable, but TV helped him forget about it.

The man was happy, but his neighbor was pissed because he'd seen how much potential the man was throwing away. He knew the man had much more to give the world. More pain was needed for the man. A couple days later, the man was driving home from work when his transmission blew out. His neighbor had been under the hood of the man's car the previous night tinkering with some parts. The man didn't have the money to get his car towed, so he had to pull over to the side of the road and walk fifteen miles home.

While he walked, the man cursed his life, cursed his problems, and blamed God for taking everything that seemed good away from him. Once home, the man was so happy to be there and threw himself on the couch to watch TV. He still wasn't ready to see the greatness inside him. It wouldn't be unleashed until the man made changes. Later in the evening, his neighbor checked on him but was still displeased with the man. The man soaked in his sorrows for the night while he attempted to fall asleep on the couch. With no money, no food, and no car, the man was down and out. Yet, he still thought a TV was necessary. More pain was clearly needed.

The next day, the man woke up to find that his furnace was broken. This was the worst thing the man could have happen in the wintertime. The man never once became suspicious of his neighbor because he thought his life was all bad luck.

Fixing this problem would cost the man $500. He only had about four dollars in his bank account, and payday was a week away. His fridge was empty, he had no car to get to work, and he was too lazy to take public transit. The problems in his life were mounting quickly. Finally, he'd had enough of struggling. He had no choice but to cancel his cable and his

Netflix and return the TV to the store. He decided to keep the computer, though, which allowed him to research some new jobs. He was now in his darkest time. Little did he know the light was about to shine.

Embarrassed, the man had to ask his neighbor to drive him to the store to return the TV. This made his neighbor smirk because the neighbor knew the man's life was about to change. They didn't speak much on the drive. It was clear the man was upset. Arriving at the store, his neighbor said just one thing to the man: "Think about the lesson to be learned instead of just the problem." Those simple words left the man thinking for the night.

After a rough day, the man would usually go home and enjoy his TV, but that was no longer an option. He wasn't able to go anywhere. He was freezing because the furnace couldn't be fixed until the following morning. In his anger, he questioned whether God was even real. He'd spent time praying, he'd spent time in church, and he'd once given money to the church, but things weren't turning out the way he'd wanted. He went to sleep lashing out in his anger toward God.

When the morning came, he tried to go through his normal morning routine but couldn't. He went to turn the TV on, forgetting he no longer had one. What he did have now, though, was some extra money. He thought about his neighbor's words and reflected silently on his life for a while. He realized he'd drowned out his own mind for years with wasted activities. He hadn't given himself a chance to just think in a long time.

He was scared of the power of his own thoughts. He realized he'd let his life go to a dark place, which wasn't God's fault. He reflected on all the opportunities he'd had throughout his life that he'd ignored. He'd had an opportunity to minister to some youths, but he'd turned it down. He loved to give back, but he hadn't had time. He'd had a job opportunity that was more aligned with his passions, but he'd turned it down because he would've had to take a few courses. He hated school. He'd had a scholarship offer to continue playing football—his first love—at the Division I level. He'd turned that down because he hadn't wanted to be far from home and his girlfriend at the time. He pondered all of the "what-if" moments.

Focusing on the lesson, the man realized God did have a plan for him, but the man had made many choices that didn't follow that plan. Every time he'd had the chance to get back on the right track, he'd chosen to do something he thought would fit better. Eventually, God left him alone and let him spiral out of control.

How the man spent some of the money from the return of the TV:

- Groceries: $100
- Furnace repair: $500
- Bus pass: $100
- Books: $35
  - *The Magic of Thinking Big* by David J. Schwartz
  - *The One Year Uncommon Life Daily Challenge* by Tony Dungy
  - *The Icarus Deception: How High Will You Fly?* by Seth Godin

The Magic of Thinking Big was to change his mindset. *The Uncommon Life* was to challenge him and his walk with God. *The Icarus Deception* was to help him understand that life is not about being comfortable. Reading these three books changed his perspective on life.

The man stopped making excuses and set out to do the things he'd always been meant to do. He'd always enjoyed painting and drawing, but early on, he'd become discouraged. Throughout his life, many people pushed him to give up on art because there was no money in it. So, he'd stopped pursuing what he loved and started pursuing what he thought others wanted him to do. He'd made decisions solely based on greed and money. He'd taken whichever route he'd thought was the quickest way to the top. The power was in his hands, but his own lazy behaviors had blocked him. He'd built up a way of feeling busy when he really wasn't. It just made him feel better about not doing anything. All of that was about to change from the inside out!

Ten ways the man changed his life for good:

1. He gave more than he ever received.

Online, he found out his local community center was looking for some volunteers. There were art classes for children; he volunteered to help with them, so he could use his talents to give back to others. He saw children who were just like he had been as a child: talented but misguided. They were going through many of the same troubles he'd gone through at that age. He poured his experience into them while they worked on something they were all passionate about.

The man was eventually offered a part-time job at the community center. After months of volunteer work, the program had grown, and they knew he'd had a large part in that. He was now being paid to do something he loved — something he'd have done the rest of his life for free. Although his previous jobs had paid more, the man had gone home every day empty because he knew he wasn't making a difference with his work. He'd spent the money he'd made solely on things to impress people he didn't care about.

What he gave now was much more than art. He gave students hope, he gave them lunches when they were hungry, and he gave them money. Whatever they needed, he was willing to give, even when he couldn't really afford to. His whole mindset changed from "What can you do for me?" to "What can I do for as many people as possible?"

2. He conquered the morning and sacrificed the night.

He'd get up in the morning and spend the first thirty minutes with God. It was something he'd once made excuses about because it hadn't been that important. It had become easy to push to the side. When he began to look at others' lives, he realized it was easy to figure out what was important to them. All he had to do was find those things that they'd never push to the side.

Some people would never put aside family, but they'll easily push God aside. Some people would never put aside money, but they'll push their significant other aside. For this man, he hadn't pushed aside entertaining himself, but he'd pushed pretty much anything else to the side.

He'd been what many would say was "not a morning a person," but he realized that was something he'd made up, so he wouldn't have to do anything in the morning. He now set his alarm for early in the morning, but put it far from his bed. When it went off, he had to get out of bed to go get it. Once his body was cold and his feet had touched the floor, he was up. There was no point in crawling back into bed.

After his thirty minutes with God, he spent time doing what he loved. He would work on his art for about thirty minutes. This is when his mind was fresh, and the ideas just seemed to flow well to him. He'd never known this because, from a young age, he'd counted out the mornings in his life. He started to see that, when he committed to working on his paintings and drawings every day, his talents grew exponentially.

There were times when he had big due dates coming up for his job and for some of the art projects he was working on. He'd stay up as late as necessary to get things done. He realized it was better to show up the next day tired with work completed than to show up with lots of energy but his work not ready. He was willing to sacrifice sleep to do what he said he would do.

3. He pursued what he loved.

He started following the things he knew he loved. His art was just one of those things. He also loved God, so he pursued his relationship with him. He had a girlfriend whom he'd been with for a long time for the wrong reason. He finally gathered the courage to break up with her. He went after the woman he truly loved. Before, he'd only pursued what he thought he wanted. Once he started to pursue what he needed, things fell into place.

He also became more interested in loving others. That meant loving his friends and family to the best of his ability, but it also meant loving his enemies. When people thought about him, he wanted his loving character to be the first thing that came to their minds. Through it all, his ability to endure increased; love made that possible. It's hard to continue doing something when we don't love what we do. Choosing to fall in love with the idea of love brought him a long way.

4. He quit quitting.

He'd become the master of quitting things when they became difficult. His life had been a constant cycle of starts and stops. He now set his sights on finishing everything he started.

He saw others who'd work at the same thing constantly for years. Many times he'd believed they were crazy for doing so. When he looked at those same people years later, they were successful with their pursuits because they'd started and never stopped until they reached that successful moment.

The man decided he was going to be an artist, and he never looked back. He didn't wonder if he'd made the right choice or look back to see if his old job would take him back. Did things get rough? Yes. Was his journey smooth sailing? No. But, because he was now fully committed to his goals, his obstacles weren't a problem. He'd once been good at quitting. It was now time for him to get good at holding on.

5. He earned his entertainment.

Eventually, he had enough money to get Netflix and another TV, but he was a different man. He had no plans to go backward. Instead, he created a system in which he'd keep his entertainment time under control while also encouraging positive work.

He had to earn the right to do things that he wanted to do but didn't need to do. For example, if he wanted to watch an hour of TV, he'd first have to do five hours of artistic development. If he wanted to go out to eat or go to a party, he had to impact the lives of five others.

Every five lives affected earned him an hour of fun time. It seemed ridiculous to others, but he knew if he wanted more fun, all he had to do was help more people.

6. He decided the blame game was for losers.

He stopped blaming God for what he didn't do and started praising God for the many things he did do. He always had a choice over his attitude, and he decided to use that to his advantage. What had happened in the past was in the past – no more blaming other people.

When he looked back at his life, it was clear the problem wasn't in other people but in himself. It wasn't that other people saw the world in the wrong way; he needed to change how he saw other people. Losers blame other people because it's the easiest thing to do. Winners take the road least traveled, no matter how hard it may be.

7. He realized "only if" wasn't real.

He thought of the number of times he'd said,

"I could follow my dreams only if I had more money."
"I could be a much better employee only if my boss would get off my back."
"I would blow up only if someone would take a chance on me."

"Only if" had kept his life on the treadmill. His feet had moved, but he'd gone nowhere. Once he got off the treadmill, he was grounded and could make choices that helped him move closer to his dreams. It took his making a change. Then, others adjusted to the changed person.

He'd always said he'd go after his art dreams only if he had enough savings. He'd wasted years working because he'd been convinced he couldn't make enough money with his art to do what he really wanted to do.

Working had never gotten him closer to his dreams though. The only way to do that was to throw away the "only if" about money and to work toward what he wanted. It may not be the most secure route, but it's worth it.

8. He worked to be the best of the best.

One night, after he'd earned five hours to go out and do something fun, he brought his date to see a magician. Somewhere between the magician's cutting himself in half and escaping from a tank of water where he's sure to die, a strong concept hit the man. This is the misunderstood concept that ruins many pursuits. The man looked around and saw five thousand other audience members. Because each ticket cost $25, that was $125,000 in gross revenue.

That was more money than the man had ever made in a year, and this magician was doing it in one night. He had always wanted to be an artist, but the one line he heard the most from others was "You won't make any money doing that." Yet, he was sitting in a theater watching a magician make over $100,000 a night in a profession in which he'd probably always been told the same thing. The magician could do this because he was good at what he did. Those at the top of their fields are paid well if they're labeled as the best.

9. He honored God with his talents.

When the man was younger, he'd been a talented football player. After giving up a Division I scholarship, he'd tried to play at his local junior college but had suffered a blown anterior cruciate ligament (ACL). At the time, he'd been upset about this and had found himself in a horrible place.

When he thought back on that moment, he realized he'd had a God-given gift he'd used to honor only himself. Football had been his way of building up his name, so he could be popular. Popularity had meant more women would want him, people would give him more things for free, and teachers would be easier on him in school. It'd been all about him and what he could get. He hadn't used his talent correctly. As a result, it had been taken from him.

The man's art gave him a second chance to use his God-given talent. This time, he was going to use it correctly. He wanted to make sure that when people saw how he lived his life and how he worked, it would encourage them to grow in their faith in some way. He knew it would be a struggle every day, but with the strength of God, he knew it would be a battle he'd win.

10. He became a flashlight.

One day, the man was going through some old receipts, and he noticed the one for his furnace repair said "self-inflicted" damage. The man was confused. He called the company and asked questions until he understood. It suddenly hit him that his neighbor had been the one ruining his things. He knew his neighbor was the only one who'd had access to his home to do it.

The man was upset because he couldn't understand what would make his neighbor do such things. He felt they'd always had a good relationship. He thought they'd understood each other well. Over the years, they were best friends, or so the man thought. He went immediately to talk with his neighbor about this, but he kept getting no answer. This only increased his anger.

After not seeing his neighbor for a few weeks, the man found out his neighbor was in the hospital with a bunch of complications. Sadly, before they ever had a chance to talk about this matter, his neighbor passed away. In his mid-sixties, the neighbor had a heart attack and left behind only an ex-wife.

At the funeral, many friends of the man's neighbor got up and spoke of his earlier days. The man found out his neighbor had once been a football star, but he'd given it all up chasing things that came not to matter. Many people had tears in their eyes because they believed the man's neighbor had had more potential than he'd ever lived up to. The neighbor had realized he'd wasted much of his talents, so he'd dedicated his life to helping others avoid making the same mistakes.

The man was in shock at how similar their stories were, and it made sense that they'd been friends all this time. People told story after story about how the neighbor had seen greatness in them and had helped them change their lives. His neighbor had been willing to go to the most extreme measures to help people see the truth.

The man finally realized his neighbor had done those things to help him not make the same mistakes he had. The neighbor had never done those things with the intention of hurting him; he knew the short-term pain would be a long-term gain.

His neighbor had had many pursuits, including law school, but had dropped out. He'd also tried multilevel marketing. The man guessed there were some other pursuits that weren't that important to mention at the funeral. Then, the neighbor's ex-wife got on stage and dropped a bomb on the man. The neighbor had always been interested in and talented with magic. However, everyone close to him, including her, had told him it was a stupid dream because there wasn't money in being a magician. This brought tears to her eyes because she'd stopped her husband from doing something he loved.

The man sat there shocked long after the funeral was done. He realized his neighbor had been so close to him because the man was much like he'd been in his younger days. Ironically, what his neighbor saw in him was the same thing the man saw in the kids at the community center. His neighbor had saved his life by ruining the things he loved and thought he needed. If it weren't for all the pain his neighbor had been through, he would've never understood the man needed saving. All the man could remember is his neighbor's favorite quote: "There is darkness everywhere, so go light it up."

What happens to the man next?

The story could go on, but what happens next is up to your imagination. Whatever you want to happen is what happens next. Strangely enough, our lives work the same way. The story is about the journey. It took the man a lot of mistakes and a lot of pain to reach the point in life where he knew what his purpose was. Success was sure to be his because he could see what he needed, and he was willing to work at it and not let anything derail him.

You might want to hear the story ends with the man's making a million bucks as an artist or his making over $125,000 in one night with his work. If that is the ending you're looking for, you're missing the point. If because of him, even one child turns to God and doesn't give up on his or her dreams, then the man found a successful moment. If one of his students goes on to live some of the dreams he had, then by default, he's the reason for a successful moment. We get caught seeing success as what happens to us, but success paints a much different picture if it's about what others do as a result of us.

Stage: Breaking.

Defeat is a state of mind; no one is ever defeated until defeat has been accepted as a reality.
–Bruce Lee

The steadfast love of the Lord never ceases, his mercies never come to an end; they are new every morning; great is your faithfulness. "The Lord is my portion," says my soul, "therefore I will hope in him." The Lord is good to those who wait for him, to the soul who seeks him. It is good that one should wait quietly for the salvation of the Lord.
–Lamentations 3:22–26

Speak it into existence: All the struggles of my life are preparing me for a greater purpose. I will embrace the pain and learn how to become better, so I can be the person I am supposed to be.

PART 4

Applying This Book To Your Life

Application to Sports and Beyond

What do we do now? We can read all we want about persistence, but when life gets hard, quitting still can look like such a beautiful choice. The negative thoughts will creep into our heads, but we can't let them slide out of our mouths. Negativity can get to our minds, but we can't let it get to our hearts. What goes into our hearts gets pumped to the rest of our body.

I remember talking to my wife (fiancée at the time) when I was really down one day. She'd had no idea what to say to me because I am rarely ever negative. Most people who know me know I'm a positive person. I still want to quit sometimes though because I'm human. I do my best to make sure the things and people around me put me in a position that makes quitting as difficult as possible.

There were many times I had doubts while writing this book. I often thought, "What if my writing isn't good enough? What if I don't know enough about the Bible to make sense of what I'm saying?" I remember wondering if I should even mention God because I'd probably sell more books if I didn't. In reality though, how could I quit when I was writing a book like this?

I created a plan to help me stay the course. I stress to you the following plan does not mean it'll be easy by any means. It just means it will be more possible than ever.

Get Into the Word and Apply It

Do not lay up for yourselves treasures on earth, where moth and rust destroy and where thieves break in and steal, but lay up for yourselves treasures in heaven, where neither moth nor rust destroys and where thieves do not break in and steal. For where your treasure is, there your heart will be also.
–Matthew 6:19–21

The Bible can be confusing. Many times, we read the words, but they don't hit our hearts. Spiritually, I was in a position in which I honestly felt in the dark my last year of college. I didn't know the difference between the truth and a lie, and I was confused. I was upset with God for a while because I felt he'd left me hanging. But, I never gave up on him because he never gives up on us.

The whole time God was breaking down my heart. First, he was telling me I needed to clean up my act for good. "Whoever walks in integrity walks securely, but he who makes his ways crooked will be found out." (Proverbs 10:9) My dad always told me when I was growing up that what was done in the dark would always come to the light.

I was really good at sinning and then asking for forgiveness and acting like everything was cool. True repentance means we ask forgiveness and then turn in a different direction. We work hard to make sure we remove that issue from our lives for good. We can easily make life about finding faults in others, but it's really about finding out what is in our own hearts. When we get up in the morning and look at ourselves in the mirror, it's about what we know is inside us. We can get really good at seeing ourselves for whom we want to be, but once we see ourselves for who we really are, new doors open up to us.

We always have to ask where our treasure is. Even while I was writing this, sitting alone in my room, tears filled my eyes because I had lived my whole life with my treasure in the wrong places. My treasure wasn't in heaven; it was in an athletic career, women, money, ambition, and many other things that won't matter in the end. It's not that those things are bad, but putting those things ahead of God will destroy us from the inside out.

A false balance is an abomination to the Lord, but a just weight is his delight. When pride comes, then comes disgrace, but with the humble is wisdom. The integrity of the upright guides them, but the crookedness of the treacherous destroys them.
–Proverbs 11:1–3

The time I felt I was in the dark spurred me to read the Bible more than ever. During my last year of college, I brought my Bible with me everywhere. When I say my treasure was removed from this world to heaven, I mean, for the first time in my life, I didn't care how I performed as an athlete. The moment was not the end of my career, just a change in where my heart resided.

The darkness never wins. It wasn't long before my world became light. But, what good is light if I just shine it on my own life? We need to make the Word the most important part of our lives. Be confident that, if someone asks you a question about the Gospel, you can answer it. If you can't answer it, dig into your Bible until you find the answer with confidence. To put this in simple terms, God represents the rock. Anything we build off of it is destined to fall apart. Start your purpose with God, and end your purpose with God.

Have Someone Hold You Accountable

My friend Akeem Haynes is a Canadian sprinter from Calgary, Alberta, Canada. We both made the Olympic team in 2012. Before that trip, however, we went to Mexico for the Under 23 North American, Central American, and Caribbean Athletic Association Championship. We were roomies, and it was our first time meeting each other. From there, we traveled together to Monaco, Germany, and finally England. We became great friends on the journey. What really cemented our friendship though was a common pain we shared. That pain happened to us at the Olympic Games, but that story is told later in this book.

We hold each other accountable to putting God first in our lives in all that we do. We understand each other's pains because we went through some of it together. We constantly talk about life because we know we'll just make a joke out of it and help each other bounce back. Akeem likes to write and motivate others too. In many ways, we're on the same level. He's been vital in my progression from a boy to a man. This just happened naturally for us. We never went to each other and asked to be held accountable.

We all need someone to encourage us, but we also need someone who keeps it real and tells us what we need to hear. Without this person, it's so easy to fall back into old ways. We never want to have to tell our accountability partners that we gave up. That could have an impact on them and make them give up. We don't want that to happen. The worst idea we can ever get is that pain is best endured alone. Nothing changes us faster than exposing our issues to others. We have a person we want to be, but whenever we slip up, we try and hide it because of what people might say. We strive to uphold this perfect image, but when we hide things in the dark, it allows us to continue our behavior.

We always remind each other that, no matter what happens, God is always on our side. We may not get what we want, but we help each other understand God has a bigger plan.

The best way to hold yourself accountable is to partner with someone you trust. You should be on the same levels in life, and it shouldn't be a loved one. We're never meant to suffer alone. Call on your brothers and sisters in Christ and stick together.

This is why we, as athletes, have training partners. It's not impossible to train alone, but we need someone who understands our pain to help pick us up when we're down. On those days when we only have one rep left, our training partner will encourage us to keep going, no matter how much it hurts.

We can also have people who hold us accountable from an understanding that turns into a friendship. I have a friend who wrestled at Iowa State while I was there. His name is Kyven Gadson. Kyven and I don't talk all the time; we don't play the same sport and may not even have the same interests. What we do have is a common love for Jesus Christ and a mutual respect we won't tear down.

We have a similar fire. Because of that, we always build each other up. When I first became his friend, he was struggling with a shoulder injury. I felt his pain because I'd been in his shoes the year before: an athlete with great expectations who just never seemed to be healthy. I used my pain and poured it into him. He endured to eventually become an All-American. I won't tell the rest of his story, and I didn't ask him to write one for this book because I know he has his own book in him. When I saw him get through that pain, though, it inspired me to be better. It made me want to go to the Olympics because I knew that, if I did it, he'd be inspired to do it also. Seeing him do it would only bring more joy to my life.

That is the beauty of accountability. It makes everyone better. It never tears anyone down. It's not about being best pals and doing everything together. It's about being brothers or sisters in Christ and always seeing the greatness in another person. When Jesus talked with people, he might have convicted them of their sins, but it was only because he saw what they could become. You must find someone to hold you accountable — when you fall, they'll catch you.

Let us hold fast the confession of our hope without wavering, for he who promised is faithful. And let us consider how to stir up one another to love and good works, not neglecting to meet up together, as is the habit of some, but encouraging one another, and all the more as you see the day drawing near.
–Hebrews 10:23-25

Speak it into existence: I will find someone to hold me accountable, and I will hold him or her accountable as we spur each other on to love and good deeds.

Mentor Others

Do not reprove a scoffer, or he will hate you; reprove a wise man, and he will love you. Give instruction to a wise man, and he will still be wiser; teach a righteous man, and he will increase in learning.
–Proverbs 9:8–9

One of the most effective ways to ensure you never lose hope is to mentor someone else. I don't care who asks me a question because, if I can help, I will. No matter how annoying or how many times a person contacts me, I'll try my best to be there for him or her. I give people my number, so they can text or call me anytime. I do this primarily because I really love to help, but my second reason is that I understand how important it is to have people who look up to you. It's not about feeding my ego; it simply makes quitting much more difficult.

Imagine if someone's been coming to you for years for marriage advice. That person looks up to your relationship as an example, but then that person finds out you just got divorced. When you look up to someone, but that person gives up, it hurts you and the other person. If you're the person being looked up to, you have to face the other person and explain a bull crap reason for giving up. I say bull crap because, when someone looks up to you, no matter what your reason for quitting, it'll sound hypocritical and stupid.

I've always strongly believed we're all in a position to mentor another person. No matter where we are in life, someone is out there working to be right where we are right now. I proved that with this book. I didn't ask every superstar I could think of to write for this book. I asked people who've been broken over and over. People who may not be household names, but every day they still make a difference. They may have thought their story was insignificant, but it's now being read by someone and because of that story, the reader won't give up.

One gives freely, yet grows all the richer; another withholds what he should give and only suffers want.
–Proverbs 11:24

Speak it into existence: Someone wants to get to my position. I will find that person and give him or her everything I can while expecting nothing in return.

Remember the Life After Death

A couple of years ago, I wrote an article on Cover Ground about the famous life after death. It all started when John Carlos came to Iowa State to talk to a few athletes. If you don't know who John Carlos is, look him up on the Internet right now.

Carlos pointed out a kid who was an athlete on the track team and asked him what he wanted to be when he was finished with school. The kid said he wanted to be a runner. Carlos looked at him confusedly because he wanted more from the kid than that. Carlos wanted to know what the kid had to offer the world other than his athletic talents. This student-athlete truly was lost though; all he knew was he wanted to run. At the time, that's all the kid could see. He'd never had a plan for his life after death, and it came back to bite him hard later. If you haven't figured it out yet, the life after death is our lives once sports are long gone.

My point is that everything connects in life. It's not about being an athlete, yet it's all about being an athlete. It's about what the experiences of being an athlete have built us into. If we hold tight to what being an athlete has done for us, then the truth is we'll never stop being one. How could we ever stop?

Being an athlete teaches us patience, hard work, perseverance, teamwork, and so much more. Those traits in themselves benefit not only athletes but also all humans. In other words, being an athlete gives us the tools to pursue God or anything that comes from God.

At some point, we're all called to move on from sports, and we'll no longer be athletes. That's not always a case of quitting. It's never good when we see people who've forgotten what being an athlete has taught them. They become so wrapped up in their pursuits they forget what God provided to them through sports.

We can't forget what sports has given us. It's more than hope; it's the will to fight for hope. It's more than hard work; it's the ability to give everything we have. It's that feeling when we know this might be our last game ever. It might be our last opportunity to be surrounded by our team. It's that feeling that sums up years of sacrifice and pain.

It's that feeling when we dig so deep that 100 percent is not enough. One hundred percent is a joke on that day; we laugh at the thought of giving a mere 100 percent. We think of the missed opportunities. We think of the days when we could've given more. We're ashamed because, on that day, we'd give anything to have all those other days back.

When we can take how we felt on that day and pour it into the rest of our lives, we'll have no problem holding on.

When we can remember all the coaches and mentors who poured everything they knew into us, then we'll have no problem holding on.

We'll remember all the times we were hurt and had to watch from the sidelines. We'll remember the broken bones, bloody noses, torn ligaments, concussions, bruises, jammed fingers, bone spurs, pulled muscles, contusions, cuts, and stiches. When we remember the pain, we'll have no problem coming alongside others when they're hurting.

When we remember the tough losses, and the inches we were away from victory, we'll have no problem coming along someone who's ready to quit and whisper, "Try one more time."

When we end a season and can look back and think of the friendships we made, the bonds that'll never be broken, and the inside jokes that only certain people can understand, we'll easily understand it was never about winning or losing.

All along, it was about giving our all and using every bit of talent God blessed us with. It was always about loving others while working as hard as we could to honor God.

Now there are varieties of gifts, but the same Spirit; and there are varieties of service, but the same Lord; and there are varieties of activities, but it is the same God who empowers them all in everyone.
–1 Corinthians 12:4–6

So, whether you eat or drink, or whatever you do, do all to the Glory of God.
–1 Corinthians 10:31

Speak it into existence: Once an athlete always an athlete because of what God has taught me through the years of being one. In the same way, I will glorify him as an athlete just as I will glorify him after.

Use the Pain

We're going to hurt some people, and some people are going to hurt us. No person is going to beat us up as much as life will though. It's unpredictable and unfair. We try so hard to master it, but every time we think we have it all figured out, we're reminded of how broken and imperfect we are. This is why we need Jesus. He completes us. He fills the gap between who we are and the perfection we hope to attain but never can.

We're often like cars without gas. Cars don't go anywhere without gas; people don't go anywhere without pain. Some of the pain hurts so badly; just the thought of it brings tears to our eyes.

We've already been through the pain, so why not use it? Don't we make meals out of the food we have left in the fridge? Or, do we insist on buying more and letting what we already paid for go to waste? We have to use what we already have, and pain is something we have in abundance.

Using our pain is essential for endurance because it helps us get away from being self-absorbed. To use our pain, it first takes acceptance, and then it takes having a greater purpose. To help educate another person using our pain, we have to let go of how it hurt us and understand how it made us better. Once we understand our pain, we can manipulate it.

Get the most from your pain

Would you ever fill up your car with gas and then never drive it again? No way! I remember so many times during my childhood when my dad drove a car that was on its last legs — busted down old cars. He once had a car so jacked up the horn only worked when he turned left.

Dad hated having to fill up the tanks of these cars because he knew they could be nothing more than scrap parts at any time. He didn't want a full tank in a car that couldn't be driven anywhere. My dad tried to get everything he possibly could out of his cars, but he also wanted to use every drop of gas he had left. Some people have the luxury of knowing they have money, so they don't have to get the most out of things. That is the beauty in being broke though. It's amazing how pain, which is often seen as a negative, can have a beautiful side to it like that.

When we're broke, the pain teaches us to make every dollar we have go as far as possible. It had to have been painful for my dad to see other people always have new cars while his were breaking down. I learned a lot from those moments though. I learned about getting the most out of life. My dad borrowed a car from a friend at one point. Of course, as soon as he got the car, it began to have problems. When these issues began, the car had a full tank of gas. My dad said he'd siphon the gas out of the tank and hold it in his mouth if he had to.

He was joking, but it was a point I took to heart. The lesson for me was about getting every last drop out of what we invest in. There's no reason to leave one drop of gas in any tank. If we want it bad enough, if the pain has hurt us bad enough, we'll suck that gas out and hold it in our mouths. Then, we'll funnel it into another vehicle. We won't waste anything. Try to approach life like that. Treat the 86,400 seconds you're given each day in that way. Get every last drop out of them.

When we play sports, if all we see is the chance to win, we're not even getting half of what we could get out of it. If that's the case, we've left gas in the tank. If we only see getting every last drop as being what we can get for ourselves, there's still plenty of gas left in the tank.

Every day of practice and every game or competition provide you with an opportunity to lift up and encourage another person. That feels better than winning, and it was the beauty of much of my pain as an athlete. I realized that, after every single game or meet, someone was pissed off with his or her performance, so I always tried my best to encourage that person. That felt better than winning. That's sustainable through life. Winning is never sustainable. Even the greatest of the greats lose at some point in life.

God never took any shortcuts in making each of us. We were made in his image. Every practice and competition provides the opportunity to go out there and take no shortcuts. That too is sustainable. We can choose not to take shortcuts for the rest of our lives. We can't win for the rest of our lives though.

Turn your pain into greatness

How do we use the pain? How do we take something that hurts and use it to propel our lives forward? Before we can use the pain, we must first accept that it exists. We can get caught up in believing that pain is weakness, something that only quitters look to. Pain is really the opposite of that. Winners admit to pain and find ways to make it work.

When Michael Jordan (MJ) played in the famous "Flu Game," he didn't act as if nothing was wrong with him. He knew just how bad he felt, but he turned it around and used it to his advantage. Instead of saying, "I can't play because I'm sick," he played knowing his game with the flu was still better than that of his opponents playing healthy. MJ thought about the parents who'd used all the money they had to buy a ticket, so their kids could see him play. He accepted the pain and used it to destroy his opponent. Just when the other team thought MJ was up against the ropes, he came out swinging and caught them by surprise. MJ proved he could endure.

Learn from the pain you cause others

We can even use the pain we put on other people. I have plenty of examples of this in my own life. I have hurt women by being dishonest. I have hurt a lot of them by being greedy. My old way of thinking looked something like this. If someone pointed out my faults to another person and caused that person to be upset with me, I'd immediately go after the person who'd opened his or her mouth, instead of looking in the mirror to see if it was actually true. My mindset was focused on who was doing me wrong, no matter how much wrong I was doing to others.

Thinking like that never breed's growth; it only creates further destruction. The issue was never the woman; the issue was never the other people who told the truth. I realized I was the one telling lies, so I was the issue.

These pains changed my life because they showed me how good God is. Many of these girls have forgiven me, and every one I asked even helped me with this book. That is love, to go to someone who hurt you deeply and help them out regardless. I thank God for putting forgiveness in many of our hearts.

Take the pain you've dished out to others and do everything you can to make it right. Let the person you used to be drive you to keep pushing toward the person you're becoming. Pain is the best way to change because it hurts. Sometimes, the worst type of hurt is the one you put on others' shoulders. When you can look back and smile on those situations because they're so far from the person you are now, that's a successful moment for your soul.

This all applies to being a better athlete because it relates to everything in life. If we want to be diligent as athletes, we must be diligent in everything we do. We can't go home and behave with no diligence and expect that it won't show up in our training. If we want to be truthful with our teammates and coaches, it requires our being truthful in everything we do.

If we want to know what we're really like, we have to look not only at what we do when the lights are on us but also at everything we do. We must look at all of our behavior: How we respect others, how others respect us, what we do with our free time, how we act around strangers, how we act around friends, how we clean, and how we talk to family. We must especially look at how we handle adversity.

All these things add up and build the character we need as athletes to endure anything. We can't separate parts of our lives because they all rub off on each other. If we can't remember to read our Bible every day, we'll forget to do important things in other aspects of our lives every day. When we have trouble hanging on to our pursuits, we must look back at our history of endurance. Do we quit often? When we allow God to work in us, he'll change the fiber of our being.

Know that all pain comes with a lesson

From my middle school through university years, I suffered a broken tibia that required two surgeries, an avulsion fracture of my hip, three fractures of my L5, two pulled hamstrings, a pulled groin, and tendinitis of the sesamoid bones. I'd also had one of the worst cases of mono some doctors had ever seen.

I used to ask myself all the time why this stuff kept happening to me. But, when we ask "Why me?" we always ask the wrong question. The correct questions are "What can I learn from this, and how can I use this information to make another's life better?"

When we start asking those questions, we begin to see different results in our lives. From all my injuries, I asked what I could learn. From all the therapists and people I'd met in dealing with the injuries, I'd already learned a lot about the human body. I'd learned plenty of reasons why those injuries happened in the first place. I read books, and I almost became obsessed with learning more about athletic injuries. I studied yoga, Pilates, stretches, weight training, massage therapy, and anything else I thought could benefit athletes.

I learned to stay healthy by holding myself accountable for my own body. Just like the problems I'd caused with women, injuries were no longer the responsibility of someone else. Injuries were something I could always control if I chose to work at it. It didn't matter whether that was true. What mattered and always will is the frame of mind we adopt in life.

How can I help other people? is the second question I asked. From this question, I created Cover Ground and began writing to help athletes. I shocked myself with how much I actually could help. Ironically, if it weren't for Cover Ground, I wouldn't have had the confidence to write this book.

When people asked me questions or they were feeling down about an injury, I knew how to help them. What started as one of my issues turned into a way I could help other people. The result: Other people could learn from my mistakes. Others had an athlete whom they could go to with many questions, knowing I understood their pain.

When things go wrong, ask the correct questions:

1. What can I learn from this?
2. How can I use what I've learned to help others?

Use the pain; don't go through it all for nothing

"My grace is made sufficient for you, for my power is made perfect in weakness." Therefore I will boast all the more gladly of my weaknesses, so that the power of Christ may rest upon me. For the sake of Christ, then, I am content with weaknesses, insults, hardships, persecutions, and calamities. For when I am weak, then I am strong.
–2 Corinthians 12:9–10

Kill Your Fears

For God gave us a spirit not of fear but of power and love and self-control.
-2 Timothy 1:7

Success seems to be connected with action. Successful people keep moving. They make mistakes, but they don't quit.
-Conrad Hilton

We must remind ourselves on a daily basis that fear is not of God. His goal is not to make us scared of how we're going to make it. His goal is to make us faithful that he will get us through anything. Fear blocks us from doing what we're supposed to do. It paralyzes us and prevents us from taking action. Instead of thinking we're enough, fear drives us to focus on why we aren't enough. The only way to ensure we never lose hope is to make sure we're ready and willing to walk through that fire of fear.

Our goals are on the other side of a busy highway. Crossing the traffic won't be easy because we know a passing car could end our lives. We sit at the side of the road waiting for the right time, but we quickly realize there is no right time—there never will be. We just have to push ourselves out there and run on faith.

We can't stand to be in this spot for another minute. We've been in the same place for a while, and it's crowded. The only way out for us is to cross the highway. Cars have killed some people who've tried to cross. That scares the rest from trying. No one has any idea what's on the other side because the few who've made it have never come back, nor have they tried. Maybe we'll get across and find it's not all we thought it'd be. Then again, if we cross, we'd at least know, and it may lead us to a better place.

When we finally have the courage to take that first step, we jump out into traffic, starting and stopping to let cars go by. We have faith no one is driving on the line or changing lanes. Before we know it, we feel grass. We feel like we've finally made it!

We forget that traffic goes in both directions, meaning we have to do the same thing all over again. This is what endurance is really about. Taking the first step is tough, but a lot of people still do it. It's hard but not hard enough to weed out the weak. As in the journey of 633,600 inches, we have to look at how far we've come instead of how far we have left to travel.

Being in the middle of the road means there's the same distance on both sides of us now. One side leads to freedom; the other side leads to comfort. We're never meant to be scared of the unknown. We fear the unknown because that's where greatness resides. Greatness doesn't lay its head to sleep every night in the places we're most comfortable. If it did, we'd all be great by now.

Greatness is in the places to which we are terrified to travel. Greatness taunts us because we can see it, but we can't touch it. We can hear it saying to us, "How badly do you want me?" We allow fear to destroy our hope. Fear disconnects us from life because we're no longer who we're supposed to be. It's like our souls never stop walking forward. Our souls don't feel fear; they just know progress. It's time we catch up to our souls.

Ultimately we know deeply that the other side of every fear is freedom.
–Marilyn Ferguson

Feed Your Hope

Blessed be the God and Father of our Lord Jesus Christ, the Father of mercies and God of all comfort, who comforts us in all our affliction, so that we may be able to comfort those who are in any affliction, with the comfort with which we ourselves are comforted by God. For as we share abundantly in Christ's sufferings, so through Christ we share abundantly in comfort too. If we are afflicted, it is for your comfort and salvation; and if we are comforted, it is for your comfort, which you experience when you patiently endure the same sufferings that we suffer. Our hope for you is unshaken, for we know that as you share in our sufferings, you will also share in our comfort.
–2 Corinthians 1:3–7

Hear my cry, O God, listen to my prayer; from the end of the earth I call to you when my heart is faint. Lead me to the rock that is higher than I, for you have been my refuge, a strong tower against the enemy.
–Psalm 61:1–3

Every time in our lives when we're ready to give up on something that we aren't supposed to give up on, it's because our hope has been starved. God controls all hope and encouragement. If we lose those things, we're more likely to lose our connection to him. If all the water in the world ran dry, we'd have to use rainwater. The problem is, if it doesn't rain, we won't have any water.

Without water, people become dehydrated, food can't be cooked, crops can't grow, and animals die. Water is vital for life. There'd be no point in going to our friends for water or hoping we'd magically find water. Our hope would be in the wrong place. Our hope needs to be in the rain, the source of all the water. Even if we saved up and stored water, eventually we'd run out if it didn't rain.

This is what our endurance often looks like. We run out of it, and we turn to the wrong people. Your mom may be the first person you turn to, but what happens when your mom gets smacked by life and loses hope? That is the wrong place to turn.

Turn to God. He'll be more than happy to provide you with more endurance. He doesn't want you to die of dehydration; he doesn't want to see the land run dry. What he wants is to see you turn to him to fulfill your needs.

For me to write this book, my hope didn't come from me. My hope was that God would power me with enough endurance to see this book to completion. When I put my hope in him and prayed for him to put hope in others, then I went to my friends and asked them for any hope they could spare. Put your faith in the source not the beneficiary of the source.

PART 5

The Athlete Stories

There is no greater agony than bearing an untold story inside you.
–Maya Angelou

Count it all joy, my brothers, when you meet trials of various kinds, for you know that the testing of your faith produces steadfastness. Let steadfastness have its full effect, that you may be perfect and complete, lacking in nothing.
–James 1:2–4

The people behind each of the following stories took the time to write their stories and send them to me. I can't thank them enough for doing this! This book wouldn't be the same if they weren't such amazing people. I could have interviewed them and written their stories myself, but I knew the stories would be much more powerful told in the words of the people involved. I provided the same guidelines for writing to everyone. It's such a blessing to see how differently each person tells his or her story. We can all learn something from them.

Taylor Goetz

Hometown: Ankeny, Iowa
Sport: Volleyball
Age at time of story: 18- 21

Any athlete would probably agree that quitting is one of the worst things you can do. Athletes don't quit, and if you do, then you aren't strong enough, and you're a loser. The truth is, I did quit, and that's the hardest part of my athletic career I've been through.

My name is Taylor Goetz, and I play volleyball at Iowa State University. Coming in as a freshman, I was like any typical athlete: Big headed and thinking I was going to be the one to do something big in the four years I play in college. I was going to make this program better; I was going to start and be one of the best. It's funny how a mindset can be so different when you're living for yourself instead of for God. Well, God quickly pushed me off my high horse by giving me the most difficult two years of my life. My freshman and sophomore years brought me to rock bottom. After I quickly realized I wasn't going to play and I wasn't as good as I thought, my confidence was knocked right down to the floor. I'd lived for volleyball my entire life. When I realized I not only wasn't succeeding, but that I also had no confidence toward the game whatsoever, I knew that something in my life was missing. How could a game bring me to such a low point? There had to be something bigger than getting my fulfillment out of volleyball. Looking back now, I know that God was just starting me off on a journey that would change me and help me to see him, my Savior.

Throughout freshman year, I started going to the volleyball Bible study. Something about that hour of the week created an absolute peace in my heart, and it set me on fire for God. The following verse is one of one of the first verses I memorized.

Not only so, but we also rejoice in our sufferings, because we know that suffering produces perseverance; perseverance, character; and character, hope. And hope does not disappoint us because God has poured out his love into our hearts by the Holy Spirit whom he has given us.
–Romans 5:3–5

This is one of my favorite verses. It changed my mindset for sophomore year. I took it literally on the court. Every day when I'd feel frustrated in the game, I'd just think about persevering and not giving up. Although I wasn't the best or most athletic on the team, I could be the hardest worker. And starting with that led to the other characteristics in the verse. God's word is truly amazing because, once I began to have the mindset that I'd work hard and persevere through any drill, practice, or mental slump I was going through, I realized I was becoming a better person — my character was transforming.

This part of the transformation happened more on the inside than on the outside because I've never been one to openly act out in a way that would strike people as having bad character. But, the thoughts on the inside of me are what changed; I became less negative. This was the ultimate turning point for my career. The mind is so powerful, and whatever thoughts you feed yourself daily will become reality. I didn't even realize how many thoughts went through my head each day that had no benefit to me whatsoever. As I started calling myself out on these thoughts, I made it a point to cast them to God and change the negative thoughts to ones that would encourage me. In 1 Peter 1:5-7, it says, "Cast all your anxieties on Him, because he cares for you." So every time my mind would go in a negative direction, I'd give it up to God and be done with it. The most beautiful part of this to me comes next:

hope.

Hope was the part of this journey that was hidden from me for a long time. Although my relationship with God was building, I was still having a hard time fully giving up everything on the court to him. I still felt as though the court was where the devil had the most hold on me, and I couldn't shake that feeling. With a lot of thought, I decided the best thing for me to do was to stop playing volleyball. At the end of the day, I realized I'd lost my passion for it, and I felt my life needed to go in a different direction. Ultimately, I did what every athlete is trained not to do from the moment they start playing a sport: I quit.

I didn't play my sophomore spring season, and in a time that I thought would bring me a lot of growth, I became lost. I now didn't have the identity of being a volleyball player. The entire spring I went in and out with my relationship with God because the ways I knew him and relied on him were taken away from me. I didn't go to Bible study anymore because I didn't play anymore. My relationships with my teammates were completely different, and I had too much free time. I'd try to get involved in different things, but for some reason everything kept falling through. I was at a point in my life where I was having a hard time feeling God's presence.

To make a long story short, God was just preparing me again for something incredible. At the end of spring season, when the team had just wrapped up its last game, I received an e-mail from my coach asking me to rejoin the team. Athletically, the team had every player it needed, but my coach asked if I'd rejoin because the team needed another leader with character. As I read this e-mail, I knew in my heart that God was at work. I've never felt his presence so immensely as I did when I read that e-mail. I realized God was using volleyball to build our relationship again, and he wanted me to lean on him even though I didn't fully understand what he was doing with me.

It was as if the first time around I hadn't fully gotten it, and I knew he wanted to give me another chance to finish what I'd started. He wanted me to completely surrender to him this time. God was bringing Romans 5:3-5 back into the picture because I'd experienced perseverance and character, but I had yet to experience hope. The mindset of the season for me began with the word "hope."

My junior season came, and after preseason, I was voted one of three captains on the volleyball team. I worked hard at building relationships with my team. My reasons for being there this time around were completely different. To me, although I might not have had the attention, the playing time, or the popularity that came from being a star volleyball player, I was there to be a leader in different ways. Hope gave me a joy, a joy that couldn't be taken from me. Of course, certain things didn't necessarily make me happy, and I had my days when I struggled, but those things couldn't shake the joy from me, or the hope given to me by the Holy Spirit. My mindset was a lot broader now. I had an eternal perspective knowing that ultimately volleyball means nothing. When it's my time to be judged, God is not going to care how many games I played in, how many assists I had in the season, or what my win-loss record was. He cares about me. He cares about my relationship with him and how I can reflect his light onto this earth.

My passion isn't supposed to be volleyball; it's supposed to be bringing God the glory he deserves. Although it was hard to see it when it was happening, I can now look back and see specific examples of how he's been present at each step of my journey. God is always at work, and he's always present. He loves us not for anything we do in our athletic career. He has a plan.

Brian Dzingai

Hometown: Harare, Zimbabwe
Sport: Track and field
Age at time of story: 27

To give anything less than your best, is to sacrifice the gift.
– Steve Prefontaine

It was December 2007. I was in the middle of my base training and had just graduated from Florida State University with my master's degree. I had a standing offer letter from Deloitte to start working in Atlanta in January 2008, yet I was in the midst of training for my second Olympic Games. I had come off probably my best year on the International Association of Athletics Federations (IAAF) circuit in 2007 and was still unable to renew my contract with Nike, so taking the Deloitte offer was the logical solution. This was an opportunity to begin earning a steady and reliable income. It made sense.

My family was in the United States for my cousin's graduation, and they were imposing upon me to stick with Deloitte. However, deep inside, I wanted another opportunity to take a crack at the Olympics. Back in 2004, coming off my senior season in college, I had gone to the Olympics in Athens and had performed dismally. But, I had still finished the year as the seventh-fastest individual in the 200-meter dash that year.

I'd always known if Coach Ken Harden and I planned it right, we'd have a legitimate opportunity of making the final. That's all we could ask for, an opportunity to be in the Olympic final. I called Deloitte; they were surprisingly ecstatic and deferred my start date to October 2008.

The spring of 2008 rolled around, and I was training well for the upcoming summer. Being an international student comes with all sorts of immigration complications. For the past four seasons, I'd traveled back and forth to Europe in the summertime when I was competing, which gave me a chance to fly back to Tallahassee and get some quality training with my coach every two weeks. However, because I'd graduated, the situation had changed. I either was misinformed or I misunderstood the instructions I'd received from the international student office.

I decided to make a trip to Juarez, Mexico, which shares a border with El Paso, Texas, to renew my American student visa. Unbeknown to me, Juarez was, and probably still is, one of the most dangerous drug towns in Mexico. I'd planned my trip well and had a guide who took a group of people to the United States consulate in Juarez. This was by appointment basis only.

When my turn arrived at the booth to be interviewed, my visa application was denied. Not only was it denied, but the consular office also went ahead and canceled my current visa, as my presence there was in violation of my current visa status. What did this mean? As of that moment, this meant that, with the little I had (i.e., sixty dollars, an American Express card, and my backpack, not to mention I was wearing just shorts), I had to find my way back to Harare, Zimbabwe, via Mexico City from Juarez.

My whole world had collapsed. What was going to become of my Olympic dream? I started thinking that maybe I should have stuck with the Deloitte offer. What was going to become of my car and my other personal belongings? The time was about three thirty in the afternoon. At that point, I had no right of entry back into the United States. I promptly made my way back to the border. I remember this vividly. The border was busy around rush hour with people commuting back and forth to the United States and Mexico. The border officers were irritable at that time of day.

When my turn came to speak to one of the officers, I started stuttering, trying to explain my situation. He wasn't trying to hear my story and told me I had to figure out a way to get myself back to Zimbabwe. I left and went and booked a place at a local Holiday Inn. I lay on my bed gazing at the ceiling. My Verizon phone wasn't catching any reception at that point, so I couldn't call anyone. I clearly remember that, for the first time in my life, there was nothing any individual could do to help me. Nothing. I couldn't call anyone. I couldn't reach out to anyone. I was in this foreign land in which I knew no one.

Trust me, I became a prayer warrior. I prayed in my hotel room for at least forty-five minutes, asking God to intervene and make a plan in a time when everything seemed impossible. I decided to go back to the border after seven o'clock that evening, knowing the rush hour craze would be over. Perhaps the officers then would have the patience to listen to my situation. When I arrived, I remember telling myself to pray. There was a restroom, and inside those restrooms the toilets were pit latrines. That was by far one of the worst restrooms I'd ever come across. I knelt down and prayed, asking for God's intervention.

I went back and joined the line. When my turn came, I was directed to a different officer than the one I'd dealt with earlier. I asked the new officer if he'd allow me to sit back down, so I could deal with the same officer from earlier. I didn't want to make it seem like I was avoiding the prior officer, trying my luck with somebody else. The new officer agreed. When my turn came again to go to the earlier officer, I told him my story again and again. He wasn't keen on helping me out. I begged him to call a supervisor in case he could do something to help me out. As he was telling me no, a supervisor walked by and noticed I'd been talking to this officer for a while. He walked up and asked what was going on. I told him my story and how I'd been misinformed and all I was trying to do was to prepare for the Beijing Olympics. This man simply went online and corroborated some information I'd told him about my being an athlete. He immediately gave me a thirty-day B-1 visa. He told me to get back to the United States, sort out my affairs, and leave the country. God is good. My prayers had been answered.

I knew that, once I was back in the United States, with the help of a lawyer, I'd be able to extend my stay and figure out the best visa to apply for. I returned to the United States without having to extend my B-1 visa, was awarded an H-1 visa through Deloitte, and was able to travel freely that summer.

This is only two-thirds of the story though. When I returned from Mexico, I found out the Zimbabwean Athletic Federation was trying to ban me from participating in the Olympics because of an incident at the World Championships in Osaka. (I'd demanded professionalism from the president of the federation.) Their timing was strategic, as they were trying to make it difficult for me to appeal any ruling. I tried to fight them and even received word from them that the IAAF had been notified I wasn't allowed to compete in Europe, but I still competed all summer long, including in a few of the Diamond Leagues. Unbeknown to me, they had zero jurisdiction on the Olympic Games and couldn't effectively ban me. The rest is history: I went to Beijing and placed fourth.

Upon returning from my Beijing performance, I was awarded a green card based on my "extraordinary ability." That process took less than six weeks. God is good, all the time. All the time, God is good. God provided all of the support because no man could get it done for me.

This experience made me a tougher individual, and I believe what my coach always said to me, "B, there is always a way." I really believe "impossible is nothing," and "I can do all things through him who gives me strength."

I can do all things through Christ who strengthens me.
–Philippians 4:13

Anonymous Woman #1

Sport: Athletics
Age at time of story: 19–24

In God I trust, I will not be afraid.
–Psalm 56:4

Psalm 56:4 is on my back because God always has our backs, no matter what we're dealing with. We just need to trust and believe.

I didn't necessarily have a hard time, more so a drastic change in lifestyle. Things had affected me outside of track that essentially affected my training and performances because of the mental aspect of it all. And, I didn't know how to deal with the situation. Instead of finding the answer in the Word and trusting in God, I tried to find love in the clubs, in men, in drugs, and in alcohol.

In college I was faced with many challenges, as many student-athletes are. First, I had my first real heartbreak my second year of college. I didn't know how to handle what I was feeling. Many girls can attest to a serious breakup. It seems like the pain will never go away. Roughly around the same time, my mother called me to tell me that my father was leaving her. This was something I wasn't so surprised about because of their history, but it was certainly still painful.

My mother would call me constantly to confide in me, so I pretended to be brave because I felt I needed to be strong for her and help keep her together. But the more I tried to keep her together on the phone, the more I couldn't keep myself together off of the phone.

At the time, I did believe in God and had grown up Christian, so to speak. I'd been baptized at thirteen and went to church every Sunday, but I didn't focus my life on living a Godly lifestyle. I didn't have the tools I needed to have faith and trust in God. I wasn't polished, which means not knowing the Word and not trusting and having the knowledge that God is the answer and that he'd see me through.

I looked everywhere else for comfort and healing except to him! I was desperate to get rid of the pain quickly, and I did that by first drinking alcohol until I was intoxicated and going out with my girls on a Saturday night. Then, it turned into Fridays and Saturdays, to eventually starting on Thursday nights, and even Wednesday nights sometimes. But, all of it wasn't enough because there was still a deep hole inside my heart.

I looked to men for comfort, bringing home a guy here and there, hoping the pain would disappear. It became a "thing" for me. My lifestyle was so out of control I didn't even recognize myself anymore. I'd been living this lifestyle for a good year, just lost, digging a deeper hole as the days went by and getting to a point where I had zero passion for school, and I had zero passion for track.

I'd lost my morals, and I'd lost any ambition to succeed in life. When I went home for summer break, I'd decided not to go back to school. I knew my life wasn't healthy, but I knew I wouldn't be strong enough to change my lifestyle if I went back to where it had started.

Every Sunday I'd go to church with my mother. And you know those sermons where you feel that the message is speaking directly at you? Well, that is how I felt, every single Sunday. I was on my knees crying during and after every message, feeling the built-up pain and anger.

I was angry at my mother, at my father, at my ex, but mostly, I was angry at myself for not treating myself with respect and having sex with different men and for abusing my body with alcohol and drugs. I realized so many people go through hurt and a lot worse than what I'd dealt with. It wasn't an excuse for me to spiral the way I had. My issues were small compared to the rest of the world's. How had I let things spin out of control?

After I took a semester off from school, my coaches allowed me to come back on full scholarship. Getting my education and doing my best in track was important not only to me but also to my family. Still, at that point, I wasn't polished with the Word and wasn't living a Godly lifestyle.

At that time, I was dating my future husband, not knowing it was going to turn into such a blessing. We both were athletes, striving to become professional athletes post graduation. We both worked hard at what we did, and we were both so supportive of each other that it was easy for us to fall in love. He became my number one fan and my best friend.

After graduating, I focused on my training in hopes of making the 2012 Olympic team. At that time, my boyfriend was playing his professional sport in another state. The long distance was challenging for us, but we knew it was only temporary. Our goals were our main priorities.

I attended a new church, one that felt like home, and it's where my faith began to make great progress. I'd never felt the Lord's presence more than I did in that church. The pastor was so gifted you knew the Lord was speaking through him; the anointing he had was incredible. My love for the Lord began to grow more and more. Along with my working on my faith, my boyfriend and I began to do Bible studies together over the phone and when we were together. Doing this, we noticed our relationship had gotten so much stronger over time, and our hunger for the Lord kept growing.

Now we're married, and we both still are doing what we love and doing it not for ourselves but for the Lord. Each day is a battle in this ungodly world, but I continue to try to live Godly, study, and grow and to have faith.

He heals the brokenhearted and binds up their wounds.
–Psalm 147:3

Brendan Morgan

Hometown: Pickering, Ontario
Sport: Football
Age at time of story: 18–21

The most challenging thing I had to go through as an athlete was walking onto a Division I football program. In 2010, after failing to receive any scholarship offers out of high school, I decided to walk onto the University of Virginia's (UVA) football program. At the time, my mother was my main support and still is today. She provided me with not only the funds but also the hope and courage I needed to make such a bold decision. When I told her I wanted to play Division I football, she did everything in her power to help me achieve this goal. She gave every last dime she had and even took extra jobs to fund my dream. There are a lot of people in this world who claim to have your back, but not many would break theirs in order to see you succeed. That's exactly what she did.

My first year at Virginia was pretty nerve-racking. I remember the first day I walked into the football locker room; I could sense an air of hostility. I recall one player turned to his teammate and whispered in a contemptuous manner, "Who's this?" Despite the lack of acceptance I'd experienced on my first day, it didn't deter me in any way. I'd soon be able to practice, and I knew that was where I'd earn my respect. On my first day of practice, I was unable to wear equipment and was told to stand by my position coach and pay attention.

Having played running back all throughout high school, I'd originally intended on playing that position at Virginia. But after spending a practice following the running back coach, I was a bit put off by his personality and his favoritism toward certain players. As a result, I decided to change my position to wide receiver the very next practice. This position seemed to be the most fitting. For one, it seemed to be the most popular position for walk-on players, so I figured it was where I'd be able to earn a scholarship.

Boy, was I wrong! I had played only a bit of slot back in Canada, and I figured I had enough skill to play wide receiver. However, it turned out there were a lot of fundamental skills I was unaware of. Over-the-shoulder technique catches, catching balls from the jugs, routes, and alignments were some of the many tasks I faced as a receiver. However, over the course of time, I was able to develop my skills and make a name for myself. Things were looking up for me. In fact, I managed to win the Freshman Fridays workout completion, which involved a series of competitions exclusively for the freshman class and took place Friday mornings during the season.

After redshirting my first year, I was looking forward to playing my second year, which was virtually unheard of for walk-ons. That summer, I went home and worked my butt off. I returned to Virginia that fall. To my surprise, my position was changed to running back. Now for those who might have forgotten, upon entering UVA, I'd originally intended to play running back but decided to change my position because of the coach.

I had mixed emotions concerning my position change. It was somewhat disappointing because I'd worked all summer bettering myself as a wide receiver. I also was still unsure about my new position coach. Nonetheless, I continued to stay positive and worked hard day in and day out and soon began to reap the fruits of my labor. That season, our team went 8-5 and was invited to Atlanta, Georgia, to play against the University of Auburn in the Chick-fil-A Bowl. Unfortunately, we lost that game, but it was a game I'll never forget. That very week, due to my efforts on scout team kickoff, I was bumped to the starting position, so I finally played in my first college football game. To think that my coaches believed in me enough to start me in a game against the former NCAA national champions was unbelievable and added fuel to my fire. I thought I was at the top of my game, and nothing was going to stop me. Just when I thought things couldn't get any better, they did.

Following the Chick-fil-A Bowl, I remember one particular practice during which I felt I'd made a name for myself: It was the day we had the Weenie Bowl. Now as condescending as the name may sound, the Weenie Bowl was a big deal for me and other players who didn't play on a regular basis. It was an opportunity for us to showcase our talents and endorse our value on the team. That day, I made it very clear I belonged. I broke a seventy-yard run for a touchdown off a cutback on a zone read play and burned a couple of players in the process. It was magical. Everyone was going nuts, including my head coach. A few days following that practice, I was called up to meet with my position coach. I sat down in his office, and he told me that he and the other coaches were impressed with my effort and assured me I'd receive a scholarship after the spring granted I continued on the right path. I was ecstatic, but I didn't boast about the news. The break was coming up, and I knew that upon my return, I would have to be more focused than ever.

Upon returning to school after the break, I was once again called up to my coach's office. To my dismay, I was told that my position had been changed to cornerback. This came as a shock to me for two reasons: (1) I'd been doing so well at running back, and (2) I'd never played corner before. Nevertheless, I approached this situation as I had all others in the past—with a positive attitude. Playing corner was one of the toughest challenges I faced at UVA. My coach was a dick, to say the least, and I just couldn't seem to get the hang of the position.

As time progressed, I continued to have trouble adjusting, and I could see my scholarship slowly slipping away. Nearing the end of the school year, I was called into the defensive coordinator's room. I was told I wasn't going to receive a scholarship because of my lack of development in my new position. It was a hard blow and one that resonated throughout. To make matters worse, my mother didn't have enough money to continue to pay my tuition. At that moment, it was clear it was time for me to leave Virginia. I called my mother, packed my bags, and made my way back home.

Despite my being unable to receive a scholarship, the situation taught me to be fearless and always to strive for my dreams, no matter how large they may seem. At times, the task seemed unreachable, but because I was patient, I didn't give up when times were hard. Rome wasn't built in a day. As a walk-on, I understood there was a process I had to undergo to create a name for myself.

Unlike most of my teammates', my name was not nationally known; however, I never looked at this as a negative but rather used it as motivation. Every day, I put my all into my craft and never lost sight of my goal. I made sure I got better, and I made sure people noticed. In the Bible, it says that with faith the size of a mustard seed, we can move mountains. Although, I have undergone many trials in the past few years I still believe this is true. No matter how big, how wide, how far, or how deep our dreams may appear, as long as we commit our efforts to God, he will deliver them.

Commit your works to the Lord and your plans will be established.
–Proverbs 16:3

There are situations in our lives that may seem catastrophic and devastating, but we must understand they're all part of a greater plan. No matter how difficult something may seem, if it's what you desire, achieve it. Things aren't always going to come easy in life, but remember, no matter how difficult your dreams may be, don't let your circumstances determine your future. Just because I'm not at a Division I program anymore doesn't mean I can't become a professional football player in the future. As long as I work hard and focus on God, he'll guide my future and create a way, even if it may seem impossible.

Justine Charbonnet

Hometown: New Orleans, Louisiana
Sport: Track and field
Age at time of story: 18–22

Before college

August 25, 2005, was the day that started my journey to discovering the bigger picture of my life. It was also the day that began my journey to the realization that, in the midst of some of the most terrible situations, the greatest things can come out of them. August 25, 2005, was Hurricane Katrina.

My family and I were separated from our beloved city of New Orleans and forced to start over in this unknown place called Texas. What was one of the biggest adversities I've ever had to face turned out to be one of the biggest blessings God could ever give me. I discovered a love and talent for track and field once I got acclimated into the Houston school system. From there, I was able to meet one of the best coaches, friends, and role models a girl could ever ask for: Coach Ham.

He taught me not only the fundamentals of sprinting and jumping but also the fundamentals to being a great person and role model. I was able to start my freshman year on varsity. My events included the 4x1, 4x2, 4x4, 100, and 400 and the long and triple jumps. I'd had a very successful high school career and was always known in Texas as "the fast little girl from the woodlands with all that long hair."

When it was time to start looking for a college to continue my running and jumping career, my family and I were still new to the whole recruiting and college athletics thing. Of course, being from Louisiana, running for Louisiana State University (LSU) would be a dream come true. Little did I know God had bigger things in store. Every year, our high school regional meet was at Baylor University, and every year while we competed, the Baylor coaches were away in Des Moines for Drake Relays. In 2009, an epidemic swept Texas: the swine flu. When the swine flu hit, word spread that all regional meets would be canceled and the top times from the districts would move on to state.

I was devastated. Our district was one of the easier districts in the area to compete in, so although we won our events, our times and jumping distances weren't the greatest. Because of the swine flu, I wasn't even going to get the chance to fight for a position at the Texas State Meet. Could this get any worse?

A couple days later, we got word the decision had been given a second thought, and our regional meets would continue on but would be pushed back a week in order for the swine flu to calm down. In the junior year regional, I had the meet of my life, and here's the best part of all: All the Baylor coaches were there to see it! The swine flu, which at one time seemed to have ruined my life, ended up giving me the opportunity of a lifetime: a track and field scholarship to Baylor. God works in such mysterious ways. Now, let's fast-forward to life as a college athlete at Baylor.

Freshman year

I came in thinking I could do whatever I wanted, eat whatever I wanted, stay up as late I wanted, and still have what it takes to be a Division I sprinter and jumper. I couldn't have been more wrong! I'd never gotten dead last in so many races in my life, and I was jumping distances the best jumpers could probably have reached just by standing on the board and stretching out their feet into the sand!

I was an embarrassment to myself, to my coaches, and even though they won't admit it, to my family. I was more focused on being a part of the social scene and entertaining a relationship I had no business being in. I compromised all the things that were important to me and didn't even realize it. On top of all of this, I'd gained a lot of weight for a track athlete and was at a huge risk of getting my scholarship taken away. I had finally reached my ultimate low.

One Monday while I was at Fellowship of Christian Athletes (FCA), our chaplain Brother Wes talked about how, when we reach a point in our lives when we realize we can't handle everything ourselves, we need God to intervene. He said it was at that point when we've reached our lowest place in life that we finally can just stop and surrender everything to God and allow Jesus to come in and help put back together the pieces of our shattered lives. I knew at that very moment God was talking to me.

I went back to my dorm room and just sat and broke down. My mind was filled with so many questions: How had my life gotten to this point? How had I allowed myself to get this low? Did God even care about me anymore? How could he have taken something so special away from me like this?
My roommate, Tiffani McReynolds, (one of the most successful freshmen track hurdlers ever) walked in and saw me crying. She said, "Come on." Right there, we turned off the lights, got on our knees, and opened up the personalized Bibles Baylor gives every student-athlete, and we prayed for my situation. I gave the Lord my life and all its shattered pieces right then and there and asked him to please help me get through this difficult time.

After the conference meet, the end of my season finally came to a close. It was now time to face my biggest fear I'd been dreading since my first poor performance on the track: my meeting with the head coach to discuss my scholarship. I said a long prayer before I mustered the courage to walk into that room and await the verdict for my future. As I sat down, our head coach explained to me I'd been underperforming and had gained a lot of weight. As I waited for those words "You're released" to come out of his mouth, for the first time I saw the miracle of God's grace toward an undeserving sinner coming to fruition in my life.

My coach said I'd now gotten freshman year out of my system and knew the consequences of my actions. I'd lose some of my scholarship, but I'd be given a second chance to work harder than I ever had before to redeem myself and become a worthy member of the team. Right then and there, I knew God had a purpose for my being at Baylor. I didn't know exactly what it was yet, but it was something worth my needing to be there. I walked out of that office forever a changed woman; you better believe that summer was about to be a summer to remember.

That freshman summer, I worked relentlessly to lose the extra weight, get into shape, and get my endurance and speed back to where it needed to be. I was constantly calling Coach Ham to figure out what else I could be doing. It was also the first summer I worked Team Waco, the Waco summer track program for all the Waco area kids. It was a blast teaching them the fundamentals of sprinting and jumping and watching them develop into better athletes throughout the course of the summer. Motivating them to work hard to be the kind of athletes they want to be really inspired me to work even harder on myself and to get to where I needed to be, so I could be a role model for them. Critiquing and helping them with certain things also made me more aware of things I could fix in my jumps and sprints.

Sophomore year

I had come a long way from that day sitting in my coach's office, but one thing I still lacked was confidence in myself. I felt I always had to prove myself worthy to my coaches, my teammates, and even to God. I felt if I wasn't running a certain time or jumping a certain length, then I was a failure to them all. I put a lot of unnecessary pressure on myself to become the athlete I really wanted to be, and although I was improving, I still wasn't where I wanted to be.

I spent most of my indoor season stressing and beating myself up about my performance and allowing the anxiety of possibly losing my scholarship to take control of my life. I'd reached a point where track was no longer a gift from God but rather a heavy burden I was forced to live with. It got so bad my coaches had to talk to me because I was no longer a fun teammate to be around or a fun athlete to coach. I'd lost my true passion and simply wasn't having fun anymore. They'd ask, "Where is the bubbly girl from the woodlands we recruited?" At times, I wondered the same thing.

That's when God really started to work in my life. He provided me with people and Bible studies and small groups that taught me more about the love of Christ and helped me realize my worth goes far beyond my performance on the track. I was so comforted by the things I was learning about Christ's love for me that I really started getting into his word more and more. I even started going to early morning worship service on Tuesdays with some of my teammates where I learned how to truly pray for not only myself but mainly for others. I was starting to spend a lot more time with my God and doing things for him and his purpose for my life instead of trying to do everything my way. I began to get really involved with our FCA community service. The more I shared the love of Christ with other people, the more I felt and saw the realness of his love for me. When I spent time ministering to God's people, my problems, which once seemed to consume my life, became less and less important to me.

At that point, when I looked at my life, I knew I was created to serve and love people. In the process, God was allowing me to do what I loved through things like track and field as his gift to me. When I looked at track, I thought about my Team Waco kids and the joy they found from jumping in the sand and the thrill of pushing their bodies to their maximum speed in hopes of getting to the finish line first, all simple things I'd so easily taken for granted. I thought about how my life started from Hurricane Katrina and how I'd gotten to where I was. I realized I'd taken God's love for me for granted as well.

Jesus had to use the very gift he gave me to pull me back to him when it was taken away. Allowing me to reach the ultimate low was the only way he could get my attention. I'd become so wrapped up in being a college student and a college athlete that I'd forgotten about my first and most important position: a Christian. I had become so consumed with my relationships with coaches, teammates, and boys that I'd pushed aside the most important relationship in my life: my relationship with Jesus Christ. When I was able to finally make that relationship the center of my life and my main priority, the rest of the pieces of my life started falling into place.

That outdoor season, I was able to let go of my pressures and have fun, and I even ended up being an All-Conference performer. Through finding Christ, I was able to find the confidence in myself that had been hidden by my fear of incompetency.

Junior year

If I'd thought Christ had revealed all of himself to me my sophomore year, then I was wrong. He was clearly just getting started! Throughout the off-season training period, we really stressed to the incoming freshman the importance of nutrition, hydration, sleeping, and allowing your body to recover. That was the year I really understood the purpose of my test (freshman and sophomore years) was for me to become a living testimony to share with those around me. I found myself able to relate to people struggling on our team and to give great advice to those making bad decisions. I could share with them my struggle and my story of pretty much what not to do. More importantly, I was a living example of how to overcome the adversities they faced and how to turn them around into a positive situation.

When it got close for our season to start, we voted for captains. To my surprise, the team chose me! As I stood in front of my team to make my acceptance speech, I could see the flashback of my 180-degree transformation from the day Tiff and I got on our knees to pray a prayer of surrender in the dorm room to my now standing before my team as a leader, a role model, and a captain. If that wasn't the work of Christ, then I don't know what is. Throughout the season, I learned to trust God and the plans he had for my life because I knew they'd always somehow be greater than the ones I'd planned.

While doing community service with our FCA, we spent a lot of time doing Bible studies at the homeless shelter. As some of the people opened up about their problems, I'd almost be ashamed of the things in my life I'd considered to be the end of the world.

As student-athletes, we can become so involved in our sports and our college lives that we forget how good we actually have it. When I shared the trials I faced in college, which were nothing compared to the things these people faced, they were still touched by the way God was working in my life. I will never forget this one man in particular; he was from Oregon. I had shared with our small group how I had dreamed of going to the Track and Field National Championship meet in Eugene, Oregon, but because of my trials, I never thought I'd be capable of making it there. He shared with the group how beautiful his state of Oregon is and how I must keep fighting so I could make it there and see the beauty myself.

One night, I went to Wal-Mart, and a man was outside wearing a Santa Clause suit and jingling his bell for Salvation Army donations. I folded my dollar to stick it into the red slot of his bucket. As I looked up, to my surprise it was Mr. Oregon. I asked him how he'd been doing, but what he said to me is something I'll remember for the rest of my life. Despite all his problems and all the things he'd had to worry about in his life, he told me I was going to make it to that National Championship in Eugene, Oregon, because he was always praying for me. Sure enough, by the pure grace of God, our 4x1 team qualified for nationals — getting the very last spot by .007 seconds!

The amount of joy I felt in that moment is indescribable. To see so many obstacles overcome to get where I was then was nothing but the hand of Christ's selfless love on my life. Even though we didn't make it to the finals, just being able to get there and see the transformation spiritually, physically, and mentally that I was able to make through Christ's strength were greater to me than any national title.

Senior year

This is what I like to call the "let go and let God year." Reflecting on my journey, I'm so blessed to have made it this far and to have had the guidance and outlets and people who poured into me to help mold me into who I am today. Now, all I can do is be a light for all of the younger people on my team, so they may experience the same fulfillment in Christ I have.

At the beginning of the year, our sprint coach asked us to e-mail him our goals and tell him why we run and what motivates us. I told him the goals I had for my last season, but most importantly, I told him what keeps me pushing and working my hardest every day. I work hard, and I push myself, so I can be an inspiration to those on the team who face adversity and trials. I want them to see someone who's just like them and to know they can do whatever they truly set their minds to. Christ's strength is inside all of us, but we have to feed that spirit for it to grow.

I want my life to be an example of the great rewards that come from being obedient to God and trusting in his plans for your life. If it takes my testimony and the things I had to overcome in life to empower the teammates around me, then I'm more than glad for the things I went through.

This past Christmas break before my last season started, I told God my relationship with him is my first priority, and I wanted him to do whatever he needs to in my life to make sure our relationship is where it needs to be before I graduate in May.

After my first indoor meet, I really irritated my Achilles tendon and had to sit out for a couple of weeks. During that time, I was truly tested to see how much I actually trusted God. The first couple of days, I was really frustrated and anxious about getting back to competing, but the more I tried to force running or jumping, the worse my condition became. When I got to the point when I could barely walk, I was finally forced to accept my condition and surrender to God's plans.

This was my first real time in rehab; my eyes were opened to a whole new world of patience and perseverance. I was able to learn strengths and weaknesses I never knew I had. I gained a lot of close friendships because of the time I spent with some of my teammates in rehab. I was able to pour into people and encourage them in a way I hadn't been able to before because I hadn't fully understood what they were going through. Most importantly, because of this Achilles injury, I was, and still am, forced to be completely dependent on God every time I step on the track to run or jump. I never know how my

Achilles is going to feel each day, and I have to look to the Lord's strength to pull me through and to not get discouraged.

I can't even begin to tell you how much my relationship with Jesus has improved and evolved because of this injury. I am so thankful for every adversity I face now because it's a constant reminder of Jesus' love for me. He just wants to spend time with me to help me get through it. He uses my problems as an opportunity to show his great power. I'm so grateful for all he's done for me during my journey with him at Baylor. I know he brought me here, so he could draw me near to him. I know everything in my life happens for a reason and for a greater purpose. I hope my story will inspire you and encourage you to seek the Lord in all the storms of your life. At the end of every storm is a rainbow waiting to reveal itself.

Wilfred Sam-King

Hometown: Freetown, Sierra Leone/Winnipeg, Manitoba
Sport: Athletics/track and field
Age at time of story: 17

Track and field, also known as the fundamental sport of all sports, is my escape from the hardships of life. I was born in Gala, Sierra Leone, a small country in West Africa best known for its horrid civil war and blood diamonds. My mother, sister, and I fled the country to Gambia (a neighboring country) in 1997 when the rebels attacked the nation's capital, Freetown, where I grew up. My father stayed behind because he was and is an influential entrepreneur and leader in Sierra Leone.

He stayed behind to protect his livelihood, his businesses. My mother, sister, and I were sponsored to a city named Winnipeg, in a province named Manitoba, in a country with a maple leaf on its flag. Much of the Western world doesn't know the true prominence of the United States of America. Even some of the highly educated refer to North America as just "America," as in one singular country. Winnipeg, Manitoba, Canada, although unheard of to many, became my new home.

Moving because of war as a young child was difficult, but at the same time, it was a blessing in disguise. I still have vivid memories, smells, sounds, and even tastes of my experiences from back in Sierra Leone, some of those good but most bad. Growing up through the Canadian education system in multicultural classrooms, I understood pain, suffering, happiness, and joy a little more than the other children.

There were times I'd feel alone and unhappy because others would speak of their fathers. There were times I was discouraged because I couldn't help comfort my mother when she'd get a phone call about her loved ones who'd been killed. Between the ages of 6 and 12, I found the perplexity of being in a developed nation but being raised with humbling Sierra Leone ideals to be most difficult at times. Material objects are the desire of any child it would seem in the Western world, whereas in some underdeveloped nations, family and survival are the main desires.

During these difficult times, I knew I had to express myself, which to this day I'm very good at; however, as a child with my mother working two jobs, my sister somewhat distant at times, and little to no communication to my father, I needed an outlet. That outlet started during recess. The class bell would ring, and 200 screaming children would go outside to play—but I would run! I'd run as fast as I could until the world around me was just a blur, run as fast as I could until there was no sound but the wind. I'd run as fast as I could until my heartbeat drowned all my sorrows and pain. I didn't know at the time what I was doing was relieving my burdens, all I knew was it felt great.

Fast-forward to my senior year of high school in Fort Richmond Collegiate; I was student body president and captain of the track, soccer, and handball teams and graduated with honors. My mother purchased me a ticket to visit my uncle in the Netherlands as a graduation gift. I was also to meet up with my father in the United Kingdom to discuss my future. I arrived in the United Kingdom, saw the sights, felt the atmosphere, and met with my father.

He told me I needed to stop running and focus only on my academics during university. I'd already accepted a track scholarship to the University of Manitoba for September 2010. I was torn, bitter, and upset. All I could think was "How could I not run?" My father and I have never had a prolonged relationship, or a relationship at all, and that void would only grow if I disobeyed him. A man I'd only been around for no more than two weeks of my life since we'd left Sierra Leone was trying to take away my one physical stronghold. My mother, an ordained minister, told me, "Put your trust in God."

This decision of not running was out of the question. I knew deep down I couldn't stop, but I had no idea why the notion made my heart fall to my stomach. I left the meeting with my father. He gave me money to go shopping, and then the next morning, he left for Dubai. I knew it might be another five to ten years before I saw him again. The pain I'd felt as a small child came rushing back, and once again I had no one to speak to or to console me.

We flew back to the Netherlands. I tried running the streets of my uncle's small suburb to clear my mind, but this time there was no school bell that rang to bring me back to reality. I am a sprinter/hurdler who runs for a maximum of twenty-three seconds, but on this day, I ran for two hours. I got lost multiple times, tears ran down my cheek, my teeth clenched, and anger and sorrow overflowed my veins. Finally, I stopped, sat down by a monument, and closed my eyes to find darkness and calm, but the bright oranges of the sunset lit up my eyelids and made me smile. I prayed my favorite prayer: "Lord give me strength, wisdom, and understanding." Clarity came upon me. Although my father and I share the same name, we're not one and the same, nor does he decide my future.

What I was most hurt about was that God had given me a gift, a way to tune out the world and help me cope, and running had become an essential part of who I was. Where my father wasn't, physically and emotionally, the Lord was, in a form that was very real. I'd made my decision. I wouldn't tell my father I was continuing my running. I would just trust in God. Today, I've used track as a tool to build friendships and networks and to enjoy the simplicities of life. I know I'm destined for great things, whether it's on a large scale or small. I knew I could never go against something God had put in my life that has granted me so many blessings.

So Father, give me the strength
To be everything I'm called to be
Oh, Father, show me the way
To lead them
Won't You lead me?
–*Lead Me* by Sanctus Real

A father of the fatherless, and a judge of the widows, is God in his holy habitation.
–Psalm 68:5

Hannah Willms

Hometown: Waterloo, Iowa
Sport: Track and field
Age at time of story: 22

For I know the plans I have for you, declares the Lord, plans
for welfare, and not for evil, to give you a future and a hope.
–Jeremiah 29:11

I have been a Christian since I accepted the Lord into my heart
in preschool. I was blessed being raised by a Christian family
and attending a Christian school until high school. It wasn't
new to me to have someone suggest turning to God and
prayer for a time of need. I'd heard it many times before, but
the true meaning didn't really sink in until I was faced with
the most difficult time in my life. My junior year of college, I
discovered what turning to Christ really meant, and what it
truly felt like to give my entire heart to Him.

Sports have always been a huge part of my life. I don't
remember there ever being a time when I wasn't involved in
at least one. Throughout my childhood and high school,
sports had always come naturally to me. I'd always excelled in
the needed skills and played beyond my own age level. In
high school, I was blessed with ability in both volleyball and
track and field. In volleyball, we'd been state runner-up two
years, and in track, I'd won fourteen state titles and placed
fifth in Junior Worlds for Team USA. Everything felt so
natural to me. I'd never had to think too much; I just enjoyed
the moment and was happy.

I was offered an opportunity to participate at the collegiate
level in both sports, but I chose to play volleyball at Iowa State
University (ISU). In 2010, my freshman year at ISU, I was
redshirted and given the option by my coach to high jump for

the track team. It was something I'd practice a couple of times a week and then be thrown into one or two meets. I could then still be involved in both sports I loved. Spring season came for volleyball. I was committed 100 percent to getting better at that sport, so as planned, I was practicing a couple of times a week for the high jump. The first meet came that I got thrown into, and I jumped five feet eleven inches, just two inches under my best jump from high school of six feet one inch. So far, everything was working out perfectly. Near the end of the indoor season, I qualified for the NCAA championships in the high jump and finished, placing twelfth. This earned me the honor of second-team All-American as only a freshman. I was so excited to see what my college career had in store for me in the upcoming years. After the indoor season of track, I was back to volleyball where I was training to be the starting outside hitter for the next season, so I couldn't compete in outdoors for track. Spring season was going great, and the coaches told me I was "the next big hitter" for our team.

Fall came, and that's exactly how things started out, but in a matter of a few weeks, everything changed. I went from starting every game, to starting half the games, to not playing at all. I'd been a starter my whole life, in every sport, so sitting on the side was not something I was used to, and not something that set well with me emotionally. I went through a rollercoaster of emotions that season: being happy, then sad, then mad, and then not really caring about anything.
I felt as if all my confidence had been stripped away, and I wasn't ever going to be good enough. Eventually though, I accepted the fact I wasn't going to play in every match and forced a smile the rest of the season. We ended the 2011 season in the Elite Eight in the NCAA tournament. I was very proud of what we'd accomplished, but I was ready to move on to the track season.

My sophomore year, 2012, I decided I wanted to do more in track than just high jump. I wanted to compete in the heptathlon, a series of seven events, five of which I'd never done. Once I told my volleyball coach this, I was given an ultimatum. If I wanted to do both track and volleyball, I'd be allowed one hour of track a week. As much as I loved volleyball, I loved track too and saw that in my future after college. So, I decided to retire my volleyball shoes and concentrate just on track. I thought, "Perfect. Now I can really focus on running and jumping and excel even more than I did in high school."

Track season came, and things went completely in the opposite direction. I was now training for not one but seven events after not competing for a year, and my body had changed that past year while I was training strictly for volleyball. Because of this, I was now slower and was jumping a foot under my personal best. I was told my performance had gone down because of the "bad weight" I'd gained that past year in volleyball. So, I thought, "Easy solution. The more weight I lose, the better athlete I will become." After that season, I told myself I was going to get back to being the athlete I'd once been.

I thought I could fix myself, and I thought I could control my future. In my mind volleyball was gone, my track abilities were gone, and school wasn't going as well as it could've been, so to gain back control of my life, I had to make sure every decision led me in that upward direction. Instead of turning to God for strength and comfort to direct me, I took things into my own hands and tried to fix myself. I disconnected from everyone and everything. I planned out each day to an exact schedule, and if that was thrown off at all, I'd become upset and disconnect myself even more. I became anxious about eating, studying, and practicing, and eventually it led to disordered eating and a lack of any social interaction. I wouldn't hang out with friends on the weekends because I had to make sure I got that extra few hours of sleep. I wouldn't go out to eat or get ice cream because that wasn't something that was going to help me get better. I became easily irritated when friends or family ever commented on any of these things, which led to more isolation.

I knew I needed help, but I wasn't convinced until we had a track meet in which I ran a 400-meter race ten seconds slower than I once had. I finished the race with the worst feeling of weakness and could see the worry in my dad's face. From that moment, I knew something needed to change.

My dad and I are very similar in a way others don't always understand; we're very point-blank when it comes to conversations. We see things as black and white and no in-between. He's always been someone I can go to when I need an honest answer. That evening after my track meet, we had a conversation that led me to where I am now. He told me sports are only a little part of who I am, and there is so much more in life than being an athlete.

After that day, I started praying more than I ever had before; I prayed for peace, happiness, courage, and guidance. I was becoming so much closer to God knowing my guidance was from him and that he would lead me down the path of his choice. I surrendered everything up for God to direct my life in a way that was pleasing and honoring to him.

This was the verse I'd turn to every time I had a doubt, worry, or question about my life and the hardships I faced. This verse calmed my heart and gave me all the answers I ever needed.

Trust in the Lord with all your heart, and lean not on your own understanding.
–Proverbs 3:5

Through this transition of giving my heart to God, I've become a stronger, more independent woman who now isn't afraid of any obstacle thrown her way. Some may get the impression I'm lackadaisical or don't care if I lose or jump badly, but that's not the case at all. Yes, I still get disappointed when I don't compete as well as I wanted, but in the end, I know I tried my hardest, and it is was it is. Everything I know in my life is happening for a reason I may not understand right now. But, with my life and heart given to Christ, I know it'll all work out in the end, and I will be happy.

Strength and dignity are her clothing, and she laughs at the time to come.
–Proverbs 31:25

Yves Batoba

Hometown: Keller, Texas
Sport: Football
Age at time of story: 19

Now glory to him who is able to do immeasurably more than all we ask or imagine, according to his power that is at work within us.
–Ephesians 3:20

In September 2010, a few weeks into the beginning of football season at Oklahoma State, I made the best decision of my life by recommitting my life to Christ. I had several teammates who reached out and explicitly explained the Gospel to me. As I dug into the book of John to learn more about Jesus, I began to love God more and more. With this newfound faith, I just wanted to completely make God the center of my life, which led to my breaking up with my then girlfriend in March of the following year because our relationship wasn't exactly focused on God.

A couple of months after we broke up, she was diagnosed with ovarian cancer and a tumor in her brain. Since graduating high school, she'd had to take care of herself because of her dysfunctional family life, but now that she'd discovered the cancer and tumor, it was up to me to take care of her. She had a friend she could stay with during some days of the week, and she had me to stay with on the other days of the week. So, here I was, a nineteen-year-old sophomore in college balancing a full-time academic schedule, a football schedule, and an ex-girlfriend who relied on me for help.

Every day, I'd talk to her to see how she was doing, when she was eating, how treatment was going, etc. During this time, I saw her condition get worse by the day. There were days I skipped football practice, meetings, and workouts because the sport I'd once loved more than anything else just didn't seem important. I was struggling in school, but I couldn't care less because my only concern was to make sure she was okay. The toughest part was when she went to the hospital to get the tumor removed and ended up being in a coma for three days. I was the one who had to make the decision whether they should pull the plug.

After she woke up and the tumor had been removed, she only had to worry about beating cancer. I spent most of the summer with her. Then, she went back home with me to Texas for Thanksgiving and Christmas. It's by nothing but God's amazing grace she's still around today, looking and feeling as healthy as ever! In fact, she even auditioned to be a Houston Texans cheerleader. Although she didn't become a cheerleader, she made it all the way to the final round. She lives in Tulsa on her own now, and we still keep in touch. Every time I talk to her, I'm reminded of how seeing God work through that moment in my life shaped me into who I am today.

My family has always played an enormous role in my life, especially during that time, but most of my support came from my three roommates/teammates who are also believers. They were always there to help with any task or talk about what was going on. There was a very specific time when they all came into my room and told me that, as bad as the situation was, I couldn't allow it to ruin my life. I was throwing everything I'd worked for up to that point away. I've never been an overly emotional person, and I definitely don't like to show vulnerability, but I remember being completely in tears when talking to them that night.

Athletes think differently than everyone else. Just like in football, there's not a team that ever goes into a game believing they're going to lose. Despite the sorrows and hardships I faced, I never allowed myself to believe she wouldn't kick cancer's butt as long as I encouraged her and was strong for her.

The good thing about hitting rock bottom is there's nowhere to go but up. At that time, as a recommitted believer, the only thing I had to cling to was God. Every time I went to Bible study or church or even had a fruitful conversation, I'd write everything down to look over later and share it with my ex. Every time we were together, we'd read the Bible and pray together. If it weren't for that tough time, I don't think I'd be as strong in my faith as I am right now. It really taught me to depend on God for everything.

I was in a very unique situation. It's not common to remain extremely close with your ex, especially when you really don't have a choice. When growing spiritually with someone of the opposite sex, it's easy to confuse all of the emotions we feel toward God with emotions we feel for each other. It's important to be honest with yourself about what you feel and to be consistently honest with the other person to reduce confusion. My best friend, Rebekah, gave me the quote "honesty is better than truth." It reminds me that, even though factual truth is important, it's more important to be honest about the circumstance and everything surrounding it.

I have told you these things, so that in me you may have peace. In this world you will have trouble. But take heart! I have overcome the world.
–John 16:33

We can rejoice, too, when we run into problems and trials, for we know that they help us develop endurance.
–Romans 5:3

As you go through your spiritual journey with Jesus, it's certain that times will get difficult. As long as God is the center of everything in your life and you give him every worry you could possibly have, you can't lose. These hardships are what strengthen your relationship with God and allow you to receive unexplainable peace.

The peace of God, which goes far beyond all understanding.
–Philippians 4:7

Jenn Volcy

Hometown: Toronto, Ontario
Sport: Soccer
Age at time of story: 17

Eventually, all of the pieces will fall into place. Until then, laugh at the confusion, live for the moment, and know that everything happens for a reason.
–Albert Schweitzer

When I was growing up, my mother always told me not to worry about anything because God had a plan for my life. The words sounded nice, and they were comforting at times, but I didn't always believe her. These words always seemed like more of a consolation prize than anything else; no one ever wants the consolation prize.

During my junior year of high school, I tried out for a new club soccer team. I'd played soccer for years, and it was the only sport that I truly loved. At the time, this team was everything I wanted. I'd be playing for a bigger, wealthier club, which could afford to send the team to showcase tournaments across the border. I won't say I necessarily had a plan to play college soccer, but I wanted to travel and play the game I love; I wanted to do that with this particular team.

Throughout the trials, I traveled with the team to Philadelphia. I played in one showcase tournament, and I was allowed fewer than forty minutes of total playing time. Needless to say, this was rather disappointing. Following that tournament, I was notified I hadn't made the team and that I'd be a better fit for another team, the "B" team. Nobody wants to be told he or she is a better fit for the B team. I was so disheartened and disillusioned. I wasn't good enough. The coaches fluffed it up with a lot of comforting words. They told me the other team would help me develop my skills and build my confidence. They told me it would benefit me much more than playing for their team ever would—once again, a consolation prize.

I started my season with my new team. Suddenly, I started receiving e-mails and phone calls from American coaches. They wanted me to come play soccer for their teams. I was confused as to how they knew who I was. I'd never sent out any player packages, and I'd never made one of those fancy athletic online profiles. I asked one of them, "How did you find me?" He told me he saw me play in Philadelphia and that I was very talented. I had potential, and I was good enough. Although I'd never had any plans to play college soccer, I accepted a scholarship to a Division I school in Louisiana. This was something I'd never imagined for myself, but it happened. I absolutely loved my four years in Louisiana because I learned so much about myself while also figuring out what I wanted to do in life. Louisiana solidified my dream of becoming an attorney. I had amazing mentors at my university, and the faculty most definitely pushed me to follow my dreams and pursue a legal career.

What does this have to do with the B team, you might ask? Simple. As I sit on campus at my law school today in California, I realize I probably wouldn't be here were it not for those few "wasted" months my junior year. At the time, I didn't understood why God wasn't giving me what I wanted. It wasn't until recently that I looked back and realized maybe God had bigger plans for me, and that was the road I had to take to get here.

Do not worry about tomorrow, for tomorrow will care for itself.
–Matthew 6:34

Now, I understand. Had I not tried out, I wouldn't have traveled to Philadelphia where those forty minutes of playing time granted me the chance to play college soccer. I never would've gone to Louisiana, and who knows where I'd be right now? I probably wouldn't be in law school. I know now that life happened the way it did for a reason. I was there for as long as God intended me to be, and I don't regret it.

I should mention that playing with the B team wasn't the worst thing in the world. As it turned out, I was reunited with so many girls I'd played with growing up. I never really did connect with any of the girls on the A team, but on the B team, I was surrounded by friends. Looking back, I ended my senior year of high school playing the game I love with the people I love. I created more memories with a team I "fit" with. Most importantly, I took the path God set out for me, and I've never been happier than I am today. I don't worry so much anymore when life doesn't go the way I plan. I guess my mother was right.

Dontae Richards

Hometown: Mississauga, Ontario
Sport: Track and field
Age at time of story: Approximately 16–17

I'm confident many of you will agree with this statement: One of the hardest things I've ever had to go through as an athlete is injury. It seems injuries have always managed to hit me when I feel like I'm on the verge of something big, maybe not big in terms of something spectacular but big as in something special at that stage of my track career — something big to me. Immediately, I can think of a few upsets I've had on the track because of injury. My track career was almost over before it began.

My grade eleven season was the first time my newly developed passion in this sport was really tested. But, let me back up for a moment first. My high school wasn't known for its athletics when I got there, nor was it known for them when I left, but I promise you we had a lot of talent hiding in that windowless building. We had ballers, soccer stars, and football players who just never seemed to get the exposure they needed to get to the next stage of their athletic careers.

In track and field, your talents speak for themselves and aren't lost in the win and loss record of your team. Apparently, in 2004, some of that talent included a young man named Tyrone Halstead (T) and me. T and I trained together that first year of high school, and I dare say I was a little faster than he was in grade nine. We cleaned up our freshman year and won everything, including the provincial 100-meter and 200-meter races. After that season, Tyrone joined a track club while I decided I was doing just fine without training and wanted to play other sports.

The following season really motivated me to take track seriously. My training partner had a full year of training under his belt, and my pride took a hit most of the year. In the end, I lost the 100-meter dash, but I came back the next day and broke the 200-meter record. I think it was that moment combined with losing that lit a fire inside me. I decided to join Mississauga Track Club that summer and trained all winter leading up to the school season.

I thought grade eleven was going to be my year. I was coming off an Ontario Federation of School Athletic Associations (OFSAA) record, and I'd officially started training for track. I thought I was going to do some real damage. A couple of races into my season, I noticed a pain in my groin. About halfway through my season, I couldn't run without shooting pains in my left leg. I had it checked, and I was diagnosed with osteitis pubis. This injury not only killed all my hopes of running well that season but also affected my next year. At the time, I was angry at the amount of time I'd spent training that was about to go down the drain. Of course, I consulted Google, which was a terrible idea, and read that, on average, it takes other athletes almost a year to recover; in some cases, it can end their careers. Fortunately, I'd caught it early.

The other major setback that comes to my mind right away was in 2011. I'd just made my very first national team, the International University Sports Federation (FISU, also known as the World Student Games). I'd just switched training groups and made my first national team after missing World Juniors because of a hamstring strain. I remember being crazy excited to show off what I could do. I got all my friends to find streams or live results links from home, and I talked with my coaches and grandmother about how pumped I was. Most people said, "Do your best. It's your first time, and it's a new experience. Just go out there and don't worry about anyone else." I was far from nervous or concerned with other runners.

The atmosphere in China was ridiculous! It was a new stadium, and it held eighty thousand screaming track and field fans. The first day, the first two rounds out of four were held. I showed up that day ready to roll. I got out in my heats and ran a personal best to make it to the next round. In quarterfinals, boom! I had another best, and I was running the semifinals the next day. I made sure I cooled down well and stretched and had a good dinner that night. I got lots of sleep and woke up feeling better than I had the day before. I thought, "All I have to do is execute well and make this final and anything can happen. I can come away from my first international competition with a medal." I ran the semis, and after a bad start, I tied my best time and made it to the finals! I made it through the mixed zone to get my stuff. I did a few strides to stay loose because I only had about an hour until the finals.

An hour later, I was lined up behind my blocks about to go. I thought, "Get out, stay low, relax." I couldn't have been more excited to run. The gun went off, and I was gone! But, I thought I felt something in my leg. I thought, "That was weird, oh well." I took a step on my left leg, good. I pushed with my right. I thought, "I'm cramping." In another couple of steps, it got worse, but I'd clearly left the guys to my left and to my right. I was beating everyone to 25 meters, so maybe I could just hang on. I pushed again on my right leg, and I felt my body say, "Nope, not today." I decided I'd limp my way through the finish line. I won't lie; after I got my bags, I found a nice quiet spot back at the track, threw some water on my face, and bawled my eyes out for ten minutes; not because I was in pain, which I was, but because, for some reason, I felt I'd let my family, friends, and myself down. I was frustrated and thought about all the other times I'd gotten hurt before big races and how much I'd changed and had taken care of myself, but it seemed like nothing had changed. When I returned to Canada, I got an ultrasound that came back positive for a 4.5 centimeter tear in my hamstring.

In both of those experiences, my grandmother definitely provided most of my support, along with a couple of my best friends. There are only two or three people in my life who I can say have seen all of my highs and stuck around throughout all of my lows. They—and especially my grandmother—have been a major part of the reason I've never given up. I'm someone who hates to lose. I understand there'll be times when I'll be new to something, will lack experience, or will simply be outclassed, but I'll definitely not just roll over and lose. I'll take my loss, try to learn from it, and come back harder!

Keeping that in mind, when I think of all the people who've supported me throughout everything and how great the feeling is when I know I've made someone proud, I'll never give up. In my situations, it would've been easy to get down on myself. I recall being angry for a few days, thinking and wondering if I'd done something wrong, if I'd missed part of my warm up, if I'd forgotten to take my vitamins, or if I hadn't gotten enough sleep. The fact is, in most situations, once you've taken control of everything you're supposed to as an athlete, these things just happen sometimes.

Going through what I thought were life-changing, heartbreaking injuries has molded me into the athlete I am now and definitely taught me two things: how to be patient and how to remain positive. As an athlete, you'll be thrown many curveballs by life, and the important thing you can do is just roll with them and have some faith. You'll eventually get better, and you'll compete again. In my case, I took the time to work on all the little things I may not have had the time or energy to work on with my training schedule.

For instance, I worked on my flexibility, and I worked on developing smaller muscles and my stability. That was an easy way to turn a negative into a positive. You just have to stay on top of your recovery process, listen to your therapists, and trust that everything will work itself out. You're not the first person to get injured, and you'll probably get hurt again at some point. That's just the nature of sports.

You've got to remember that the way you plan things in your head is 99 percent of the time never how they turn out. That doesn't mean the end result is different, just that the path you plan to take isn't the one life will put you on.

I can do all things through Christ who strengthens me.
–Philippians 4:13

Kelsey Calvert

Hometown: St. Louis, Missouri
Sport: Soccer
Age at time of story: 19

Somewhere behind the athlete you've become and the hours of practice and the coaches who have pushed you is a little girl who fell in love with the game and never looked back...play for her.
–Mia Hamm

Signing my letter of intent was one of the greatest days of my life. I had arrived; I was going to play college soccer at a Division I program. I'd waited my entire youth for this moment. Finally, after a childhood of practicing on fields where the grass came up to my knees, sliding in the mud while my friends were at prom, and attending countless tournaments like the one in Mitchell, South Dakota, where after a game, my parents took me to see the famously named Corn Palace (literally, a palace made of corn), I was in college! I had all the gear, I had the name on the back of my jersey, and I had the athlete status. I was untouchable.

I walked to my morning class, Women's Studies 203, and sat down next to my friends, who were all male athletes. The class was 90 percent male. Our professor began a discussion on women's athletics. I looked at the other female athletes in the class and rolled my eyes; mark me down for a 100 percent today.

A boy in the back of the class casually raised his hand to start the class discussion and said, "Yeah, girls are garbage at sports." Uh, what? I turned around to see if he was just kidding, but he was dead serious, and in fact, most in the room were laughing. The comments continued: "Female athletes are dikes." "Women should be in the kitchen." "The female's body wasn't designed for athletics." For the next hour and a half, the comments kept coming like water out of the floodgates.

I was in shock, and for the first time in my life, I doubted whether I truly deserved to be a collegiate athlete. Had I gotten this opportunity not because I was talented but because by law I "had" to be given it? I thought of the immeasurable moments the game had given me, the state championship I'd won, and the times I'd played a full ninety-minute game and then stayed after to play some more; these life lessons, these moments suddenly didn't matter because I'd become just a number, just a girl.

I went to clear my head the only way I knew how — on the field with a soccer ball at my feet. After I'd been alone for hours, the words of my classmates became haunting and, in fact, crippling; the opposition can be overwhelming. Gathering myself and wiping my tears from my face, I walked inside. My mind still heavy with thoughts, I opened my locker to see what I'd written on a piece of paper just a year before: "Athletes who are mentally tough simply cannot have their spirits broken." It was simple logic. "A non-athlete is easily discouraged. Perseverance and positive attitude are a choice." I learned a valuable lesson that day: There isn't a person in the world who can affect your spirit unless you let him or her. I remain confident during adversity. I'm a girl, and I play sports. I dare you to prove me otherwise.

It took a lot of prayer, phone calls to my Dad, and time alone with the ball to endure the words I heard that day. I never gave up because I remembered the little girl inside me who used to wipe up on the boys at recess, the girl they'd put in the all-boys league because she was too aggressive. I did it for my five-year-old self. This situation prepared me for much of what I would face once I graduated. Men dominate corporate

America, and I really don't care. I work in corporate America, and I'm a woman.

So do not fear, for I am with you; do not be dismayed, for I am your God. I will strengthen you and help you; I will uphold you with my righteous right hand.
–Isaiah 41:10

Drake Swarm

Hometown: Bettendorf, Iowa
Sport: Wrestling
Age at time of story: 20

Once you have wrestled, everything else in life is easy.
–Dan Gable

The tough thing about being a collegiate athlete is the season grind. The term "grind" is used a lot nowadays, but few truly understand it. I believe that through my lifestyle I encounter the grind during the heart of wrestling season.

In Division I wrestling, the season lasts from mid-October to March while adding preseason training from the start of the school year to October. In wrestling, you have to undergo many challenges in your daily life, such as your lifting schedule, mandatory class lectures, wrestling practice, diet, and on top of all that, school and homework.

My daily schedule consists of waking up around five o'clock in the morning and driving to our mandatory team lift. As a team, we usually lift on Monday, Tuesday, Thursday, and Friday at six o'clock in the morning. After I lift, I run to our university dining hall and grab some breakfast. Because my weight class is 125 pounds, I try to maintain my weight around 132 to 133 pounds, so a strict diet is essential.

After breakfast, I attend two to three classes a day, which are located on different parts of the campus. During the breaks between my classes each day, I grab a quick lunch and attend my required tutoring sessions. When I'm finished with my tutoring appointments, it's usually practice time. As a team, we have practice on Monday, Tuesday, Thursday, and Friday at three thirty in the afternoon. Typically, a practice will end around five to five thirty, and then I walk to the dining center again to eat some dinner. After dinner, I return back to the athletic academic center to fulfill my required study hall hours. By then, it's usually ten or eleven o'clock at night, and I head home. This is my grind that I encounter on a daily basis during wrestling season.

My situation has molded me into the person I am today. With the support team that God has blessed me with, which consists of family, coaches, and friends, I can go through a rough day and still see the positives. When things get tough, I try to get tougher. That's what the grind brings to my life. I know some results won't come when I want them to, but everything has a reason, and God's timing is perfect.

Be on your guard, stand firm in faith, be men of courage; be strong.
-1 Corinthians 16:13

Jarrett Hamilton

Hometown: Toronto, Ontario, Canada
Sport: Soccer
Age at time of story: 18

It was August 2008, and the confidence I had in myself had never been greater. I'd just finished playing with the Toronto Football Club (TFC) academy and had received a full Division I scholarship to play at Oral Roberts University in Tulsa, Oklahoma.

After my first couple of training sessions with my new team, my confidence grew even more. I'd solidified myself as one of the best players on the team, and I was only a freshman. The coaches bolstered my confidence even further by putting me in the starting lineup during practices, so I could begin to gel with what would be the core of the team. Again, I was feeling great; nothing in the world could bring me down, or so I thought.

It was now our final exhibition game of the season. We'd previously played two exhibition games, and I'd done very well, scoring a goal and two assists. In this last game, I was easily the best player on the field for the first half. The other team was very frustrated with me, as I was creating opportunities all over the field. The second half was underway, and I decided to go on a run with the ball by myself. I beat a couple of guys, and I had one more to get by before I'd be on a breakaway to the net. Well, that defender had other ideas.

I'd never been hit or body checked that hard in my life. I remember flying in the air and being unable to control how I was going to land. Then, pop! I wasn't exactly sure what had just happened, but I knew I was in a lot of pain, and my left arm was going numb. A teammate started to freak out, and my worst concerns were reality.

I had dislocated my shoulder. The medical staff tried to put it back in, but it was so badly dislocated, they had to take me to the emergency room. I was then drugged up, and they popped my shoulder back in. Then, they gave me a crap load of pain meds to take home. I was kind of out of it because of the drugs, but I remember my coaches showed up after the game, and they had my mom on the phone. She was crying hysterically, saying she was going to come all the way to Oklahoma. I told her everything would be fine, and that was a bit unnecessary.

That's where the struggle began though. I couldn't play soccer anymore. I'd struggle to wake up to go to class because I was in so much pain. After class, I had to watch my teammates practice. There was nothing I could do about it. I took my rehab very seriously, but I knew, no matter what I did in rehab, it wouldn't put me back on the field. I was miserable. I was eighteen, in a new place all by myself, with no friends nor family, and I couldn't play soccer. The one thing that kept me happy and sane was gone. I struggled with this for weeks. I'd call friends and family, bawling my eyes out, saying I wanted to come home and I couldn't do it anymore because I couldn't play. I missed out on trips to Las Vegas, Memphis, and other places, but the worst was yet to come.

About two weeks into my recovery, commenced maybe the darkest period of my life and any faith I had at that time. I began to blame God for what had happened to me. I couldn't understand how he could take this away from me. If something made me so happy, and I was doing so well, why do this now? I couldn't comprehend why this happened to me. I couldn't understand how he could see I was so high yet want me to be so low. I eventually lost faith in God completely. I refused to believe he existed. Yes, it was that dark in my life.

About six weeks after my initial injury, I could begin practicing again. But, it wasn't the same. I didn't feel right. I was still in a bit of pain, and I was completely out of shape. I fell deeper into my dark hole.

When I was eventually ready to play, I was no longer a starter, and I started off getting twenty to twenty-five minutes a game. This was very frustrating because I wasn't playing well, and my coach and I both knew I was completely healthy and capable of so much more. My first season was pretty much a complete waste. My shoulder didn't properly heal until after the season was done, which is when it finally got the proper rest it needed.

It's crazy when they say things happen for a reason. During the off-season, I was so motivated to get back to where I was before the injury. I ran more, I worked harder, and I put in way more work in the weight room. By the time spring season games came around, I was back to being the best player on the team. I had regained a lot of my confidence, and I only wanted to get better. In my next three seasons, I was a three-time All-Conference selection, a two-time All-Tournament team selection, and an all Mid-West regional team selection, and I led my conference in total points my junior year.

I haven't shared this story with anyone in such detail before. But, there is no better platform on which I can share it than in this book. This situation helped me become who I am today. My faith in God has been restored, and I know now that, no matter how difficult or dark your life may look or feel, you have the power to change your attitude and take action to make that change. I feel good about sharing this story because I know there will be some injured athletes who'll read this story. If you're going through what I went through, I hope my words can inspire you to change your outlook on your situation for the better.

I waited patiently for the Lord; he inclined to me and heard my cry. He drew me up from the pit of destruction, out of the miry bog, and set my feet upon a rock, making my steps secure.
–Psalm 40:1–2

Jamie Adjetey-Nelson

Hometown: Windsor, Ontario
Sport: Track and field, decathlon
Age at time of story: 28

I never wanted to be another great athlete. I always wanted to be the best me I could be.
–Jamie Adjetey-Nelson

I can't remember the exact day, but it was about to be the hardest day of my life to date. I know it was late May. I was finally sleeping well after about two years of having sleeping problems because of a medical condition. I was in the zone, preparing for Olympic trials. And like on most days, I went through my routine. I awoke three minutes before my alarm, meaning I was on a good sleep cycle. I reached over to check my phone messages, and I had a text message from one of my brothers: "Yo, [one of my other brothers] was shot last night in Alberta."

I leapt to my feet and called the brother who'd texted me. He told me my other brother had been shot and had been transferred to a hospital in Calgary. He was the youngest of my mother's children. I had the responsibility to find him. Was he okay, or was he in recovery? Or even worse, was he dead? I made the calls and was getting frustrated with the nurses, who were only doing their job. Finally, I got someone who told me my brother had gone into surgery, but that's it. My mother was the emergency contact. I had to call her and let her know the details. That's the last thing I wanted to put on my mother. I gave her all the information I knew, and all I could do was wait.

I couldn't stay home and let it weigh on me, so I went to my morning practice. I continued normally the best way I could. I'm not the best Christian, but I live the way my mother taught me, and she is a very devout Christian. I said a prayer asking God to save my brother.

I went through the motions at practice, so I could rush home to hear how my brother was doing. When I got home, my mother told me he was out of surgery and in recovery. Still, I had no details of how or what had happened. He hadn't put himself in some of the best scenarios, but he's my brother. I have grown with him, and I love him. I was concerned but optimistic. I believed it would all work out. During practice two of the day, I just tried to get through. I didn't want to lose a step, so I went through the motions but didn't push it too much. My mind wasn't fully there.

I got home after practice, and I told my girlfriend of eight years what had happened. I'm strong, so I hadn't cried yet. My eyes filled with water, but no tears fell. Lumps caught in my throat, but I hadn't bawled. My sleep that night was horrible. I was waiting on more details. I was waiting to hear from my brother. I needed to hear his voice. I needed confirmation he was alive. I awoke the next morning, and like a creature of habit, I went through my daily prep for training.

It was a beautiful spring day in Windsor. I was walking to the track, and it was one of the most beautiful days I could remember. My phone was usually on silent because, when I walked to the track, only training got my attention. However, that day, my mind was on my brother. I was at the parking lot of the St. Denis Centre when my phone rang. I answered the phone and heard my brother's voice. He was in tears; I could hear him crying. I heard the cracking in his voice. I said his name, and he said, "Jamie."

He said, "I'm paralyzed. I can't feel my legs. The doctors tell me that I am never going to walk again." The break hadn't happened yet. I said, "You don't listen to those doctors. You are an Adjetey-Nelson. You have the same genetic makeup as me. You are going to be okay. Don't worry about what he said. You will do what you have to do. You are an Adjetey. We are strong. Pray." I continued not to let him hear the pain I was feeling all over. We talked briefly because I didn't want him to dwell on it and the drugs he was on made him sleepy. I told him I loved him and God was on his side. Then, we stopped talking.

I hung up the phone. I saw my coach in the parking lot, and finally, I broke. I'm a 203-pound, 6-foot-2-inch beast of a man, who'd been brought to tears in pain. My coach hugged me and asked me what was up, and I told him. He knew I needed to be with my family, so he told me to go home. As I turned and walked away, sobbing, distraught, and unprepared for what my brother had told me, I dropped to my knees and prayed. I didn't pray for me to get through this; I prayed to make a deal with my Lord. "God, please, let my brother walk again. If it means my never getting to the Olympics, please let him walk again. I don't need to be there. Let him walk please!"

My brother was eventually airlifted back to Windsor after a little more than a week. My brother, 6 feet 5 inches and 300 pounds, was in a bed that barely held him. We began to talk. He told me he couldn't even control his bowels nor clean himself.

Like my coaches have done for me, I set out a plan for him. I let him know anything was possible. I never knew how well I could do in sports until I tried, so it was his turn to be at his best. He was doing his Olympic training. Day in and day out, he did his therapy. He told me of his progress and how well he was doing. I reminded him what I'd said when we first talked: He is an Adjetey-Nelson, and he has talents he didn't know.

A month and half went by. You can guess what happened. My brother was standing. He was using a walker. It was a miracle! He had his legs back. The better his health became, the better I slept at night. My training got better. He was preparing for the rest of his life, and I was preparing for one of the most important meets of my life.

Calgary, Alberta! Canadian Olympic trials, two days, one event, the decathlon! After day one, I held about a fifty-point lead on a tough competitor, and I was feeling okay. There are always ups and downs in a decathlon. I was ready to fulfill my destiny and compete at an Olympic Games. Day two got off to an awesome start. I was vaulting and throwing well. I managed to get a huge best in the javelin throw. The only event left then was the 1,500 meters. As an athlete, I know there are no guarantees in sports, but I was feeling great, the most confident I'd felt for a 1,500 meters in my life.

The gun went off, and the race began. I had a seventy-point lead on the other top competitor. He was going for it, and so was I. Only one of us could go, so it was winner take all. Four hundred meters in, I was feeling okay. Fifty meters later, my right hamstring started to feel weird, so I adjusted to make my stride more dynamic. At approximately 525 meters, my right hamstring cramped, and I was now shuffling. I transferred much of the work to my left leg, but at 550 meters, my legs failed. Both of my hamstrings cramped. There it was. My Olympic journey was at an end. At the time, I didn't know it was my last shot, but there it was, over just like that. I cried. I was hurt. I was disappointed but more upset for my family, my friends, my country, my support staff, and my coaches who'd put all that work into me. My Olympic dream was over.

It showed me how much this wasn't all about me. It was about the journey and how it touched others. I was so happy to reach the level that I did. But, who knows why it happened?

So much could go into what had happened, from diet to physiology to God's answering my prayers and intervening.

The better man won on that day, and he deserved to be an Olympian. All I can say is, I'm happy my brother is walking again. Regardless, I never gave up because life was hard. My brother was going through a tough time in his life and was working to get better. If he could work through struggles, then so could I. I needed to be an example to him that hard work pays off. My hope was the Olympics, and his hope was to walk. It made me see how blessed I was for all I had in my life. It made me appreciate how I'd gotten to where I was. It showed me you can bounce back from the most difficult times in your life.

It is God who arms me with strength and makes my way perfect. He makes my feet like the feet of a deer; he enables me to stand on the heights. He trains my hands for battle; my arms can bend a bow of bronze.
–Psalm 18:32–34

Hayli Bozarth

Hometown: Norton, Kansas
Sport: Track and field, thrower
Age at time of story: 22

The hardest part about accepting the saying "everything happens for a reason" is waiting for that reason to come along.
–Unknown

In June 2013, I was faced with something I had prayed about never having to face in my years as a collegiate athlete: making the decision to transfer. I had to choose between going to Boise State to be with Coach Wall, who'd been my coach the last four years and the coach I'd planned on staying with for a while, or staying at Iowa State and adapting to a new coaching staff.

I knew what my gut was telling me, but I had to make sure it was going to be doable for me, academically and athletically. After many sleepless nights, a list of pros and cons, and what seemed like endless talks with my parents and old coaches, I walked into the new head coach's office and asked for my release to transfer to Boise State to finish my last year of eligibility with the coach who'd gotten me to the point I was at in my career. I had no home, I knew I was welcome at Boise State, and I knew the coaching staff, but before I could get out to Boise, I had to endure the fall semester at Iowa State.

Just when I thought everything was getting back on track and I'd figured out how I could student teach and train at a level that would allow me to continue to improve, I had a moment that seemed to stop time itself. I'll never forget it: July 24 at about five o'clock in the evening. I was working at a youth summer camp. It was the second-to-last day of the camp. Like usual, the kids wanted to play Capture the Flag. We had multiple kids missing that day, so the adult leaders decided we'd also play to make it more fun for the kids. I was running with the flag and tried to avoid getting tagged. In that split instant, my foot slipped on the grass, and my right knee bent at a ninety-degree angle, outward. Instantly, I thought the worst! I got up and continued to walk. It seemed better until the following day when walking was no longer an option for me.

Because I'd asked for my release from Iowa State, I had to figure out to whom and where I could go to have the magnetic resonance imaging (MRI)/x-ray done. After discussing things with my parents, we decided the best thing to do was to go to a doctor we knew and with whom our family had had previous luck. This was all fine and dandy, but that meant I had to drive five and a half hours to Kearney, Nebraska, with an injured knee just to see him.

After seeing the doctor, I found out I had a partially torn and sprained medial collateral ligament (MCL) along with a low-grade ACL tear. I'd just asked for my release from Iowa State seventeen days earlier and had figured out how I was going to survive the semester and show up to Boise State prepared. To make the situation worse, I'd be on crutches for five weeks, missing two months of lifting legs and not throwing for three months.

I wasn't allowed to drive, so my parents took me home and cared for me. I'll never be able to thank them enough because I know I wasn't a very pleasant person to be around. My coaches kept reminding me I could continue to lift upper body and do seated drill work to keep my progress in an upward direction. Coach Wall always tried to remind me how stupid it was to try to "juke" a ten-year-old because he knew how hard I was on myself and how upset I was. He also reminded me that everything happens for a reason and maybe this was a break I needed to take my training to the next level.

I truly believe the main reason I didn't give up was because I had unfinished business with myself. I'd decided just three months prior to transfer and to strive to reach new heights as a thrower. I knew if I gave up, I'd only be disappointed and full of regrets.

Another factor that played a large role in my not giving up was that I come from a small, supportive, rural farming community in Northwest Kansas. I had "put us on the map," and my family, friends, and community members knew me as a competitor who never gave up. I knew if I gave up, I'd not only let myself down but also the community and my family and friends who'd supported me since day one of my athletic career.

Looking back, I believe my situation made me who I am today. Holding myself accountable for the workouts during the fall and doing the rehab on my knee that strengthened it back to 100 percent before I moved out to Boise in January were the most challenging phase of this struggle. Because I held myself responsible for this, I believe I showed myself "this is who I am." If I could get through that six-month struggle, I can get through anything. Every time I step in the ring, I just want to please God and have fun because I never know when the opportunity will be taken from me for good.

"For I know the plans I have for you," declares the Lord, "plans to prosper you and not to harm you, plans to give you hope and a future."
–Jeremiah 29:11

Justin Burns

Hometown: Toronto, Ontario
Sport: Powerlifting
Age at time of story: 24

Weakness is a choice. I choose strength.
-Unknown

Strength athletics is something most people don't quite understand. But, I'm a powerlifter and have been since I set foot inside a weight room. I was in awe of how strong some of the men were. All I ever wanted was to become as strong as I possibly could. This may have been a weird goal for a fifteen-year-old boy, but it was what I wanted. So, that set me on a journey that went through another sport I fell in love with— football. I was quite the athlete for a kid who weighed 240 pounds at 5 feet 7 inches, and believe me, that wasn't muscle.

I used powerlifting to enhance my football skills throughout my high school career, and it worked. I became one of the best offensive linemen in the province of Ontario and won a number of awards. By high school's end, I was very successful in my athletic career as well as in my studies, having become an Ontario scholar and achieved honors twice. I was a young man destined for a great life. Little did I know that four years later, I'd be faced with the biggest decision of my life. But, a little backstory is needed.

After finishing high school, I'd decided I needed a year to mature and get my life together in terms of which career path I wanted to take. I'd turned down scholarship offers to University of British Columbia as well as St. Mary's University because I was very indecisive and didn't want to jump into something I'd regret.

I used that year to train. I wanted to get as strong as I possibly could to try to become the best lifter in Canada. I'd broken six national records as well as one world record, so I'd say I sat at the pinnacle of my weight class and age grouping. It seemed as if no matter what I did, I couldn't fail. Boy, was I wrong about that!

So, once the year was over, I decided football was no longer what I wanted to do. I leaped into the trades and became an electrical apprentice. I did this for three years with little satisfaction; my motivation had quickly gone downhill. One day, it all came crashing down around me. I lost my job, and powerlifting seemed to be a chore I no longer wanted to complete. I'd gone from the picture of confidence and strength to a defeated child in less than three years.

I became extremely depressed and retreated into my shell. I'd never been dealt a setback quite like that in my life, and I had no idea how to take it. I clearly took it in absolutely the wrong way and became a person I swore I'd never be. After I'd spent a few months in self-loathing, my mother, of all people, asked me one very simple question: "What was your first love?" That question brought me all the way back to the first time I'd set foot into a weight room. It was strength. Strength is what I loved; strength had been the focus of my whole life until I took the misdirection.

Am I acting strong? Is this how someone strong acts when things go a little south? These were the questions I had to ask myself. The answer, of course, was no! I needed to make a change, and fast. My mom bought my personal training certificate program and my strength and conditioning program to get me started in the right direction. I completed both programs in less than three months and was primed to begin helping people become the strongest they could be. I tried looking for a career path that focused on strength, but no company wanted to offer my services to their clients.

I asked myself, "Why spend my effort and time making someone else's dream come true?" So I began what is now known as "Untamed Strength Systems," and to this day, it's growing slowly but surely.

Hardship is dealt to even the most undeserving of individuals, but to endure and prevail is strength and courage. No matter how hard you get beaten down by life, all that matters is that you pick yourself back up, dust yourself off, and keep on moving forward!

Strength is so much more than just the physical. Being mentally strong is more important than physical, in my opinion. If your mind knows you're going to accomplish something, your body will follow — it has no choice. Weakness is a choice. I chose strength. What will you choose?

Be strong, and let your heart take courage.
–Psalm 31:24

Kendra White

Hometown: St. Louis, Missouri
Sport: Track and field
Age at time of story: 19

The Pursuit of Happiness should probably be the title of my life's journal. It began the summer of 2012 when I had to make the hardest decision of my athletic career: stay at the legendary track powerhouse, Louisiana State University, or transfer to another college. To provide some background, I had a far-from-great freshman year. I wasn't competing well, I only had one true friend, and being so far from home made things even worse for me.

Going to practice every day was a personal struggle; I felt as if I didn't belong. I was putting in hard work yet not getting any positive results or recognition. Now, some may call it the freshman woes, but I knew in my heart that something wasn't right about my being there. I wasn't growing as a person, and I was losing passion for the sport I love so dearly.

While at home during the summer, I contemplated transferring: Why did I want to leave LSU, what were the pros and cons for my schools of interest, what if I didn't like the new school? Finally, after a lot of thought and prayer, I decided I'd start a new chapter in my life at Iowa State University (ISU).

Now, many speculate why I left and chose ISU over other schools, but honestly, I didn't know why I was led there. I just let God be my captain, and I chose to follow his lead. It was this big decision that brought me closer to him because, once I got to ISU, there was a completely different atmosphere. My entire team and coach were like a family; they genuinely cared for one another and welcomed me like they'd known me before I even arrived.

Things seemed to be off to a great start! I was training well, my coach had become more like a Christian mentor, I got along with everyone on the team, and on top of all that, I was doing well in most of my classes. Nevertheless, Satan always attacks you when things are going smoothly in your life. I strained my hamstring and therefore wasn't competing as well as I wanted to, and I couldn't concentrate in class. The type of student-athlete I am (like most who love their sport), I wanted to be better! My coach kept me motivated with the constant reminder that God does everything for a reason, and through him all things are possible. I can recall several occasions when he'd talk to me about keeping my faith and trusting God's plan to work on his time. Many of these talks ended with prayer for physical, mental, and spiritual strength.

With my coach's sincere, continuous support, I never gave up on my goals, placing at conference, making it to regionals, and then qualifying for nationals. It was his support that kept me focused as I stepped onto the track that hot day in Walnut, California. I got down into my starting blocks with one thing in mind, "God, you do everything for a reason, so I'm letting go of my doubts, and I'm just going to run for you." It was because of my prayer at the start of that race that I was able to finally have a breakthrough performance as I crossed the line with my second-fastest time ever in the 400-meter dash.

It was because of the same prayer that the next weekend I ran even faster at Drake Relays in Des Moines, Iowa. It was because of the same prayer that the time I ran qualified me to run in Texas at the NCAA regional meet. I was so ecstatic after both races that I just gave God all of the glory by praising him at the finish line. My coach met me after both races with a giant hug and "great job!" For his support, I'm so very appreciative and grateful. I'd found happiness again! I was competing well while upholding a 3.0 grade point average. I was enjoying life at ISU both on and off of the track because my relationship with God was now flourishing because of Coach Wiens and his constant watering of the faith I had planted inside me.

Looking back on this situation, I can truly say it molded me into not only a better athlete but also a better Christian. When I'm anxious about something, I remind myself that God has me covered, so there's no need to doubt or worry. This experience taught me to appreciate every trial I go through because, as I overcome it, I know my character is being built up even stronger. Hence, if I hadn't decided to leave LSU, then I would have never had the chance to work with Coach Wiens and get the push to grow as much as I have up to now. I would've been disobedient to what God wanted, which was for me to live for him and not others. Now as I compete every weekend, I say a prayer as I get down into the blocks and give God the glory when I finish the race because I know I wouldn't be where I am today if I hadn't put my trust in him.

Jesus replied, "Because you have so little faith. Truly I tell you, if you have faith as small as a mustard seed, you can say to this mountain, 'Move from here to there,' and it will move. Nothing will be impossible for you."
–Matthew 17:20

Brittany Gomez

Hometown: New Braunfels, Texas
Sport: Softball
Age at time of story: 8

You never said I'm leaving, you never said goodbye.
You were gone before I knew it, and only God knew why.
A million times I needed you, a million times I cried.
If love alone could have saved you, you never would have died.
In life I loved you dearly, in death I love you still;
In my heart you hold a place, that no one could ever fill.
It broke my heart to lose you, but you didn't go alone.
For part of me went with you, the day God took you home.
–Unknown

Ever since I was little, I knew I wanted to play softball for as long as I could. When I was younger, my parents put me in with the boys to play baseball, but they never gave me a reason why.

I come from a family in which no one had ever gone to college. The closest anyone in my family had gotten to college was when my aunt attended a small two-year school in the middle of nowhere, Texas. I can proudly say that, because of the support from my family and friends, I now play softball at Iowa State University, a game I've loved my whole life. There's not one day that goes by that I don't remember what my family and I have overcome so that I can be where I am today.

When I was eight years old, I was told unforgettable news. My grandma was diagnosed with brain cancer. She'd raised me like she was my mom, being my number one supporter and my hero. I didn't want to believe she was actually ill. With all the bad people in this world, why would this happen to my grandma? Why did this have to happen to a woman who attended church regularly and brought me along with her? Why did this have to happen to a woman who was like a mother to all her younger siblings and anyone in need of help? Why did this have to happen to a woman who brought her family together and was nothing but caring to anyone she'd ever met?

After I was told the news, time seemed to slow down. One day she was her happy and regular self, and the next it was as if she had no strength to get out of bed. I'd leave school to go visit her in the hospital, and the smell of it would consume every part of my body. She was one of the strongest people I knew, and after chemo it killed me seeing how weak she looked. The day she bought a wig was the day I partially understood what was going on.

I will never forget the day I was called out of elementary school to visit her at the hospital for the very last time. I remember holding my dad's hand, walking down the hall to a room where she lay in a bed with family surrounding her. I didn't yet know what was different about that hospital visit until I was told to tell her goodbye. My uncle lifted me up to give her a kiss on her cheek, but this time instead of her face being warm, it was cold.

Although I wasn't a Division I athlete at age eight, my grandma played a huge part in my going on to become one. She taught me that no matter what you endure, keep at it and work through it.
She'd go through chemo over and over again just for the possibility of some hope to pull through. No matter how much it hurt her, she'd still do it for the chance of staying on this earth. She stayed strong even until her last day with us.

The hardest thing I went through as an athlete was being here on this earth while my hero was passing. There was absolutely nothing in this world I could do to stop it. There's never been a day I don't wish she were still here with us physically to watch my younger siblings grow and go through life. Despite that, I'm glad she's no longer suffering and is finally at peace and watching over our entire family.

My parents and my grandpa helped me understand what had happened and that she was in a better place. My hero was gone, but I couldn't give up. I could be selfish all I wanted and cry my eyes out night after night wondering "Why me?" but that wouldn't bring her back. My parents made me understand the only thing I had control over was me. I needed to live my life for her.

I want to be that woman she was to others. I've never forgotten about her, and I never will. My goal is to make her proud of me for anything and everything I do in my life. Change may be painful at times, but I feel my life is completely different than it could've been if she were still here with us physically. I've gone through a lot of different things in life since she passed that I know she had something to do with while watching over her family.

I only knew her for eight years, but those were the best eight years I could have ever asked for with her. Because of her, I work hard each day to become a better person, someone she'd be proud to call her granddaughter. Because I've gone through something as tragic as this, I sympathize more with people who've gone through the same thing. Because of her, I strive to be better for my younger siblings, and I hope I portray a little bit of her in me. I know if I ever need anything, I can always talk to her because she understands.

I'm not saying I don't have those random nights when I completely break down and miss her miserably, because I do. What I'm saying is that, even if you've gone through something like this, there's always one thing for sure you have control over—you. If you don't like the way something is going in your life, make a better choice. I can now talk about my grandma to others without tearing up, although I still can't bear to watch home videos with my grandma in them.

No matter what you endure, don't give up. Do it for the ones who look up to you, but most of all, do it for you. If you've gotten this far already, don't throw in the towel. Keep your head up and keep pushing. You won't regret it.

This verse was in my grandma's house:

The LORD is my shepherd; I shall not want. He maketh me to lie down in green pastures: he leadeth me beside the still waters. He restoreth my soul: he leadeth me in the paths of righteousness for his name's sake. Yea, though I walk through the valley of the shadow of death, I will fear no evil: for thou art with me; thy rod and thy staff they comfort me. Thou preparest a table before me in the presence of mine enemies: thou anointest my head with oil; my cup runneth over. Surely goodness and mercy shall follow me all the days of my life: and I will dwell in the house of the LORD forever.
–Psalm 23

Justin Coleman

Hometown: Beatrice, Nebraska
Sport: Football
Age at time of story: 20

In the end, we only regret the chances we did not take.
-Unknown

Going into my senior year of high school football at Beatrice High School in Nebraska, I thought I had it made, as I'm sure many young athletes do. I was coming off a junior year in which I was selected to the all-state team. All I had left to do was put up some numbers similar to those of the previous year, win the state championship, and accept my football scholarship to Nebraska. At least, that's what I thought, but that was the farthest thing from the truth.

My final year at Beatrice High, I was fortunate to again be selected to the all-state team, and I made it to the state championship game, but still no Division I offer. At that point, I thought no one knew talent when they saw it. The recruiting process dragged on for me, and I went into February's signing day accepting a partial offer to the University of Nebraska at Omaha (UNO), a Division II school. Going to a Division II school meant I expected to play in the shadow of Division I football and assumed my dreams of one day playing in the NFL were out the window.

During the next two years of playing at UNO, I was fortunate to find my way onto the field and even started my sophomore year. Our coaching staff and strength staff did an amazing job of demanding the highest from the entire team, and the organization's development of players at the Division II level was next to none.

I say all this out of respect to those who taught me so much in my two years at UNO, while I was still hung up on the fact I was never offered a Division I scholarship. My work ethic improved drastically over the two years, and I began to hold myself accountable for the smallest of things, still clinging to the hope I could get an NFL tryout after my time at UNO.

Following my sophomore year, the week prior to spring ball, I was notified the UNO football program was being cut. The next morning, I got a call from my head coach who confirmed the rumor; UNO no longer had a football team, and if I wanted to continue to play, I'd have to transfer somewhere else. Just like that, the rug was swept out from under my feet, and I didn't know what to do. I could finish my degree at UNO and keep my scholarship while kissing football goodbye or begin another search for a new football team. Quitting football was now a real option because transferring to play elsewhere meant giving up my scholarship and earning my way onto another team.

I went back and forth on the decision and spent the months of March and April in limbo. This extra time to think and the struggle turned out to be the best thing that could have happened. I had no choice but to renew my faith and believe it would work out. I stopped asking myself for all the answers because I had none. After two months of weighing my options and contacting numerous schools to see if they'd let me play football for them, I decided to transfer to Iowa State.

I moved to Ames to begin working out with the team in May 2011, and that only marked the beginning of my struggle. I didn't know anybody, and nobody knew me, not the coaches, strength staff, or players. My living situation was just as bad because I moved in with two other random roommates I'd found on Craigslist. I knew walking onto a Division I football program in the Big 12 would be an upward battle, but I was going to give it everything I had.

From day one, my motto was "be relentless." I wasn't trying to shock the world in one day but rather outlast the rest and put myself in the face of the decision makers day in and day out, so they wouldn't forget me.

That summer, I walked to all my workouts as I found my way through Ames and spent a lot of time questioning my decision. The workouts were so tough on me both mentally and physically because I was in a situation I'd never been in before. Because no one knew me and knew what to expect of me, I had to earn my keep from the get-go. All I had in mind during every day of the workouts was to do what they asked in an attempt to impress someone. Each rep I took that summer, I did with the intention of getting better. Every lift was to be more powerful, and every run was to get more explosive. I remember being in so much pain and questioning my decision to play football to the point I would do reps of up-downs saying to myself, "God wouldn't have put me here if I couldn't handle it."

Before, I'd always thought I had the answers and I was working as hard as I could. The reality was I didn't have the answers, and I could've been working so much harder. The process of going to UNO, followed by walking onto Iowa State, turned out to be a blessing in disguise. I wouldn't have had it any other way. My faith was truly restored, and I began making Friday night pregame chapels mandatory for myself because I knew the things I was capable of with my trust in the Lord.

I was fortunate to make the travel squad while still redshirting in my first year at ISU. The following year, I traveled and was on all four special teams as a junior, while backing up two returning starters at receiver. In 2013, as a senior, I was awarded the scholarship I'd been working for.

I'd proven myself enough through my motto of being relentless, and the payoff was finally here, taking a massive weight off my shoulders. Now, all I had left to do was play, and that's exactly what I did. I began the season with a starting spot at receiver while still contributing on special teams. Through the season, I was grateful for the opportunity to play at Iowa State and tried never to forget just how I got there. It was a long and unconventional road to the playing field, but I don't believe I would've ever played in the Big 12 had I been given a scholarship right out of high school. So, even when we have different ideas for ourselves, we have to learn to always trust God's path and timing.

Do not be rash with your mouth, and let not your heart utter anything hastily before God. For God is in heaven, and you on earth; therefore let your words be few. For a dream comes through much activity, and a fool's voice is known by his many words.
–Ecclesiastes 5:2–3

Anonymous Woman #2

Life's not about waiting for the storm to pass, it's about learning to dance in the rain.
–Vivian Greene

Hometown: Toronto, Ontario
Sport: Track and field
Age at time of story: 15

After entering high school in 2007, I made the decision to hang up my old soccer cleats and trade them in for my first pair of spikes, after I'd played soccer competitively for the preceding eight years. For the majority of my first year of training and competing as a sprinter, I was constantly approached by coaches, officials, and senior athletes telling me how much potential I had and how far I'd be able to go in the sport of track and field.

Although some people might argue this is what everyone wants to hear in their first year competing in a new sport, to an overachieving fourteen-year-old, all this did was cause me an ample amount of anxiety. Going to meets and hearing coaches tell their athletes to chase me down and make sure to beat me was far from anything I'd had to deal with thus far in my life. My race-day anxiety elevated with each meet, until it got to the point where I couldn't eat and could barely sleep for days leading up to competitions.

With the help of my mother and coach, I was able to get my anxiety in check in time for the provincial championships in June 2008. After winning one gold and three silver medals, I felt invincible and more eager than ever to continue to develop as a young sprinter and to grow as an athlete.

Fast-forward to 2009. One bad step in a hurdle race caused me to compete with an extremely painful foot injury for the majority of my second season. Against my better judgment, I continued to compete, for the sake of not letting down my family, teammates, or coach, and in a desperate attempt to live up to all the pressure that was placed on me only a year prior. Based on my performances from my previous season and the progress I was making in the current season, I was looked at as someone with potential to win four more medals at the provincial championships in 2009. Unfortunately, by the time the championships came around, my foot injury had only escalated, which I later discovered was a broken first metatarsal and a fractured fourth metatarsal. I'd known it was bad and definitely had accepted a fracture as a possibility, but I hadn't realized how bad it actually was. Still, despite the great amount of pain I was feeling, and icing my foot at every possible second, I competed in heats for three events at the championships and qualified for the finals in all of them.

While I was getting prepared for my first final, my coach looked at the state of my foot, which at this point could barely fit into my spike, and told me he wouldn't let me go over a hurdle. He'd allow me to run the finals for the 100 meters and the 4x100-meter relay, but those finals were scheduled after the hurdle final. The problem was that not running the hurdle final would cause me to be disqualified for the rest of the day, meaning I wouldn't get to run in any of the finals in which I'd qualified. My coach gave me the option to either not run the hurdle final, and be scratched from my other finals, or false start twice in the hurdle final, so I could compete in the other two. Weighing the consequences of both options, I decided it wouldn't be fair to the other competitors for me to enter a race and knowingly false start twice and then compete later on in my other two finals.

After telling my coach my decision, I went back up to the stands and cried. One of the worst moments of my athletic career to this day is that exact moment, sitting in the stands, in tears, watching the finals of the races in which I'd earned my place, with an empty lane. Sadness turned to anger, and I decided the anxiety, the stress, and now the disappointment were way more than any sane teenager needed to go through. I convinced myself I'd be a lot happier if I gave up completely on track and field and went back to soccer, where instead of being an individual I'd be a member of a team, and I wouldn't have any pressure on me or any expectations to live up to.

On the way home from the competition, I broke down to my mother, who's been and continues to be my greatest support system in everything I do. I told her the pressure was too much and the only way to never experience the same disappointment again would be to keep myself far away from track and field. Like any mother would, she told me how ridiculous my plan was and spent the next little while lecturing me on why this was a terrible plan. She told me that, although this may seem like the worst thing that could have possibly happened, it was all in God's plan and that a situation like this would all be for nothing if I didn't learn from it. Like any rational 15-year-old, I screamed and yelled and was 100 percent convinced my life was over, my mother knew nothing, and she was obviously out to ruin my life along with whatever higher power had caused the injury in the first place.

After some time, I finally came to my senses. I accepted the fact that, as per usual, my mother was right, and she helped me realize two things. First, the only person who was putting pressure on me was me. All of the pressure I was so concerned about and stressing about was from me, meaning that it had always been within my control to regulate. Second, she made me realize that, regardless of how I performed, I would never be letting anyone down as long as I gave my best effort. These two very simple concepts were something that I'd never considered until that point. It showed me I had no reason to give up.

With my newly found optimism, I told myself this was nothing more than an obstacle and, like everything else, the hurt was only temporary, but it wouldn't be any easier if all I did was wallow in my misery. The amount of disappointment I felt also made me know that, aside from the pressure everyone else was putting on me, I had to do this for me. Instead of always trying to please everyone else, and perform well to meet others' expectations, I needed to learn how to run for myself, for my goals, and ultimately for my own satisfaction. In doing so, I'd never be disappointed in myself if I tried my absolute hardest.

Looking back at the experience, I wouldn't say I'd ever want it to happen to anyone else, and to be completely honest, I would much rather it had never happened to me in the first place. With this in mind, however, I'm very appreciative for the support I received from my family, friends, teammates, and coach as well as the new mindset it gave me, and for their help in my growing into the person I am today.

This experience has changed my perspective on adversity for the better, as it is a constant reminder that everything is only as bad as you make it and that all hardships will pass in time. Instead of letting one negative event get the best of you, try to accept that every misfortune comes with a lesson. It's entirely up to you whether or not you're willing to figure out what the lesson may be.

Not only so, but we also glory in our sufferings, because we know that suffering produces perseverance; perseverance, character; and character, hope. And hope does not put us to shame, because God's love has been poured out into our hearts through the Holy Spirit, who has been given to us.
–Romans 5:3–5

Joshua M. Radford

Hometown: Topeka, Kansas
Sport: Track and field
Age at time of story: 18

Throughout high school and middle school, I was heavily criticized by my peers because of my height, race, and social status. I grew up in the inner city of Topeka, Kansas. The neighborhoods around my house were run down, drug ridden, and rarely clean. For me to make it out of there, my mother knew I'd need to go to a school and receive a great education. Little did she know the price of that great education would come at the expense of what made me different.

When I was growing up, my family never had a lot of money. Although my mom's job paid well, she was driven into debt after our house was broken into during my seventh-grade year. However, she was the type of mother who wanted to give her children everything. My sister and I are two years apart, but we were both adopted at two months old from separate families. Early on, my mother tried to teach us that being financially savvy and driven toward success would be the key to making it out of the lifestyle we lived. She was my biggest influence and supporter throughout my life.

The year my house was broken into was the same year the criticism started to take full effect. My most vivid memory from that year would have to be what happened after a football practice.
A teammate and I were talking about how cool it would be to compete in college athletics, and after overhearing our conversation, one of my football coaches came up to me and said, "Well, Radford, you don't have to worry about that

because you'll most likely never compete in collegiate athletics at any level, let alone even have the grades to get into college."

From that day forward, I wanted to prove to not only him but also the world that everyone was wrong and become the best thing to ever come out of my school district. School was a struggle for me, but I always worked hard. I took my drive for athletics and applied it in the classroom.

In high school, I gave up football and started to compete in basketball, cross-country, and track and field. After being a varsity athlete my freshman year for cross-country, I knew I could go somewhere with it. I could prove everyone wrong.

My drive became stronger, and my focus on athletics was clearer than ever. I gave up basketball after freshman year to focus on track and cross-country, and in my freshman year alone, I grew from four feet ten inches to five feet five inches — a sophomore who had everyone on notice. With that growth spurt came better athletic ability, and it was just another tool God gave me to be able to achieve my goal. No matter what people said about me in high school, I knew I'd come out on top. While it was hard to even come to school some days because of the constant criticism, I knew it was the only way I could achieve my goal.

By my senior year, I had given up cross-country and focused primarily on track and field. Distance wasn't my passion anymore, so I began jumping, and that's when my life changed.
To make a long story short, jumping, long and triple jump, came easy to me. That year, I took the indoor Amateur Athletic Union (AAU) League by storm. People who'd competed against the same kids for years wondered who I was. When I told people I was a distance runner turned jumper, they laughed and didn't take me seriously. But after this scrawny little kid out jumped them, it was evident I was

that guy to beat, which led me to my biggest accomplishment, my National Championship.

The weekend of the 2012 AAU National Championship was a crazy one, to say the least. I was projected to not even make the finals, but my coach and I knew that, after having beaten the odds my whole life, I could still do something special. But, who knew the first day would also be my last day?

After barely making it to finals in the triple jump, I knew I still had a long way to go if I was going to place in the top three and become an All-American. Winning wasn't even on my mind. My first jump into finals was decent, and my coach told me I was in the lead at that point because the top two jumpers had scratched and the others behind them had had bad jumps. Then, my second jump in the finals, everything changed. I landed wrong on my second bound and tore everything in my hip.

It was at that moment I thought to myself, "It's all over. Everything I've worked hard for will be gone, no college athletics, no All-American status, and no satisfaction of proving everyone who'd ever doubted me wrong." But, as fate would have it, the top two jumpers completely scratched out of finals, and nobody else had jumped farther than my first attempt. It was later that night when my coach told me I'd won the AAU National Young Men's Division Championship.

However, one of the most satisfying feelings ever was going back to school the first day. The football coach who'd told me I would never be anything had ended up being my Civil and Criminal Rights teacher my senior year (ironic, right?). After I got back, I set my medals and trophy on his desk. All I said was "I did it."

While I'd accomplished many things in high school on and off the track, that moment changed my life forever. Despite my severe injury, I was recruited to Wichita State University and graduated high school with a 3.0 grade point average. After getting my diploma, I knew I'd made it. But, my story was far from over; it was just beginning.

After surgery and rehab my freshman year of college, I hung up the spikes and ended my athletic career for good. Despite everything that had happened to me up to that point, I knew I'd done the impossible. I left a mark on my high school that will not soon be forgotten. I was one of only five athletes to ever go straight out of my high school and become a Division I athlete. I never competed in outdoor season for track my senior year, never won a state championship, nor did I even make it to state for track. But, in the face of doubt, I prevailed.

Go back and report to John what you hear and see: The blind receive sight, the lame walk, those who have leprosy are cured, the deaf hear, the dead are raised, and the good news is preached to the poor. Blessed is the man who does not fall away on account of me.
–Luke 7:22–23

Cheria Morgan

Hometown: Toronto/Pickering, Ontario
Sport: Track and field
Age at time of story: 23

Why me? Why now? For how long am I going to be unable to run?
–Cheria Morgan

The moment I found out I had tears in my Achilles tendon, my mind was filled with questions about the unknown. After graduating from an American university, I'd moved back to my hometown and had begun my post collegiate track career. I had a new coach and was training with some of the best track athletes in the country. This was an opportunity I didn't take lightly. I was ecstatic about being back home and having the support of my family and was ready to jump-start my post collegiate career.

My training had started off well. I felt my fitness improve, and I found a great support system in some of my training partners. Two months after I joined the group, it was time for us to head south for our annual warm weather training camp. It was then I first experienced pain in my Achilles. As a Division I athlete who was used to competing at a high level, I was accustomed to experiencing stiffness but nothing compared to what I was feeling that day. Although the team therapists gave me permission to complete camp, there were days when I was running through pain.

Upon returning home, I was given an ultrasound, and it was confirmed I had a tear in my Achilles. It was a small tear but large enough to cause pain because of all the pounding and explosive action I did while running.

My coaches gave me some time to rest my Achilles in hopes the tear would heal on its own. After a few weeks off, I believed my Achilles had healed because I was no longer feeling the pain. As the year progressed, I received regular treatment and eventually began sprinting again. However, as my training program picked up momentum, the pain in my Achilles became more apparent. It was too late in the season to "shut it down," and as an athlete, you always want to fight through the pain. I finished my season as best I could; I placed sixth at the 2012 Canadian Olympic Trials in the 100 meters.

With the season officially over, I took the time to have my Achilles medically attended to and spent the end of my summer in a boot and crutches. I thought that would be the end of my Achilles issues, but they seemed to follow me like a dark cloud. The next year, I found myself with two tears in my Achilles. The wise decision would've been to shut down my season and fix the issue right away. Nope, I didn't do that. Instead, I chose to continue through the entire season with the tears in my Achilles. Those six months were probably the longest, most emotional months I'd gone through in a long time. Because I woke up and hobbled to the bathroom in the morning and came home after practice in worse shape than when I'd left, I knew I needed to stop running and rest my Achilles. But again, the athlete in me persevered.

By the end of the season, I was well aware I had to find the cause of these reoccurring tears in my Achilles and not just address the pain. I couldn't keep putting my body through this spiral of ongoing pain. There was more to life than track, and when all was said and done, I wanted to leave the sport in one piece. While under the medical care of one of the best sports doctors in Canada, I underwent a rehab protocol to heal and strengthen my Achilles.

As my Achilles improved and I continued rehab away from the track, I was able to reflect on my season and think about my future in the sport. With the injuries I'd faced throughout the years, I'd slowly lost the love I once had for track. I knew if I was going to be successful in this competitive sport I needed to spark that love for track and field again. I later talked to my parents and my mentors and prayed on it and made the decision to relocate. I didn't choose to relocate because of my Achilles but more so because I needed a fresh start. The more I prayed, the more I knew I was making the right decision.

I pray that the eyes of your heart may be enlightened in order that you may know.
–Ephesians 1:18

When God shined light on my situation, I was able to see the direction for my confusion. Giving up had never been an option for me; I just needed to have faith in what God was going to do. Looking back, I realized I'd always been walking *for* Christ, but this situation allowed me to walk *with* Him through the struggles in my life. I was always a believer in Christ, but learning to commit to what he wants me to do and saying, "What you show me, I'm going to do." was always a struggle for me. One of my favorite Bible verses says, "Trust in the Lord with all your heart and lean not on your own understanding; in all your ways submit to him, and he will make your paths straight." (Proverbs 3:5–6)

The moment I stopped fighting my injury and humbled myself and turned to the Lord, I was able to see the changes that needed to be made. When times get tough, we try to figure it out on our own instead of turning to the Lord. In the words of Helen Keller, "When you face the sun, the shadows always fall behind you."

I strongly believe it's through hard work and perseverance that we can achieve wonders. As I continue to work toward my Olympic dreams, I'm grateful for the journey I've experienced thus far and pray the future is bright. Why not me?

Alecia Beckford Stewart

Hometown: Brampton, Ontario, Canada
Sport: Track and field
Age at time of story: 24

Chase success; don't run away from fear.
–Unknown

My passion for sports started at age three when I was in gymnastics, but by the time I was ten, track and field had stolen my heart, and I've been in love ever since. I grew up as a Seventh-Day Adventist, and honoring the Sabbath meant Friday sundown until Saturday sundown. But, those of you who know the world of track and field know that track meets are almost always on Saturdays. My mom battled with the idea of letting me run because she hadn't been able to pursue track growing up because she'd been heavily into the church, but she saw my passion, my talent, and my drive and thought maybe it would be worth it. She consulted with the pastor and prayed on it and came to this conclusion: The Lord had given me this talent and would want me to use it. I'm so thankful my mother has been so supportive, and I thank God every day for her.

From the time I was in elementary school up through high school, my mom never missed a meet and always reminded me of the importance of keeping my faith, even if we weren't in the church to worship. To this day, I pray and just talk with God before every run, every jump, and every throw.

When I set my sights on getting a scholarship in the United States, it was all I could think about, and my actions toward that goal were relentless. I hadn't known where to start, but I found a way to ask the right questions, talk to the right people, and train until my dreams came true. It was official; I was going to be an Illini and attend the University of Illinois.

At Illinois, I saw many ups and downs but, overall, wouldn't trade the experience for anything. I was fortunate to work with an amazing coach, trainers, and academic advisors and have great teammates. I was also fortunate to be relatively injury free during my collegiate years with the right training and treatment. I finished my collegiate career with a silver in the pentathlon and a silver in the heptathlon in the Big Ten conference and just missed out on NCAA by one spot. I was thankful for it all, getting the fourth-best heptathlon score in school history, graduating with honors, and obtaining a bachelor's degree in science with a minor in chemistry. What more could a girl ask for?

Well, for me it wasn't enough because I knew I had more in the tank, and my ultimate goal wasn't accomplished yet. Becoming a doctor is my end goal, but I set my sights on continuing my athletic career and wasn't going to let anyone talk me out of pursuing my lifelong goal of becoming an Olympian. My brain would be in tip-top shape in ten years, but I couldn't say the same for my body.

Transitioning from school life and moving back home was rough because I then no longer had the support system most NCAA schools provide to athletes. Because I was a multi-event athlete, I had multiple coaches with whom I worked. I decided to work with a sprint group for my hurdles and speed work and most of my general training, while I worked with a separate coach for throws and another coach for jumps. I had great coaches in their respective fields and was excited and prepared to dominate my first outdoor, post collegiate season.

Along with doing the intensive training schedule, I had to work a few part-time jobs to support myself because I didn't have any fancy sponsors. My schedule was jam-packed, and I was always on the move, but goals are not accomplished by accident or by sitting around, so I was willing to do everything possible.

In 2011, my goals were to qualify for two national teams, score 5,800 points in the heptathlon, and perform well enough to get myself some government funding. That was the focus, but it all came to a halt at my first outdoor meet. I traveled down to Tennessee to compete and qualify for a national team. The competition was going to be in Jamaica, which made me even more excited because I'd be able to compete in front of family there. I was ready, and I felt sheer confidence running through my veins.

After day one of competition, I was in first place and had had a solid day of competition. My performances were all on pace for me to get the score I needed for the team. The next day, I woke up feeling great. I was ready to dominate the last three events that would propel my outdoor season into high gear. Long jump was great. Javelin was next, and my warm-up felt effortless. I was the fifth thrower in the lineup, and I was ready to make the spear fly. Because I had no one in Tennessee to watch or coach me, I'll never know what went wrong, but I ran down the runway, drew the javelin back for three crossover steps planted, and let that javelin fly—Bam! I went down holding my leg in pain!

My first thought was "Don't fault it; that was a good throw!" So I tucked my feet in close to my body, so I wouldn't cross over that line. My next thought was "I know I didn't come all this way and get hurt. I just sprained my knee. I'll be just fine." I didn't take any more throws and saw the medics. They advised me not to continue, but not knowing the severity of the incident, I didn't want to bow out of the 800 meters and make the trip and competition a waste. The medics taped me up, and I ran. That second lap wasn't pretty, but I managed to score what I needed to qualify for Jamaica. When I returned home, I got an MRI and found out I'd torn my left ACL and had some meniscus damage as well. I was crushed. I was in shock and didn't know what to do with myself. The pity party lasted about seven days, but after talking to my mentors and praying a lot, I was back on track. I was going to try and complete my season and accomplish my goals with a brace on.

I trained, I made alterations, I cried, I lifted, and I did all the things I would do injured or not, but it proved not to be enough. Completing and competing in a heptathlon are two very different things. I may have been mentally capable of doing it, but physically, no matter how lightweight the brace was, it wasn't going to be enough to get me competitively through a heptathlon.

The faith I had was strong enough to get me there but not to get me through. Later that summer, I had the surgery and began the rehab and rebuilding process. In 2012 and 2013, more hardships and another major injury followed, but I kept pushing on. I still was able to get new personal bests in shot put and javelin, after coming back from surgery and moving past the fear of not being good enough. I didn't give up and still haven't because I feel God isn't done with me yet. He's never given me more than I can handle and has allowed me to build a lot of character and weed out the negative influences in my life while going through hard times. I know he has a plan for me. He knows the ending, and I'm along for the journey as long as he will allow.

Finally, be strong in the Lord and in his mighty power. Put on the full armor of God, so that you can take your stand against the devil's schemes. For our struggle is not against flesh and blood, but against the rulers, against the authorities, against the powers of this dark world and against the spiritual forces of evil in the heavenly realms. Therefore put on the full armor of God, so that when the day of evil comes, you may be able to stand your ground, and after you have done everything, to stand. Stand firm then, with the belt of truth buckled around your waist, with the breastplate of righteousness in place, and with your feet fitted with the readiness that comes from the gospel of peace. In addition to all this, take up the shield of faith, with which you can extinguish all the flaming arrows of the evil one. Take the helmet of salvation and the sword of the Spirit, which is the word of God. And pray in the Spirit on all occasions with all kinds of prayers and requests. With this in mind, be alert and always keep on praying for all the Lord's people.

–Ephesians 6:10–18

Author Story: The Olympic Dream

Hometown: Markham, Ontario
Sport: Track and field
Age at time of story: 22

The key to everything is patience. You get the chicken by hatching the egg not by smashing it.
–Arnold H. Glasgow

Acceptance is not submission; it is acknowledgement of the facts of a situation. Then deciding what you're going to do about it.
–Kathleen Casey Theisen

For athletes who participate in a sport that competes in the Olympics, it's well known the Olympic Games are the pinnacle of the sport. To understand this story to its core, we'll need to take a trip down memory lane. When the Olympics were awarded to London after the 2004 Olympics, an intense goal was set in my head. I was fourteen at the time, and my brother and I made a pact that we wouldn't go back to London ever again unless we made that team. Our dad was born in England, so we'd both been there once before.

Fast-forward to 2012. It was the Canadian Track and Field Olympic trials. I'd been on fire that season to that point, and Justyn had been doing well too. In sports, nothing is guaranteed though, and a good performance on that day was required. My dad had been telling us all season we'd finish first and second at the trials. Even though I was confident in our abilities, the scenario just seemed too perfect to be something that could happen to me.

The finals were set to go, it was a beautiful day, and a group of eight guys who all knew each other pretty well were setting off on a race that would see their dreams fall apart or come alive. Bang! The gun went off, and I flew out of the blocks and led the race to about 70 meters. At that point in the race, my whole track career flashed before my eyes, all of the work I'd done, the sacrifices I'd made, and the parties I'd given up in college; I saw it all! I just wanted the line to come closer to me, but it seemed as if it were getting farther away. I felt the pressure of others building on me, so I threw my body across that line. I looked to the left—no one was ahead of me. I looked to my right—my brother was ahead of me but no one else. That meant we'd actually come in first and second.

Of all my sporting achievements, this one definitely makes me the proudest because I performed when it mattered most and I'd done it alongside family. At that point, I thought I'd already lived my ultimate story of endurance, but the truth is, I was just getting warmed up. I'd been through so much as an athlete, but finally my Olympic dream was coming true. I'd endured the rough times to reach my goal. But, little did I know my need to endure was just getting started.

I was named to the Olympic team as a member of the 4x100-meter relay pool. Now, a relay team has four people, so most people would figure that, after I'd finished second in the 100-meter dash, I'd be selected as one of the members of the team. I figured that, even if politics managed to creep their way into things, finishing second left me safe from all the drama. To figure out who would be stepping on the track and who would be sitting in the stands, we had competitions in Monaco and Germany plus weeks of practices. It's an understatement when I say I gave everything I had each practice. I ran with every ounce of effort and heart I had. It wore me down in the process. To come out every day knowing you have to prove once again you're a candidate for your dream is tough.

I'd done everything I possibly could, and I felt I'd bled my heart out to be able to run for my country at the Olympics. We had a meeting with the whole team, during which it became clear I wasn't going to run. The coaches asked us who we thought should run, but I realized they weren't really listening to our suggestions. It was more of a "let me know what you think, so I can say I gave you a chance to speak, but I already know what I am going to do" kind of moment. That was the point when you notice who has the balls to say what needs to be said and who is going to sit there in silence. I can say that was one of the toughest things I've ever sat through in my life. I spoke calmly and stated how I truthfully felt, but inside, I was steaming mad. There were about three people I wanted to hit with chairs. I am usually an extremely positive person, but this scenario left me feeling quite depressed. I spent a lot of time alone in Germany and London just thinking about things. It was one of the most unfair things I'd ever gone through as an athlete. I felt sorry for myself, and I wanted the world to feel sorry for me too. I was in constant communication with my coach, who was back at Iowa State, and I'd call him and just vent because there was nothing else I could do. I knew my epic season had come to an end.

The Olympic Games came, and I was in the stands, as expected. It was as if I were a spectator at the Olympics who got special privileges to eat and sleep where the athletes did. I later found out that, because I hadn't been chosen to run, I wouldn't get a uniform or a bib number, even for memory's sake. That crushed me to the bone. It made me feel as if I'd never even made the Olympic team. The fact I never got a bib number means that six other people were listed as being better than I, even though I finished second. That is some tough stuff to swallow. This, I will never forget!

The Lord is near to the brokenhearted and saves the crushed in spirit.
-Psalm 34:18

Jeff Cathey

Hometown: Gary, Indiana
Sport: Track and field
Age at time of story: 15

If you fall behind, run faster. Never give up, never surrender, and rise up against the odds.
–Jesse Jackson

When I was growing up, I didn't have it all. I didn't grow up in a family that had a lot of money. We were poor. I always wanted to play sports as a kid but never had the money to pay for the fees, and I really didn't want to stress my mother out by asking for the money. We were going through hard times trying to find a place to live and just figuring out what we were going to eat. It was hard to manage playing sports because I was always moving, from house to house, from friends to cousins to grandparents. I was never stable. I couldn't join a team because we were always on the move.

Another reason I struggled was because I'm from Gary, Indiana, one of the most dangerous cities in the United States. I grew up in a bad part of town called a "gangway." There was a lot of shooting and fighting that took place in my neighborhood. Members of my family were in gangs, and I was slowly but surely going down that same path. It was an easy path to choose because I was born into it. But, I saw a way out when I was introduced to sports.

I tried most sports, whether I was good or bad. There were also athletes in my family. Most either played basketball or ran track. In my city, it felt as if the only choices were to be in a gang or play basketball.

I went to a public middle school that offered sports. I started with basketball because everybody in my family was good at it. It was okay. I was decent, but I felt it wasn't my strong point. I wanted to play a sport in which I could shine, so I joined the track team. In the beginning, I wasn't that fast, and I couldn't get the hang of anything. I took some time to think about what I could do to get better. I just kept running every day. I showed good work ethic. We went on to be city champions, and I got Most Valuable Player (MVP) of the year. I was shocked! After I'd finished my eighth-grade year, I'd figured out my strong point was track and field.

About that time, my city was getting pretty bad, so my mom figured it was time for a change. We moved in with some friends in Hammond, Indiana. I started my freshman year there at Morton High School. But, shortly after the year started, my mom got a call from a cousin in Lincoln, Nebraska, who told her we could live a much better life there. So, my mom decided the best idea was to move to Lincoln.

We ended up going back and forth between Hammond and Lincoln for two years until we were stable. By that time, I was halfway through my sophomore year, right in time for track and field season. I had so much to catch up on during this time, but it was time for a change in my life. My mom was busy paying bills and making sure we had food on the table and clothes on our backs. I got a job and earned some money, so I could do club track. Lincoln was a better environment. Although it was a tough adjustment, it helped me out, giving me better opportunities and a better mindset. My track career took off.

After just half a year, my mom decided she didn't like Lincoln. I think my mom wanted to move back to Indiana because we weren't used to that kind of living. We weren't used to living around any other race but black. I was devastated to be leaving in the middle of the season but had no choice. In the stress of moving again, I didn't have time to get stable and run. Thankfully though, we moved back to Lincoln for my junior year, and I was able to start track again.

My next struggle was battling with lots of hamstring injuries. It was always frustrating for me because I'd be doing so well and then—Boom! There went my hamstring. Part of the problem was that I was cocky. I felt I could run through the injury, but that just made it worse. I never gave myself time to recover. When I had that attitude, nothing went right for me. Battling this consistent injury had me emotional, stressed out, and wondering "why me?" But my mother was always at my side encouraging me to stay positive, telling me, "Your time will come." My coach, Sara Domeier, comforted me too, saying she was praying for me and that things were going to be okay. She reminded me to stay humble. She motivated me by telling me, "If you want to be great, let this injury make you a stronger person." She never left my corner, and she's still here today if I need her.

I had to sit out two seasons of track and field. There were many times I just wanted to give up and quit. Because I was unable to compete during my recoveries, it was hard to stay strong and keep faith. But when I'd start to think about quitting, my head would flash the words "What would I do if I wasn't doing track and field?" Honestly, track and field kept me on my toes in school. It motivated me to stay on top of things and continue my education. I fell in love with the sport and just did what it took to run. Instead of letting my injuries tear me down, I just kept praying to the Lord to put his healing hand on me. I trained harder. I'd lift weights and go through therapy to get better. I was willing to do whatever it took to get better and compete.

I didn't give up in my struggles, because I saw my mother struggle. At one point, she was a single parent raising six kids. She was a strong woman. When I thought about giving up, I thought about how my mother never gave up on us kids. I wanted to make her happy and proud that I was doing something other than being in the streets. I wanted to be that positive role model in my family. I had family members who were starting to look up to me. I was the first of six kids to finish high school, the first to go to college, and the first to get an athletic scholarship. My motivation and reward are when my sisters and brothers tell me they look up to me. It's the best feeling in the world. I don't want to fail, and I don't want to let my family down.

Looking back on all of the things I had to overcome, I see that making positive choices in struggles made me a better person and athlete. Times do get hard, and I'm still struggling to this day, but I've learned to manage it as I'm growing into my manhood. So here's my advice: If you're battling some tough things in your life and in your sport, just keep praying and stay humble. It helps me more than anything. As an athlete, things are going to happen that you like and don't like. Always ask yourself "Why give up? I made it this far." Don't give up, keep striving for the best, and stay with faith by the Lord. Pray and stay humble, and the Lord will take care of the rest.

Humble yourselves in the sight of the Lord, and he shall lift you up.
–James 4:10

Michelle Nguyen Browning

Hometown: Houston, Texas
Sport: Gymnastics
Age at time of story: 20

Everybody has a story. It can be your anchor or your sail.
– Arian Foster

As a freshman in college, I was eager for a college athletic career. I had dealt with several injuries throughout middle school and high school, but otherwise, I had nothing going against me. I was naive and excited for a new level of competitiveness in gymnastics.

My parents raised me to be conscious of the privilege I'd been raised with and the blessings that I'd received, but I suppose I didn't realize how fortunate I'd been all my life until a team-bonding activity my freshman year. We were sitting around the campfire, and my teammates were talking about personal difficulties that had both shaped and scarred them. At that point, I remember thinking "Wow! I have never dealt with any real struggle." Inevitably, a year later, hardships came.

It started with coaching changes. The coach who'd recruited me decided to move on to another job. Then, in September, my dad died after a three-month battle with cancer. My grandmother passed away shortly after that. Despite the fact that gymnastics was a welcomed break from the reality of my emotional instability, it became increasingly difficult to focus my somewhat depleted energy into something that, in the scheme of things, had started to seem somewhat meaningless. Circuits and championships seemed trivial when I was dealing with the guilt of my imperfect relationship with my now passed father and the unfulfilled obligation to my mom, who was now living alone a thousand miles away.

As the season approached, however, with the help of my teammates, I found new purpose for my training: I used my love for gymnastics to feel connected to my dad, who'd been so proud of my achievements all along. My training almost served as a desperate solace I needed in order to feel some sense of normalcy. As a result, my skills started improving and hit a stride once the season started. Chronic ankle problems persisted, but otherwise, I felt near the top of my game. It felt so good to be in control of something. The season culminated when I qualified as an all-around competitor to the NCAA National Championships. I was hoping to go with my team, but the individual qualification was the next best thing. I wanted to bring the year full circle and show my best effort for both me and my dad, to whom I'd dedicated that season.

I was in the middle of training for the championships when, one day, I was having a hard time at practice and wasn't really able to catch my breath. My coaches chalked it up to a bad day and let me off easy with mainly strength and conditioning exercises. As the day progressed, I continued having breathing problems and began feeling a pain in my back and ribs as well. I made an appointment through my athletic trainer to see the doctor the next day, but late that night, my boyfriend convinced me to go to the emergency room. I was reluctant, but there was pain when I moved and breathed, so I relented.

After several hours, the doctors revealed the pain I was feeling was because of two blood clots that had traveled to my lungs. I stayed in the hospital for nearly a week, and during that time, I found out I might not be able to continue gymnastics, much less compete at the championships. For the second time that year, my world came crashing down. The sport that was getting me through was no longer something I could count on. When I was released, I was on medication and wasn't allowed to begin any kind of training or even do low-impact cardio activities. Frustration and anger were two emotions that surfaced time and time again, even though I was incredibly grateful to have made it through the medical issue.

This time taught me what endurance was all about. I felt lucky I'd been able to do something I loved for such a long time, and I knew that, if I could get back in the gym, I'd have a newfound appreciation for the ability to pursue my passion. I did my best to keep my eyes on my progress and stay grateful. I knew I wasn't entitled to anything, so each step was worth celebrating. Despite the circumstances, I knew that God had a plan for me, and I still felt blessed.

My family, my teammates, and my boyfriend were all pivotal in helping me refocus and get through the hard times. There were many instances when my own spirituality was weak, and I wasn't turning to faith for help, but even so, I had people praying for me and loving me through it. It was during this time that I was shown the truest forms of love and patience.

Many people didn't know my circumstances that year, even though it was something that was totally consuming for me personally. I think about that often because I really believe in regarding people with empathy even if everything seems to be going right for them from your point of view. Obviously, it also taught me lessons in humility and perseverance. I felt empowered and blessed when I finally returned to the competition floor the following year.

Do as I have commanded you: be strong and courageous, do not be frightened or dismayed, for the Lord your God is with you wherever you go.
–Joshua 1:9

Phillip Hayle

Hometown: Brampton/Toronto, Ontario
Sport: Track and field
Age at time of story: 18

I began running track at age twelve, and by ninth grade in high school, I'd won the provincial championships without any training, so I decided to start running seriously. I joined a local track club, and within two months, I'd broken eleven seconds for the 100 meters. The following year, I made my first national team and really started developing as a sprinter. Making it to that level so quickly really opened my eyes to the rest of the track world. I was the best where I was from, but I found that, on an international level, I was a nobody and I had a lot of work to do.

When I was seventeen, I achieved much success. I was the top-ranked youth 100-meter sprinter in the country, and I was ranked twelfth in the world. I also established a new Canadian youth record and won a bronze medal representing Canada at the 2008 Commonwealth Youth Games in India. I was on the top of the world, traveling and winning every race anywhere I went. I felt invincible, and nothing could stop me. I often referred to myself as a "beast," and anybody who lined up against me was no match. My confidence was unreal, and I earned a lot of respect from my teammates and my fellow competitors. Don't get me wrong, it didn't come easy. I was very hardworking and dedicated to running. I just loved it. Everything I did revolved around track. I remember I always used the phrase "eat, sleep, and train track and field." Many times, I would cancel plans with friends and family because I was just so focused on track. I wanted to win, I wanted to win everything, I wanted to be the best, and I was on my way to achieving that.

In October 2008, while I was competing in India, I picked up a cold, which I never really recovered fully from. I returned from India feeling fine, but within a couple of weeks, I started to feel lethargic and just plain tired. I didn't think anything of it. I just thought maybe I wasn't going to bed early enough or I'd been training really hard. I also thought it could be the effects of jet lag, not fully understanding the concept of what jet lag really was. Anyhow, I continued with training, not really thinking about it, and started focusing on my first competition indoors.

First, I had a training camp down in Florida, for which I was all too excited. The camp started off well; I had a few teammates with me, and some of my competitors came along as well. The weather was great, and I was running well in training. Near the end of the camp, I picked up another cold, but this time it was different. I woke up one morning with a pounding headache, a stuffy nose, and a sore throat. The headache was unbearable, but I tried to continue with my normal routine.

I went to practice and worked through it, probably one of the most unproductive practices I've ever had. I returned from practice and told myself I must take some medicine for the symptoms. Luckily, one of my teammates had some COLD-FX. I'd never used this medicine before, and I was a little leery about taking it, but I had no other choice. I popped two pills and lay down for a while. The next day, I felt better. The day after that, it seemed all the symptoms were gone except for the sore throat.

I returned to Canada and continued with my regular routine. A couple of weeks went by, and once again, I started feeling really lethargic and tired, and I still had that nagging sore throat. I competed in my first competition, and I performed subpar, but my coached told me not to worry and assured me I was just a little rusty and needed a few more races to get going. After my second competition and a lackluster performance, I confided in my coach about how I'd been feeling. We both didn't think it was too serious and believed maybe we just needed to back off in training a little bit.

After a few easy weeks, I started to pick it up in training again. One night after practice, I felt awful. I was exhausted. I had a fever, a runny nose, and still the nagging sore throat. I just thought I'd picked up the flu because I'd been traveling a lot from warm climate to cold climate. Perhaps, my body was acting up because of all the sudden weather changes. The flu knocked me out for a little over a week, no school, no practice, no anything. I was dead; this was not the typical flu. My throat was killing me; it was tough for me to even eat anything. I can't describe the pain I felt. I looked in the mirror one day just to try to figure out why there would be so much pain. I noticed both of my tonsils were inflamed. The left side was much larger than the right, and it didn't look normal. Because of my discovery of my tonsils and the pain I was in, I decided to go see my family doctor.

My doctor was very concerned and told me it looked abnormal and could be quite serious. She referred me to a specialist. Unfortunately, I didn't get a chance to see the specialist until a month later because he was heavily booked. When I saw the specialist, he took a quick look and immediately diagnosed me with a peritonsillar abscess, which is a complication of tonsillitis. The doctor told me that was the reason I'd been experiencing some of the symptoms for a number of months. Along with this diagnosis, through blood work, I learned my central nervous system had also crashed.

I was relieved to actually figure out what had been going on, but I was also bothered and upset that something like this had happened. The next step was tonsillectomy surgery. I found this very difficult to deal with; not only had I been very healthy throughout my athletic career but also my whole life had always been healthy. I had many questions to which I tried finding answers. I questioned why this happened and if I could have stopped it from happening.

After the surgery, I lost quite a bit of weight, being off of my normal eating habits and training routine. Being who I am, I told myself I'd take the proper steps in trying to recover and get back on the track as quickly as possible. Because it was my senior year in high school and I was coming off all the success I'd had the previous year, I rushed back into things too quickly. I tried to pick up where I'd left off and made it to the provincial championships for the fourth straight year.

I didn't go in as a favorite, but I tried to remain optimistic. I finished sixth in the 100 meters, which was my worst showing at provincial championships. I felt upset and defeated and didn't want to continue to run anymore. It had taken so much out of me just to make it back to championships, but I hadn't won. I hadn't won any races up to that point, and it was very tough for me to accept that. This was the first time I'd really struggled in my sport. I didn't want to run any more races for the year, but my coached urged me to keep going. I thought things might get better, so I agreed and kept training. After my next two races, my times improved slightly, but I was well short of what my goals were for the season. I decided to shut my season down, although my coach felt otherwise.

That was hard for me, but I felt it had to be done. I was scrambling and trying to push myself to a point that, with my fitness, I wouldn't reach. I realized that and took the necessary steps. It was tough just sitting at home, resting up and watching my teammates and competitors compete and get better. I struggled mentally, and I didn't think I'd ever be able to come back from that experience. I wasn't the same athlete anymore. My confidence wasn't there any longer, and I doubted myself constantly. My passion and love for the sport weren't the same. I tried not to think about it too much, but when everything you've done revolved around your sport for the previous three years, it was hard not to.

I've always been a religious and spiritual person, and during that time, I really looked to God for answers. I believed in my faith, and that helped me get through the experience, even when I was at my lowest point and thought I'd step away from athletics forever.

Months went by, and it was soon time to start preparing for the upcoming season. Mentally, I was still pretty messed up, so my coach referred me to a sports psychologist. I went to a few sessions. I felt it had helped a little bit, so I decided to stop going. To be honest, I didn't really feel that comfortable seeing a doctor and talking about my issues. I felt I could just work things out on my own.

I had now just started college in a new city about two hours outside of Toronto. This brought me to a new environment, working with a new coach and new everything. It was quite an adjustment, but I made it work. I had a new set of goals, and I was keen on trying to conquer them. I erased the previous season and everything that was negative about it and focused on a fresh new plan for this year. Things started out great and only kept getting better. As time went by, my confidence grew, and I started to feel strong and on top again, but I still had some doubt in myself.

The Canadian Junior Nationals came around, and it was the qualifier for the World Junior Championships. This was the championship I'd been looking forward to all year and I'd been working so hard for. I finished second at nationals and qualified for the world juniors. It was something about which I was tremendously proud, to come back from the experience the year before that had knocked me out for the whole season to finish second at nationals and qualify for worlds. I was so happy and proud of myself. That is one of my greatest achievements.

Just when I was getting back into the swing of things, my central nervous system crashed again. I'm not sure if it was from my rushing back into things or not training properly. I think perhaps the stress of school also played a factor. I tried to work through it and take things step by step, but then a domino effect happened. I kept picking up injuries here and there; as soon as one injury was healthy, I'd pick up another. This pattern continued for about two years until I was able to finally stay healthy. During that period, I wanted to quit numerous times, but somehow, I kept going. I felt awful with injury after injury and my body's breakdown. I felt mentally drained and like I couldn't do the sport anymore. I'd now finished school and was at my last straw, so I decided to make a coaching switch.

My new coaches understood where I was coming from and believed I had the potential to go further. I felt comfortable with them, even though I was still worried about how things would turn out. I just trusted the program and gave it my all. I was able to stay healthy the whole year and ran personal bests in all my events. It was a relief and fun to be running fast again. I remembered why I loved the sport so much and why I'd never given up through all those rough patches.

The reason I didn't give up and continued working is that I kept the faith that those things would come around. God was a major influence as to why I continued training. A Bible verse I held close to me in that rough time was "Be joyful in hope, patient in affliction, and faithful in prayer." (Romans 12:12) I could really relate to this verse, and it helped me stay strong. My love and desire for the sport made me persevere through that difficult time. I also have a strong passion for music, which definitely contributed to some therapeutic comfort through that period. Finally, I had long-term goals to live my dream as a professional athlete and one day compete in the Olympics.

I owe many thanks to my friends and family, especially my mother. Without her, I don't know where I'd be. She gave me endless support through that experience and was always there for me. She believed in me when nobody else did. She believed in me when I doubted myself. Sometimes, I feel this experience affected her almost as much as it affected me. She's always been my number one fan, and I can't thank her enough for everything she's done for me.

I can't help but consider that, maybe if I'd had the proper guidance from my coach at the time, possibly things would have been different. I was a young kid and fairly new to the sport. Maybe I should have educated myself more or asked more questions. Maybe I should have communicated more with my friends and family about what I was experiencing when I first started having symptoms. There are many things I could have done differently, but all I can do is learn from it and move on. This situation has made me not only a stronger athlete but also a stronger individual. I learned so many things going through that experience — definitely the toughest thing I've ever had to go through as an athlete.

I'm proud to say I still compete in this sport today, and I'm glad I've stuck with it. Athletics has taught me so many different things, and I've met so many people who've become close friends. I am definitely a lot more conscious of everything I do in relation to my sport and even to everyday life. I'm always learning and constantly asking questions. I often say if I'd had the knowledge back then that I have now, I'd be a totally different athlete, but that's the process of being an athlete. You grow and mature; you develop and learn. Things may not always go the way you want them to, but you just have to take it and move on and make yourself better. That's part of the journey. That situation has made me thankful for my health and the ability to continue running. It has made me more grateful for the gift God has blessed me with and appreciative of all things I encounter in life. That experience changed my life, and I will carry it with me forever.

Over the years I've experienced so many injuries and rough times in this sport. I could have easily just walked away, but I keep going. I always like to remember God will never give us more than we can bear, so I stay focused and work. I'm still doing this sport because I love it and I always will. The feeling of nerves before a race, the explosion out the blocks, and my spikes ripping up the track are just amazing. The drive of pushing myself to levels I've never been to before is what keeps me going. There are always going to be ups and downs, and the path to success is never easy. The most important thing is never give up and always persevere. There's always something better at the end of the tunnel, no matter how bad the situation might be.

Author Story: Down But Never Out

Hometown: Markham, Ontario
Sport: Track and field
Age at time of story: 15

Hope never abandons you; you abandon it.
–George Weinberg

Leading up to outdoor season my second year, I'd managed to get hit with a horrible case of mono. I know a lot of people have had mono, but my case was a bit different. Many doctors I saw had never seen anyone with a case of mono like I had.

Timeline of events:

- Started feeling very tired at practice.
- Thought I had strep throat because my throat hurt so badly one night.
- Went to the hospital and found out it was mono.
- Saw my throat get ridiculously swollen.
- Constantly needed a spit bucket for the white chunks I was spitting out.
- Thought my throat was getting better and that I was recovered.
- Got a huge puss-filled abscess on my neck.
- Saw the abscess had gone down and thought I was recovered.
- Had to sit by the fireplace with a fan over a bucket of ice at all times because my temperature wouldn't stabilize; I'd go from burning up to freezing in minutes.
- Had a full-body rash.
- Thought everything had gone away but realized the growth on my neck had come back.
- Had surgery to drain the growth.
- Had to have home-nurse care for two weeks.

The damage:

- Missed six weeks of school.
- Had four weeks of training while on the downslope.
- Missed six weeks of training.
- Got a scar on my neck from surgery.
- Lost twenty pounds.

I'll never forget when I went back to school; it felt so good. I'd missed everything about it, and at that point, I realized how much I loved my high school and track and field. I had about six weeks to be ready for the big show. At the beginning of my return, I'd considered the year to be a write-off. As the weeks went by, my weight increased, my drive increased, my times on the track got faster, and before I knew it, I honestly felt as if I'd never lost a step. I'd endured being as ill as I'd ever been and had come back to have the best season of my life.

The year before my provincial championships, I'd come in a disappointing third place in both the 100-meter dash and the 200 meters. Walking out of that hospital, I felt as if coming in third would be the best thing to ever happen to me. I'd have been proud of that. After I was fully recovered and back into normal training, I began to realize I could win. I'd been counted out by the time the big meet came around. You know how stories escalate; it started off as my being sick and ended with some people hearing I'd had a career-ending injury. I ended up having the meet of my life, finishing first in the 100 and 200 meters and the 4x100 relay, and we finished fourth in the 4x4. Most people remember that weekend for the wins and the medals that I collected. I'll never forget it because I showed myself just how much I could endure.

The year before at that meet, I'd gotten third place in both individual events. I'd done that on fresh legs, feeling as good as ever. The next year was a true testimony to the strength of God. I was touched with illness that should've ended my season. I was tested, but I trusted in him to return me to where I needed to be. It's very similar to Job in the sense that Job had it all taken away from him. But, once he had endured the test, it all came back to him — plus more.

But he said to me, "My grace is sufficient for you, for my power is made perfect in weakness." Therefore I will boast all the more gladly of my weaknesses, so that the power of Christ may rest upon me.
-2 Corinthians 12:9

Danielle Frere

Hometown: Muscatine, Iowa
Sport: Women's track and field
Age at time of story: 22–23

Patience with others is love. Patience with self is hope. Patience with God is faith.
–Adel Bestavros

Never doubt God's plan. It may seem things are falling apart while they could actually be falling into place. Trust Him. Keep your faith.
–Unknown

As athletes, we all go through peaks and valleys. Tough class schedules, injuries, psychological factors, family, friends, or going out and enjoying the "college life" can make or break our performances. I went through a coaching change after my freshman year. That brought changes in my technique, injuries, and an overall questioning of my faith throughout my five years at Iowa State University.

The greatest challenge was during my final year as an Iowa State Cyclone. I was having great fall training, both in the weight room and in the throwing circle, when my throwing shoulder started bothering me. It got to the point I couldn't extend my arm to throw the shot put, and the constant tension of throwing hammer and weight was uncomfortable as well.

I went to the athletic trainers and the team doctor and found out that there was no serious injury; however, my options were to get cortisone shots every few months until the end of the year or have surgery to allow room for the inflammation in the joint. After talking with my parents and my coach, I decided to have the surgery after Thanksgiving. It was important that I thought long term when making my decision because I had plans to continue training after college for the 2016 Olympic trials.

I knew cortisone shots were only a temporary fix, and I didn't want to take the chance of ruining my performances during my final indoor and outdoor seasons. I wish this decision were the hardest part of what I went through as an athlete. The hardest thing was going through therapy and trying to get myself back into throwing before my shoulder was actually ready. Because I'd missed about four to six weeks of training leading into winter break, I was that much further behind when I arrived back on campus after winter break. I found myself getting restless waiting for the green light to throw and to get back into my normal routine.

I spent much of my time talking with our athletic trainers, my coach, my parents, and close teammates about my frustrations with the recovery process. Each of them provided different support and encouragement, reminding me to be patient because I was moving along more quickly than most from that surgery. At the end of January, I was allowed to start throwing again less than two months after the surgery.

The excitement of being able to throw again was offset by the lack of consistency and repetitions, which made me feel a sense of urgency as indoor season is over the end of February or middle of March. All through indoor and outdoor season, I was up and down in my throwing distances and technique. As a rhythm thrower, I was feeling out of control and frustrated on a daily basis with my performances.

I have always held tightly to my faith in God and trusted his will, but I was being tested during that time. It wasn't until I'd missed outdoor NCAA nationals and before outdoor U.S. National Championships at the end of June when I came to terms with the whole situation. I started reading through my Bible and even reading through Bible verse tweets to get perspective. I'd been so focused on throwing far that I'd forgotten why I was doing it in the first place. My frustration was with things outside of my control, and I'd allowed myself to be impatient.

Although I'd been given support from my coach, family, and friends, I still needed to realize my own mistakes. From the time I'd had surgery until that point in June, I'd constantly recited Reinhold Niebuhr's *Serenity Prayer*: "God grant me the serenity to accept the things I cannot change, the courage to change the things I can, and the wisdom to know the difference." But, I'd never truly heard and accepted it fully. It was at that point I made a change and began communicating more effectively with my coach, so we could get me prepared for the U.S. Championships and end my college career on a high note.

All of the sudden, a giant weight was lifted from my shoulders, and there was peace in my heart. Looking back at my time in college, there were only two times when I really questioned why I was still throwing: once after my second year, and I hadn't improved from my freshman year, and then during the final two seasons my fifth year. I never gave up for a few different reasons: I can't quit once I've started something, I always believed I could be and do better, I knew God had a plan for me, and I knew deep in my gut I love throwing.

The lessons I learned from college athletics about faith, life, relationships, friendships, and how to treat people will always be far more important to me than any accomplishment in the throwing circle. Any problem or situation I went through only made me a better person and, more importantly, a better Christian. I'm a firm believer God tests us each and every day, and we must acknowledge, understand, adapt, and grow from each test. I'm now continuing to train with little to no frustration or stress because I've learned and grown in my faith. As humans, we have very little control over what happens to us. All we can do is control how we react and respond to situations.

I have faith that God is living out a divine plan through me. Have faith in God.
−Mark 11:22

Now faith is being sure of what we hope for and certain of what we do not see.
−Hebrews 11:1

Taijah Campbell

Hometown: Toronto, Ontario
Sport: Basketball
Age at time of story: 17

I grew up in Toronto (Scarborough), Ontario, in a neighborhood that wasn't the greatest environment. There were always the fears of gunshots at night and perhaps coming across the wrong person or being in the wrong place at the wrong time. As my older brother and I grew up being raised by a single mother, my mother made it her mission to never let her children fall victim to the streets. To her, the way to do this was through sports. She put my brother and me in sports for as long as I can I remember. I played soccer while he played basketball and football. Our lives were always consumed with sports, and my mother made sure that, no matter what, we were playing the next season—even if that meant she couldn't pay the electric bill on time for that month.

Until I was fifteen, I played soccer; however, my mother always knew I'd be a basketball player. A mother always knows best, I guess you could say. Obviously, I was hesitant. I was about to give up over ten years of a sport I'd loved and always known to start over. I was about to start a sport I wasn't even that good at, but somehow after much persuasion, I gave up soccer and picked up a basketball.

At first, I was as awkward and terrible as you can imagine. It was frustrating. I was playing on a team with girls who'd played the sport since they were old enough to walk, and here I was, this 6-foot 2-inch, 145-pound girl who had no idea what she was doing. The only thing I had going for me was my competitive nature. I hated losing—I still do. After about a year and a half of working at it, I noticed I'd gotten drastically better. I was starting to feel more comfortable.

I began receiving letters in the mail from universities. My mind was blown. Never in a million years did I think I'd ever be good enough to play in university. I was convinced these schools didn't actually want me and really didn't know what they were doing. I wasn't good enough. It had to have been a mistake because they didn't really want me. But, one evening while casually checking my e-mail, I noticed I had an unread message from Canada Basketball. I was nervous and confused. After reading the e-mail, I realized it was an invitation for me to try out for their Junior Women's National Team that was traveling to Chile in July 2011.

Immediately, I was anxious, nervous, and excited all at the same time. I ran and told my mother who was probably more excited than I was. So June 2011, I left for Georgian College for training camp. I was the youngest player there, still in high school while many of the girls had already completed their first year playing in university. I was terrified. There was no way I was going to be better than those girls. I wasn't good enough.

I think that training camp was the hardest thing I'd ever gone through. We practiced twice a day for three hours per session. It was eat, sleep, and breathe basketball. When we weren't practicing, we were eating; when we weren't eating, we were sleeping; and when we weren't sleeping, we were watching film. It was unlike anything I'd ever gone through before. I was exhausted; my body was as sore as it'd ever been. I was putting my body through something it had never been through before, working muscles I never knew existed. But, the other girls didn't seem to be phased by it. Finally, cuts were to be made. They were cutting down from twenty-five girls to fifteen. I was almost positive I was going to get cut from the team. But my name wasn't called. I was instead escorted into a room filled with fourteen other girls. I found out I'd made the top fifteen. As excited as I know I should've been, I was even more scared. I ran back to my room after the meeting and immediately called my mother crying. I couldn't do this. I wasn't ready for this. There was no way I was ready for this.

I also couldn't wrap my head around the fact that they chose me. A girl who barely knew anything about the sport was to play at that level? I couldn't believe it. So, I began doubting myself. There was no way I was actually going to make the team because I didn't belong. I wasn't good enough. After hours of crying and multiple phone calls and attempts to calm down, I decided I was going to make the best of the situation. I finished the training camp, but I didn't make the final team. However, I came to realize that was a growing and learning opportunity. It really put things into perspective for me. I may not have been ready, but I learned a lot about life and myself.

A quote by Norman Vincent Peale I've come to live by is "Believe in yourself! Have faith in your abilities! Without a humble but reasonable confidence in your own powers you cannot be successful or happy." We're all capable of absolutely anything, but we tend to be our own worst enemies. I encourage you to dream big and never doubt yourself, because you are enough. Let no one stand in the way of the things you truly want in life. No matter where you start your journey, you can determine your destination.

Now, at twenty years old, I've accomplished things I absolutely owe to that experience, and my mother, of course. I've had the opportunity to represent my country playing abroad in Italy, Mexico, Puerto Rico, and Russia. I received an athletic scholarship to play NCAA Division I basketball in America at Virginia Tech. I credit my mother for always pushing and believing in both of her children to do what makes us happy and work hard for everything we want. The only person who stands in your way is you.

Derwin D. Hall, Jr.

Hometown: Kansas City, Missouri
Sport: Track and field
Age at time of story: 19

Everything you need is already inside of you.
–Bill Bowerman

The hardest thing I've ever had to go through as an athlete was suffering from a hamstring injury while being ranked one of the top sprinters nationally in Division II track and field. I'd just experienced a life-altering breakup with my high school sweetheart. When I realized she was no longer in my life, I felt lost, lonely, and hurt. I decided to call out to God to help me have confidence in myself. I also prayed to God, letting him know I wanted to run for him and inspire many people with the talent he'd blessed me with.

Throughout the many days of relying on God, I felt my confidence begin to increase because I ran so well. I was ranked one of the top five sprinters in the 60-meter dash for Division II. Shortly however, that confidence turned into arrogance, and instead of representing God, I began to represent myself. I suffered an injury that hindered the remainder of my indoor track season. I relied heavily on my Bible, prayer, and motivational quotes to get me through that time.

Although my situation at that time didn't indicate it, I felt my future would be promising. I knew once I'd recovered from my injury, I'd be hungry to get back to being a nationally ranked sprinter. I felt if God assisted my increased confidence on the track, he'd administer the strength I needed to triumph over the injury.

That situation showed me an injury can cause a person to grow mentally, physically, and spiritually. My injury helped me rely on God and actually gave me a chance to experience his presence. It also showed me we should never become arrogant and boast to others; we must be humble. Eventually, before my college career ended, I was able to achieve an All-American title in the 60-meter dash. This result didn't come without much pain and prayer.

Humble yourselves, therefore, under the mighty hand of God so that at the proper time he may exalt you, casting all your anxieties on him, because he cares for you.
–1 Peter 5:6–7

Anonymous Woman #3

Hometown: Markham, Ontario
Sport: Track and field
Age at time of story: 18

Faith in God includes Faith in His timing.
–Neal A. Maxwell

It was freshman year, and I'd just moved down to Illinois to attend university and compete as a member of the women's track and field team. This time, it felt different than the college visit because I couldn't pack up my things and just go back home. I was there, in a new part of the world, where the people didn't talk like me or act like me. Most importantly, I didn't know anyone, but it seemed like everyone knew each other. I knew that year was going to be the biggest challenge for me as an athlete because I was transitioning not only from high school to collegiate-level athletics but also from everything I thought I knew to everything I knew nothing about.

I quickly befriended some teammates who eventually became like sisters to me. I remember being extremely nervous the first week of my freshman year because, to my future teammates, I was the full-ride Canadian athlete who'd jumped 1.67 meters and threw shot put. The anxiety that came with attempting to live up to that title meant performing and excelling every day. But, it wasn't those titles that challenged me the greatest—it was not knowing who I was.

Up until that point, I'd thought I knew who I was as a person, but it wasn't until I was more than 1,300 miles from home that I started to figure it out. Since I was young, I've had so many things define me, from my spiritual relationship to God to my West Indian culture and even to my athletic abilities.

However, when I went to Illinois, I felt stripped, tossed into another world of competitive athletes and people who didn't share much in common with me.

For the next three years, I was faced with the challenge of defining myself as a person and an athlete. I found this most hard because I was faced with the biggest question: Do I fuel my desires as an athlete, or do I succumb to the desires of trying everything just to find out who I really am? From freshman to junior year, I started losing my touch as an athlete. I disagreed with the politics, and the sport lost its fun. The fire inside me was slowly burning out because of all the rules and the formalities, changes in coaches and their coaching mantras, and the favoritism and exceptions to the rules. I became a silent rebellion in my own right. Everything had a time or a place when it came to track and field, so I started to become who I thought I was and started to forget who I was as an athlete.

During those three years, I started hanging out more, cramming the night before exams (because I knew I'd pass with flying colors), getting wrapped up in gossip and the drama of my friends, and enjoying the attention from males and certain love interests—simply put, being a college student. I dealt with body issues, relationship issues, and peer pressure and friendship issues and let those take priority over my responsibility as an athlete. I faked the leadership roles on the team in order to keep up appearances. Actually, I felt myself faking everything. I wasn't truly giving it my all because I didn't feel excited anymore. I was just going through the motions and falling apart, both mentally and physically.

It wasn't until the end of my junior year that I decided to get it together because, within the next year, it was all coming to an end. I used the support of my friends, family, and God to figure out what I really wanted from life, and I made a list of it all. I'd always been taught I should take it to God. That's exactly what I did. I have no clue why I hadn't done that from the beginning, but as the saying goes, hindsight is always 20/20. The result of my ups and downs is me, and I was able to accept that. At that point in my life, I became confident in his self-confidence.

In my senior year, I put it all on the line. I meshed with the athletes. I accepted the politics and became a diplomat. I was able to enjoy love and compete. I continued to grow instead of questioned everything that happened in my life. I was able to trust God! Most people say they trust God, but do they really? That moment in my life became the turning point in my faith, something I'd lost in my earlier years when I lost my dad. I didn't give up on growing as an athlete because, if I did, I knew that would become the norm for my life.

Looking back, I truly believe God made a way for me to earn a full-ride scholarship to a university in the United States, and it was in his will that I went through all of my trials and tribulations to truly appreciate his beautiful work in creating me. Although, I chose not to compete as an athlete after college, I learned a lot about who I was as a person and an athlete. Hanging up my cleats, throwing shoes, and gloves was tough, but I had to close that chapter in my life. I love track and field. It was everything. But, all of the politics made it hard to love. That's why transitioning after collegiate athletics was so difficult. However, if I'd decided to give up and not trust God, I wouldn't have become the strong, spiritual, black woman I am today. And, if you asked me if I would do it differently, I would not!

But Jesus looked at them and said, "With man this is impossible, but with God all things are possible."
–Matthew 19:26

Vinh Le

Hometown: Mississauga, Ontario
Sport: Track and field
Age at time of story: 21

Commit your way to the Lord; trust in him, and he will act.
-Psalm 37:5

As athletes, we all know the ups and downs of our sport, but sometimes, it can feel like we're stuck in a ditch or stopped at a dead end. We train so hard day in and day out in an effort to become better, but sometimes, we don't reach our goals because of setbacks, such as injury, financial problems, and family issues. I have experienced each of those three setbacks and believe me when I say none of them were easy to overcome. I'd like to share my story with you, but I think it would only be right to share some of my background information beforehand, so you can understand where I'm really coming from.

I was born in Mississauga and grew up mostly in Brampton and the Niagara region. My parents moved around a lot because of employment issues. I remember my dad always had to find a new place to work. As a result, we'd move houses. I was raised in the church. My family was, and still is, very involved with the church, so serving God has always been a big part of my life. I went to three high schools, two of them in the Niagara region and one of them in Mississauga. I faced a lot of racism growing up; I was always one of the few, if not the only, Asian kids in my classes, so I stood out. My classmates, teachers, and coaches would always initially underestimate my athletic abilities because of my race, but athletics remained an escape for me. It was a way to show others I was not to be overlooked, a way to prove the negative stereotypes wrong.

Sports basically served as a way for me to gain respect. As much as I enjoyed athletics, my parents never really encouraged it. The more I became involved with athletics, the more my parents showed a negative attitude toward it. They believed sports was the reason I'd bring home more B's and C's than A's. I wasn't one of those freakishly talented kids. I finished twelfth at my first provincial championships, and dead last the following year, and eventually worked my way up to a second, fourth, and eighth place finish at the meet by the time I was in grade twelve. From a young age, I had to work hard for what I wanted.

One of the hardest things I had to fight for was my parents' approval to participate in track and field. They only saw it as a waste of money and time and, more importantly, a distraction to my education. Eventually, I proved to them that all the time I spent practicing was worth it because I received an athletic scholarship to Long Island University (LIU) in Brooklyn, New York, when I was nineteen.

The experience I'm about describe is a recent one and, without a doubt, one of the toughest experiences I've had athletically. I'm sure we're all familiar with battling injury, and of all the injuries I've sustained, this one definitely takes the cake. I'm currently in my second year at LIU Brooklyn and believe me when I say my first year didn't go well at all. Last year, I battled patellar tendonitis the entire year and trained more as a sprinter than a jumper, even though jumping is what I was recruited for.

Despite my being very close with God that year, things didn't work out for me athletically, so I decided to rely more on myself for the following year. I made another major decision in the summer to train strictly under the jumps coach for this year. This turned out to be a great decision because my base training in the fall went well and I wasn't nagged by the pain of my patellar tendonitis. It was almost gone because I refined my technique and learned how to move more efficiently. Sounds great right? Well everything went well until I opened up my indoor season.

I'm one of those athletes who have a bit of trouble controlling their nerves during competition. Because of excitement and some anxiety, it usually takes me a couple of rounds before I start jumping correctly, which is something my coach and I are working on right now. At the time, I was extremely excited to jump because of all the new things I'd learned and worked on in practice, but that turned out to hurt me in the end.

I didn't finish my first jump because of a lack of control. With my second jump, I decided to take a safe jump, which was still technically horrible because I rushed my technique, but it was good enough to get me into the final. Then came the third round, when I decided to just go for it and give the jump all I had while my legs were still fresh. I sprinted down the runway with no control and actually seemed to execute my hop phase pretty well; that is, until I landed. I left my foot out and landed on it in a way that all the pressure and impact were forced into my heel. It was something of a freak accident because, out of all my years of jumping, this had never happened before.

Triple jumpers can experience up to 15.2 times their body weight on foot contact. (Just so you know how bad the consequences can be if you don't hit the technique right.) I realized I wouldn't be able to continue jumping in the final because of the severe pain, so I called it a day, thinking I'd have another chance to jump the following week. Unfortunately, the injury was more severe than I thought.

My coach and trainers made me take a full week off of activity and even a few days on crutches. I had weeks when I could only lift for my upper body and was restricted to pool workouts, but I still hoped I'd be ready by the indoor conference championships. The day came when I had to test out my foot to see if I'd be able to jump at conference, and it turned out to be a painful one. Although I had all these positive thoughts in my head and even acted like it didn't hurt, my heel simply just wasn't ready to jump. It was a tough reality to face because now I knew for sure my entire indoor season was done. All I could do was wonder: How could this happen to me? I trained hard all year long, I did my absolute best to do all the injury-preventing exercises I needed to do, I refined my technique, and still, just one little mistake had ruined my whole season.

As mentioned earlier, I was coming off a previously bad year, so it's not like I'd already made a name for myself. I'd started in the dumps and ended up in the dumps again, despite all my hard work and effort. What seemed to be turning out as a great season ended up being my first missed season ever. I tried to get a redshirt but wasn't able to get one. Nothing, absolutely nothing, seemed to be working in my favor. Last year, I was very connected with God and got bad results. This year, I was more reliant on myself and still got bad results. Why? Of all people, why did I have to face this reality? My teammates began talking about me; my coach even spoke about my messing up my season. Everything was horrible, and I felt alone.

Everybody wants to be your friend when you're doing good, but nobody wants to be around you when you're doing bad.
–Unknown

I'm sure we've all been there or felt that way before, but it's all part of sports and life. Despite the bad situation, I felt the only person who could help get me through was God. It was weird because I was a little reluctant at first, but as the days went on, I felt more and more of a calling from him. I realized God would never put me through anything I couldn't handle. I had to trust in him to make things better. So, I did. I began praying again before I went to sleep, I thanked God for each day, and I just felt better. I talked with my mom a lot as well. (It wouldn't be right if I didn't mention she significantly helped me through the situation too.) She constantly reminded me to trust in God, and I did my best to do so.

I eventually began training for my outdoor season in preparation for the spring break meet in South Carolina. I wanted to open up well, so I kept grinding. Unfortunately, the spring break training didn't go so well. I aggravated my heel again at triple jump practice, and it lingered in my long jump practice the day after. My coach told me to stop practice early because he saw the pain I was in. Once again, I was left with the thought of "why me?" I was so frustrated, but I picked myself back up and told myself to focus on recovering for the meet and doing the best I could, regardless of how bad practice went. I prayed about it and called my mom. Instead of flooding my mind with thoughts of why, I began to focus on trying to have a good spring break, to keep smiling and laughing with my friends, regardless of what was happening.

I told myself, "You've sacrificed too much to let a few bad practices stop you from achieving what you want." I thought about all the times I'd gone to the training room every day for treatment, all the missed competitions and practices, and all the people who doubted me, and I felt determined. With only two days to recover, I went into the meet with more positivity than I thought I'd have. I still made jokes with my friends even though I was still in pain, but I tried to focus on the things that made me feel good. The time came to compete, and although I felt some annoying pain, I focused on jumping properly. The pain began to subside as my jumps were executed better.

I ended up jumping one of my biggest season openers in the long jump. I came out injury free and realized my potential once again. I was jumping at the same level as my teammates who'd been competing all indoor season, so I knew I'd be capable of so much more once I got a couple more meets in. Of course, my technique was rusty, but the track meet showed me how much room I had to improve. No, it might not have been the best meet ever, but God saw me through it.

He answered my prayers and gave me hope again. I prayed to have a fun time jumping, and I did. I revitalized my passion for the sport, and I'm now more determined than ever to make improvements. The easy thing to do here would have been to simply give up, but I didn't. I didn't give up because I believe God has something better planned for me, that he wouldn't just leave me in a broken state. When you live for something more than yourself, when you live to show how great our God is, anything is possible. The negativity that once ruled you begins to subside and is replaced with an exciting motivation to be the best you can be. When things get tough, you have to be tougher. That resilience and strength can be found in God.

Don't tell God that you have a big problem, tell your problem that you have a big God.
-Unknown

For the moment all discipline seems painful rather than pleasant, but later it yields the peaceful fruit of righteousness to those who have been trained by it. Therefore lift your drooping hands and strengthen your weak knees, and make straight paths for your feet, so that what is lame may not be put out of joint but rather be healed.
-Hebrews 12:11-13

Author Story: When the Pressure Becomes Too Much

Hometown: Markham, Ontario
Sport: Track and field
Age at time of story: 17

One important key to success is self-confidence. An important key to self-confidence is preparation.
–Arthur Ashe

I knew the pressure was getting to me when Mrs. Haines caught me cheating on a test. She was the best teacher I'd ever had because she was no pushover but she still cared a lot about her students. Best of all though, she was one of the few teachers with whom I'd had a really good relationship. We were having one of our weekly quizzes in my World Issues Geography class. The goal by the end of the weekly quiz was to know every country in the world. I'd always studied for that class, but for some reason, I hadn't gotten a chance to for that quiz, but I wanted to uphold my reputation with her of having good grades, so I decided to cheat. I'll never forget that she'd managed to slip behind me ever so quietly and she caught me with an extra piece of paper I was looking at. She called my mom right away, which only made matters worse. What had caused all of this? It was the pressure of deciding what I was going to do after high school.

It was my last year, and my goal the entire time I'd been in high school was to get an athletic scholarship to a United States college. I remember Syracuse had jumped on me really early, and I'd gone to visit only to find they didn't actually have scholarship money for me. That was disappointing, but I figured, if they wanted me, others probably did too. My assumption was incorrect. No one else was recruiting me. The indoor season had begun, and the pressure was weighing so heavily on my shoulders because I knew I had to run fast. I was running and training horribly, school sucked, and it seemed like life itself was falling apart.

I was at a track meet for the provincial championships of Ontario. On paper, I believed that was my year to destroy the meet. A lot of my close friends, with whom I went to school, had meets of their lives, but I came in fifth and lost to a bunch of people whom I should have beat. My friends turned around and ripped on me hardcore. That was normal for us because we were typical high school boys who were quick to expose each other's shortcomings. That day, it hurt a bit more than most. It all started as good fun, but eventually, they got to me and really hurt my feelings. I went up to the stands to chat with my mom, and I started bawling my eyes out because I felt like I wasn't going to make my dream come true. The pressure of holding myself constantly to high expectations was starting to get to me and rip me up inside.

I think that was God's way of getting my attention and pulling me back in. I was so set on the things that I wanted that I wasn't communicating with him anymore. My life completely had become about me and what I wanted. I took some serious time to just reflect on what I was chasing and why. Why we do what we do is so powerful, and I think many times we forget that. We get lost in the mundane grind of each day and let go of our purpose. God put us on this planet to make a difference, but if we forget that difference, we can lose our sense of passion and self. I thrive on times when I have to just put my head down and work until I reach my destination. It all comes at a cost though. At that point in my life, I was doing it at the cost of giving God the glory.

Once I had my priorities back in order, life began to make sense again. I loved going to practice to train, school was a riot, and my competitions got much better. I ended my indoor season by signing a full scholarship with Iowa State

University. The next week, I was off to New York to compete at the USA high school nationals, where I finished third at the meet. The work I had put in never went to waste. We often begin to think that during the work period. We think about all the work we did and how it's not getting us what we want. Very few times do we stop and think about what God is calling us to do or what he's trying to teach us.

And we know that for those who love God all things work together for good, for those who are called according to his purpose. For those whom he foreknew he also predestined to be conformed to the image of the Son, in order that he might be the firstborn among many brothers. And those whom he predestined he also called, and those whom he called he also justified, and those whom he justified he also glorified.
–Romans 8:28–30

Jellisa Westney

Hometown: Cambridge, Ontario
Sport: Track and field
Age at time of story: 20

When I turned twenty, I realized my sport would require a new level of seriousness and dedication. And, with the indoor season well on its way, I needed to have a mature approach to my competition and my time management. But, if I'm honest, I was still emotionally recovering from a complete failure of a meet that had ended my previous outdoor season.

I thought my poor performance at Canadian Senior Nationals the previous season was the most difficult outcome to accept. Many people had invested in me to have an opportunity to qualify for the World Championships that summer, and I completely blew it. Since then, I've faced even greater adversities and have made some real sacrifices along the way to accomplish what I set out for myself many years ago.

Back to my 2014 indoor season: It has been a rough start. I had to end a relationship with someone whom I still loved and cared for. Though it was based on my own convictions, I sought much counsel from family and friends in order to follow through with that decision. At the time, as you can imagine, my emotions were totally out of whack. This affected my level of focus and energy leading up to the competition. I clung to my faith and the support of my closest friends to see me through. But, just as I'd begun to take hold of my focus and energy and even had started making some real progress in my performance, my season came to an abrupt halt.

The weekend before our conference meet, I got a mild concussion from a biking accident. After I'd been rushed to the hospital, with the gracious help of my neighbors, and had multiple tests and diagnoses, my new goal was to get healthy again. By the end of the week, my body had recovered well enough for me to participate in the Big Ten Championships. Although I was excited things had turned around, my momentum wasn't the same. I'd allowed apprehension, fear, and doubt to creep into my mind, and I became consumed with things that were out of my control. I'd wanted to witness a miracle that weekend, but instead, I let myself down.

Since the meet, I've been grappling with the guilt of a bad performance that I refuse to blame on my "condition." I wanted to be fearless and determined, despite the challenges of recovering from a minor concussion in such a short time. As far as I'm concerned, being able to compete was another opportunity handed to me that I didn't take full advantage of. Though I tried not to, I gave in to the doubts and excuses that played over and over in my mind.

As I continue to reflect on the results of the Big Ten and everything leading up to the meet, I'm so humbled and thankful for the people in my life who continue to support me on this journey. From my parents and coaches to my zealous neighbors, there are always people reminding me never to give up because there's still so much more ahead.

I have to keep fighting, fighting through my own fears and weaknesses as well as outside forces and uncontrollable circumstances. I can't give up because, as long as I'm still here — breathing, living, and being, there's still hope. I have to dust off my shoulders, regain my strength, and set out once again to make myself proud and fulfill my God-given purpose in this life. Looking back on my season has given me a new hunger to reach my full potential in the outdoor season. I guess that's the beauty of a two-season sport: You get a shot at redemption. But a second chance means nothing if you don't work to change yourself in the process. Eric Thomas said it well: "You're going to wake up and everything is going to change but you...so you must work while you wait!"

I truly believe Hebrews 11:1 says it best: "Faith is confidence in what we hope for and assurance about what we do not see." So, I'll continue writing my story by flipping the page of this crummy indoor season, while still acknowledging the good and bad parts of this chapter. In doing so, I will allow myself to be molded into the athlete and woman I'm destined to become.

Zachary Waslenko

Hometown: Richmond Hill, Ontario
Sport: Track and field, 100 and 200 meters
Age at time of story: 14–18

Only if you have been in the deepest valley, can you ever know how magnificent it is to be on the highest mountain.
–Richard M. Nixon

Track and field has been my passion since I was ten years old. From watching YouTube videos of my childhood hero Ben Johnson to seeing the emergence of Usain Bolt in the mid-2000s, I've felt my passion for the sport grow exponentially.

My first major accomplishment was all the way back in the fourth grade, when I broke the 100-meter city record of 13.15 seconds. From that point forward, I was miles ahead of my closest competitors. No matter whom I lined up against, I was always the favorite.

Good genetics and hard training took me all the way to grade nine, where I found myself lined up for the Midget Boys 100-Meter Provincial Final. Leading up to that point, I'd broken numerous conference records and had won the Toronto Championship, with a time that had me ranked second heading into the 100-meter provincial finals.

I went on to win my first provincial gold, earning the title of "fastest fifteen-year-old in Ontario." Just under twenty-four hours later, I'd completed the sprint double, winning the 200 meters with a time just shy of the provincial record. This accomplishment left me feeling I could achieve greatness in any aspect of my life if I set goals and stayed focused. After this victory, I went on to compete at the District D championships, with the hope of qualifying for Team Ontario for nationals later that summer. Although I won both the 100-meter and 200-meter events, I limped away with a stress fracture and missed six weeks of training.

At that point, all I hoped for was the chance to run at nationals, which was eight weeks away. Fortunately, I was able to make the national final, but it was at that point that I faced one of the toughest obstacles in my running career. Just 10 meters into the race, I felt a severe pain in my right hamstring and had to pull up and walk to the finish line. Looking up into the crowd, I could see the disappointment in my parents' faces. The ride home from Ottawa to Toronto was one of the longest car rides of my life because my entire family didn't know how to react to what had just transpired on the track.

That date was August 8, 2011, and I wouldn't run again until February 15, 2012. At that point in my journey, I didn't yet question my faith or my trust in God because I felt this was only a small obstacle and I'd be up and running in no time. Little did I know, it would be six long months of rehabilitation and watching my competition break records, as I hobbled around on one leg.

The competitiveness in me made me want to get up and run, but I couldn't. Track was my scapegoat, a way to get rid of my stress and frustration, but this was no longer an option. Worst of all, seeing my competitors flourish without my being able to compete drove me crazy.

Through the support of my parents, sister, coaches, and friends, I persevered. Special credit goes to my mom for driving me to physiotherapy twice a week for months on end.

My love for the sport was so strong; I knew giving up wasn't an option. Running had added so much joy to my life, and there was no way I'd let it go. When I did return to competitive racing, it didn't take me long to get back to my old form. After only two months of training, I successfully defended my provincial titles, winning the 100 and 200 meters.

Over the next year, I stayed healthy, trained hard, and ran personal bests. In my junior year of high school, I sustained a hamstring injury similar to the one I'd suffered in my freshman year; except this time, it was in my other leg. I was devastated and immediately began contemplating whether track was the sport for me. Because of my injury's severity, I was sidelined for over a year. Scholarships were put on hold, and major races were missed. This time I immediately began blaming God, asking him, "Why me? Why do I have to go through this again?" I felt as if my heart had been torn out of my chest because something I loved so much was being taken away from me. At first, I thought quitting was the only option, but after a few months away from the sport, I began to feel that fire burning inside me again. Truth be told, Ian Warner was one of those individuals who instilled that drive back in me and taught me that nothing good would come of giving up. Despite my facing adversity once again, I got back on my feet. Through this process, my body, as well as my relationship with God, slowly began to mend.

Now, I'm just a few weeks away from running full out, and my drive to succeed burns stronger than ever. I know track is something I was meant to do. Throughout this difficult year, I've constantly told myself that God gives his toughest tests to his strongest soldiers, which in the end will make them that much better.

Watching the Olympics in 2012 and seeing Canada win the bronze in the 4x100 relay further enhanced my drive to be part of that climb to the top. As a result of my perseverance and ability to overcome adversity, I've developed the virtue of patience and have realized the road to success has its obstacles. Most of all, it isn't until we experience failure that we can truly enjoy the feeling of success. This is essentially my story and what I've gone through as an athlete. I only hope my experience can motivate you to overcome whatever obstacle you're currently facing. Remember, never lose hope.

More than that, we rejoice in our sufferings, knowing that suffering produces endurance, and endurance produces character, and character produces hope, and hope does not put us to shame, because God's love has been poured into our hearts through the Holy Spirit who has been given to us.
–Romans 5:3–5

Faith Burt

Hometown: Cedar Falls, Iowa
Sport: Track and field
Age at time of story: 7 and 14–20

It all started in Waterloo, Iowa, at Central Middle School, where a Hershey Track and Field local meet was held for boys and girls of all ages to complete in many events. I had my eye on the bleachers, where I was going to cheer my sister on. She was one of my older sisters who'd come prepared to compete in the 100- and 200-meter dashes that day. My mom had other plans for me. She'd signed me up to run the 50- and 100-meter dashes, knowing that track wasn't my sport.

I was only seven years old at that time, but I knew I'd been born to play basketball. I was kind of a tomboy, so my attire wasn't track-worthy. I had on jeans and a white T-shirt with high-top basketball shoes. I hadn't bothered to do my hair that day, so it was all over my head, but that didn't bother me. Because my birthday's in July, I was so young that I had to run with the eight- and nine-year-olds who were twice my size. Before I raced, one of the officials explained how the cadence went and that I was to run all the way through the line after the gun went off.

I got in a runner's stance and looked at the start, which is clearly not what you're supposed to do. The best part was that I was only in the race so my mom wouldn't be mad at me for wasting her money. The gun went off, and so did I. I won the 50-meter and 100-meter dashes. After receiving the big blue ribbon, I decided track wasn't that bad after all.

Because I'd won my events, I made it to the state meet, which was held in Ames, Iowa. My mom wanted me to be prepared this time, so she got me a shirt, shorts, and tennis shoes. She even took me to the high school track to practice on my events, but we only went once. I'm not sure what good one practice did, but it sure boosted my confidence. At the state meet, I ran against all the athletes in Iowa who were trying to make it to the nationals held in Hershey, Pennsylvania.

It was kind of a big deal, but I was just having fun. I ran my heart out in the 50-meter dash and won again, breaking the state record that still stands today. My time was a 7.08 in the 50-meter dash, which is faster than the guys' record for ages eight and nine. It was another story in the 100-meter dash because I had some competition. I took second, running a 14.24 and losing to a 14.23 by Callan Jacobson. Boy, did losing crush my heart! That day, I left satisfied, with a new state record and first- and second-place finishes. Life was pretty good.

The next step was nationals. To make it to the national meet, you had to have one of the top times in the nation. The only thing left to do was to see what other kids ran. A couple of weeks later, my mom got a call for the Hershey Association telling her I'd qualified to run at nationals and they wanted to fly me to Pennsylvania. To hear news like that as a seven-year-old was amazing! I couldn't wait to take a plane, stay in dorms, visit the chocolate factory, and see the amusement park.

I'd qualified to run the 50-meter dash, and my family drove sixteen hours to see me run for a little over seven seconds. That's what you call a family who'll support you in any and everything you do. I was the baby, and having my sisters and mom there to support my track journey was the best feeling. I was so nervous, but I wanted to do my best for my friends and family. The gun went off, and there I went again, but this time I didn't cross the line first. To other people, the state meet was the big deal, but to me, this was the big deal. This meet determined who the fastest eight- and nine-year-olds were in the country. I wanted it to be me, but it wasn't meant to be. After just three track meets, I was crowned the third-fastest eight- or nine-year-old in the country. That's one of my achievements I'll remember for the rest of my life and is what started my track career.

Life lessons

After I'd decided to continue running track as my main sport, it wasn't easy. Mentally, it's the hardest thing I've ever dealt with. After nationals with Hershey, I joined a track team called Cedar Valley Track Club. With that team, I competed every weekend in the summer with AAU and USA Track and Field (USATF), traveling all over the country, competing in regional and nationals meets. I ran anywhere, from Wisconsin over to Maryland and all the way down to Florida.

I was getting beat constantly in my races, never winning against my older and bigger competitors. I lost so often I considered quitting because it wasn't fun anymore, but I couldn't because I was so passionate about the sport. My mom and sisters kept supporting me, even when I came in dead last. Before every race, my mom would read Isaiah 40:31: "But they that wait upon the Lord shall renew their strength; they shall mount up with wings like eagles, they shall run and not be weary, and they shall walk and not faint." It would remind me I wasn't running just for myself, and he'd give me all the strength I needed to make it down the track.

It wasn't until my freshman year in high school that I tapped into my pure speed. I became unstoppable, or so I thought. God had finally answered my prayers after all those nights I'd stayed up asking God, "Is track the sport for me?" and never hearing a response. My freshman year in high school, I set records, indoor and outdoor, at almost every meet. I became the talk of the town, and I did my best to stay humble about it. I remember telling reporters that I wanted to be well known throughout the whole state of Iowa, and that year I made it possible. I won the 100-meter dash at Drake Relays my freshman year in high school and was crowned the fastest girl in Iowa. I was also only the third freshman in the country to win four state titles, which was shown on ESPN in 2005.

As my success kept growing, the lessons and obstacles grew as well. My sophomore year, I was the Drake Relays champion again and won three state titles. But, it wasn't until my junior year that I was tested.

I got into trouble with the law and was suspended for three indoor meets, which put me behind in the season. Not only was I behind, but I also grew a behind and feminine curves. My body matured and changed from what I was used to running with. It was a struggle. I lost my Drake Relays title my junior year because of mind games. I talked myself out of the race and started doubting my ability. I wanted to make history, and this race was going to determine if it was possible. Everyone was talking about it, and I got too nervous. I cried before my race and didn't go with the same mind mentality I'd had in the years before.

This race affected me so much that, as I'm writing about it now, I feel the same emotions I felt after the race. I was so disappointed in myself; I never wanted to feel that way again. The race made me hungry and ready for the next year. I was going to take my crown back. I learned so much about who I was that day and about how powerful our minds can really be. My mind took me out of the race and my making history along with it.

The next year, I came back full force, ready to get my revenge, and I did. I didn't care what I needed to do to be the best. I was going to get it done no matter what. I took my crown back and ended my high school career on top—four-time Drake Champion, nineteen-time state champion, and the most decorated athlete in all sports. I made history and was inducted into the Hall of Fame in May 2013. The funny thing is, I'd wanted to make history one way, but God made it possible another way. His plan is always better.

The next step

The next step for me was running in college. I'd had big dreams of going to Baylor, but Lord knows, I was scared to even attempt to run there. I didn't think this Iowa girl would be able to hang with them, but because I didn't take that chance, I'll never know. Later, I learned life is about taking risks, and the only way you fail is if you don't try. I had people talking into both of my ears about college, and it was stressing me out. I didn't want to go to college because of how stressed I was from the daily conversations. I was going to attend California State University, Northridge (CSUN) in Los Angeles, California, but my mom didn't want me to be that far from home. She made it very hard for me to reach that dream because I had no support. She wanted me to stay close to home because I was the baby and then move about after graduating from college. Looking back, I wish I'd followed my heart and done what I was scared to do. You only live once, and you'll never get the time back.

I ended up attending Wartburg College in Waverly, Iowa, a small town. My career there wasn't want I'd expected, and the person I became wasn't who I'd expected to be neither. I was a five-time national champion and part of a five-time championship team. I'd never been an individual national champion, like I'd wanted to be, but God had better things in store for me. I left Wartburg as a two-time Drake Relays champion, a nineteen-time All-American, and a fourteen-time individual conference champion. I was also part of the winning 4x400 team that set the all-time Division III record that was twenty years old. All of those things are great memories, but they're not the best part at all.

The best part is the unexpected person I became. The level of wisdom, courage, ambition, understanding, and appreciation I gained was far better than being a national champion. The lessons I learned in college I can take with me the rest of my life, while that trophy I wanted so badly can sit in one place and collect dust. I still have a chance in life to be remembered, whether it's with track or not. I'm following the will of God. I know for sure my future will be blessed.

New beginnings

Always remember, what your heart desires God will give to you if your heart's in a healthy place. I'm a living testimony. For the last six years, I've been living in Los Angeles, California. I have no reason why I was drawn here, but I just knew I was going to end up here. Believe it or not, six years later, I'm here and ready for what this state has to offer me. My dream is to continue training and to start competing soon, and it's about to happen. God is making a way for me, opening doors no human being can close. It's my duty to praise and worship him for the future he's designed for me. I will praise him before, during, and after my blessing.

Rich Bales

Hometown: Pella, Iowa
Sport: Track and field
Age at time of story: 18–21

Track isn't a game. Life isn't a game. Faith isn't a game. These are three lessons I've learned throughout the course of my last four years competing at Iowa State University as a track and field athlete. I look back and marvel at myself as an eighteen-year-old kid coming into college, thinking I had the world figured out and success would be handed to me on a silver platter. It didn't take me long to realize that couldn't be further from the truth.

I grew up in a relatively small town just south of Des Moines, Iowa. In high school, I was a three-sport athlete who'd never known anything but success, and I came from one of the most athletically successful schools in the state. Growing up, I approached academics halfheartedly, while putting all I had into sports. Unlike most students at my fiscally affluent school, I had to work as hard as I could to help earn enough money to get by. A single mother who knew far too well the meaning of struggle, but triumphed over this struggle with hard work and persistence, raised me. It was through her I learned what it means to be ceaselessly driven and how to go after what I wanted wholeheartedly. I have her to thank for the installation of my drive.

After a successful senior year on the track, I committed to Iowa State University to run track and field. At the time, I didn't fully realize the magnitude of the decision I'd made. This commitment would be even bigger than any other I'd ever made. The summer following my senior season of track was a summer of growth in every way. I became stronger in my faith, stronger physically, and stronger in my relationships with others. You could say I headed into college thinking I had everything figured out.

What I didn't realize when I made the transition from home to college was that literally everything around me would change. The world as I knew it was flipped upside down. My friends changed, my rules changed, my routine changed, and even my church changed. I was solely responsible for myself, and nobody was there to make me do, or cease from doing, anything. Looking back at my naivety during this period of my life is a humbling experience, and I realize every value I had was challenged to the fullest.

From partying to skipping classes to being pushed to my limit at practice, I was tested every day. For the first half of the year, I succeeded. I was actively involved in a church, I attended class, and I grinded it out each day at practice. Unfortunately, by the end of the year, I began to lay my foundation in something other than God, and I was hit hard by the reality of the world. Track isn't a game. Life isn't a game. And, most importantly, faith isn't a game.

By the end of my freshman year, alcohol had become a regular addition to my weekend life, injuries had become a regular thing in track, and my faith had been put on the back burner. I was alone, hurting and throwing away the things I cherished and believed in. Everything I'd worked so hard to achieve throughout the course of my life was fading away. Something had to change.

Over the course of the next three years, a lot changed in me. I realized I'd never be the absolute best at my sport. I recognized that, to achieve my goal of gaining acceptance into medical school, I'd have to become my absolute best in the classroom. And most importantly, I realized I'm nothing apart from Jesus Christ, and the pursuit of my faith is the most crucial aspect in my life. If any of this would lead me to the

Kingdom of Heaven one day, I'd have to be the absolute best in my faith.

The following scripture, the parable of the ten virgins, spoke so much truth into my life and into my heart over the course of my college career.

At that time the kingdom of heaven will be like ten virgins who took their lamps and went out to meet the bridegroom. Five of them were foolish and five were wise. The foolish ones took their lamps but did not take any oil with them. The wise ones, however, took oil in jars along with their lamps. The bridegroom was a long time in coming, and they all became drowsy and fell asleep. At midnight the cry rang out: "Here's the bridegroom! Come out to meet him!" Then all the virgins woke up and trimmed their lamps. The foolish ones said to the wise, "Give us some of your oil; our lamps are going out." "No," they replied, "there may not be enough for both us and you. Instead, go to those who sell oil and buy some for yourselves." But while they were on their way to buy the oil, the bridegroom arrived. The virgins who were ready went in with him to the wedding banquet. And the door was shut. Later the others also came. "Lord, Lord," they said, "open the door for us!" But he replied, "Truly I tell you, I don't know you." Therefore keep watch, because you do not know the day or the hour.
–Matthew 25:1-13

These verses tell us that, if we don't prepare our hearts and lives for the day of Jesus' return, we'll be denied all of his glory on that judgment day. Those of us who've lived our lives for him will be taken into the Kingdom of Heaven, just as the virgins who'd prepared their lamps with oil were taken into the wedding ceremony with the bridegroom, while those who hadn't prepared themselves were denied.

The plain and simple truth is that—what God shows us, what life shows us, and what athletics shows us—the separation is in the preparation. I had to realize when it came down to it, for me, track wasn't a game, life wasn't a game, and faith wasn't a game. Unfortunately, these realizations didn't come without heartache and pain, but I couldn't be more thankful they became the moral of my college story.

Through my years running at Iowa State, I was plagued with injury after injury. Every day was a battle to keep pushing through workouts. Every day was a battle to get enough sleep because I was grinding away in the library. Every day was a battle to make time for prayer and time to get into the scripture. And I will tell you one thing I know for certain: It will never get easier. We're all wired to sin. We're all wired to take the easy way out. And, we're all wired to settle for what we can get. I chose the hard way. I didn't give up. I placed my trust on a solid foundation in God and relied on him to carry me through the long nights in the library and the tough days on the track. I never could have imagined the strength I'd draw from a relationship in Christ. Through his mercy, I achieved a 4.0 in the classroom a number of times. I was able to heal injuries and work hard to be my best on the track. And through him, my heart was thawed out and filled with him.

Looking back, I'm thankful for the struggles I've faced in my lifetime. If I hadn't found out what it was like to be at the bottom, the top could never have felt so good to me. My growth on the track, my growth as a student and participator in life, and my growth in my faith throughout college remain three of the most important changes I've made in my lifetime. At the end of the day, I hope that, if you take away nothing else from my testimony, you can realize that track, life, and faith aren't games. If you take the time to prepare your body, mind, and heart for the things you want most, you won't regret it. If you never give up, no matter how hard things may be or how far you may fall, I promise you'll find what you're looking for, one way or another. Track isn't a game. Life isn't a game. Faith isn't a game.

Anonymous Woman #4

Hometown: Texas
Sport: Track and field
Age at time of story: 21

What you're going through is what you asked God for.
–Unknown

I could sit here and tell you how angry I was after my freshman year when all of our coaches got fired. I could tell you about sophomore year and how devastating it was to find out my second coach was quitting and once again we had to start over with someone new. I could even tell you how I seriously wanted to transfer at that point. But I stayed. I had to be realistic and realize what God had given me. I was a student-athlete on a full scholarship with no debt to worry about. Truth is, if I'd transferred, I most likely wouldn't have gotten that kind of offer with the times I was putting on the board.

The third coach, he was the one I'd been waiting for! I'll never forget when I first met him. My teammate and I walked up to him, looked him up and down, and began flooding him with questions. I even asked him, "Are you a Christian? Do you go to church?" It was hilarious stuff! But he laughed, and his answer was yes. Out of all the coaches I've had, he's the second coach I was able to connect with on a spiritual level. He always gave me words of encouragement, praise, and scriptures. He definitely was and still is my favorite coach. I improved ever year of college, but it was about more than that with this coach. He not only told me what I needed to fix on and off the track but also taught me how. And to me, that's what makes a difference between a good coach and a great coach. Things were going great!

Then, during my senior year, I dislocated my shoulder for the third time. The doctor decided I needed surgery, which put me out of training from October to December. I remember thinking, "Ummm, hello, track season is around the corner. I can't be out that long!" But, I had to suck it up and go through with it. I was in constant, throbbing pain and wasn't able to look half decent and do my hair because I only had one arm.

I didn't let that setback be the end of my story. I was told I couldn't do any activity because a wrong movement could mess up the repair they'd done to the tissue on the inside of my shoulder. But, I'm very stubborn at times, and seriously, once you've dislocated your shoulder, you kind of have an idea what your body is capable of. And, I'd always recovered from injuries pretty well. Because I couldn't practice, I'd always sneak upstairs to the elliptical machines and do my workouts. I couldn't use my arms much, but you better believe I was going to keep my legs strong.

For three months, I focused on rehabbing and strengthening the rest of my body and staying positive. That's how I should live life anyway, right? Rehabbing is like our bouncing back from things that have knocked us down. Strengthening is making ourselves better and learning from every situation. Staying positive is knowing God is there for us and he'll never put us in a situation we can't handle.

Those three months flew by, and I wasn't ready for that indoor season at all. I looked good in practice and I felt good, but I didn't feel ready to compete. It seemed like every time I was doing well, something always came up. And just like I thought, indoor season was terrible. But to be honest, I didn't care for indoor track, so I kept my faith and kept pushing.

Since freshman year, I'd been determined and said, "I'm not going to leave this school without scoring points for my team, earning a medal, and qualifying to nationals." But, here I was a senior in college and still hadn't done any of those things.

By the time outdoor season came, I was tired. I was focused on my classes and graduating and my back always hurt. I also felt a little out of place with my team. The stress was taking a toll on me. It got to me so badly that I snapped at practice on the very coach I loved. I can't really remember why, or what the argument was about, but I was pissed. There we were at practice going back and forth, yelling in front of the team. I felt horrible because I knew he had no idea why I was upset, but I took it out on him. I was ready to give up my life as a runner.

I eventually calmed down from the situation. I wanted to quit. In fact, I went to my coach at practice the next day and tried to quit. Reflecting back on it, I can't believe I did that. But, this coach knew my love for track was far greater than anything else, and he had the nerve to tell me I couldn't quit. He made me take a week off from practice, so I could pull myself together. Deep down, I knew I couldn't let go of track; it's what I've always wanted to do my whole life. I couldn't see my life without it.

That outdoor season, not only did I run my fastest but I also stayed consistent. A friend once told me, "Once you finally get that PR you've been looking for, you won't forget what it feels like." And, I didn't. Every time I ran, I didn't accept anything less than what I was capable of.

It was time for the outdoor Big 12 conference, and I felt ready! Coach switched up my practices, so my body could handle the training. I trained with the guys mostly. The 200 meters was my race. It took me a long time to accept that. I ran a 23.68 and was number eight going into finals until someone in the third heat ran a 23.67 and bumped me out. Bummer! No surprise there, I always got ninth or tenth, just missing the finals every year. It was cold and wet. All I could do was lean over the rail and cry. It was my senior year, and I still hadn't scored any points for my team nor did I earn a medal in my race.

Then, there was the NCAA regional meet. I focused on one thing only and that was trying to drop another personal record (PR) and make it to nationals. So, I ran and actually made the finals. I was shocked because there was so much competition. But, I made the cut. My coach talked with me the next day about what I needed to hear him yell when I was coming off the curve. I was running in lane eight, so I'd be able to hear him.

It was a Saturday at the University of Texas, and the 200-meter final was happening. I was in lane eight, my body felt good, and I was ready to go. The gun went off, and so did I! As I was coming off the curve, I completely forgot about my coach, but I promise you the entire world was quiet. All I heard was his voice: "Drive...Drive...Drive!" in slow motion. Then I immediately thought, "Okay, Coach, I'm Going, I'm Going!" I felt like my body had lifted up off the ground, and I took off!

With a time of 23.63, I got fourth place in the final and twelfth overall, which got me spot number twenty-four and allowed me to qualify for nationals. I was going to nationals for the first time ever in college! I was so happy. It felt like everything I'd worked for had finally paid off. I knew I had the slowest time going in for the 200 meters, but I wanted to run my hardest when I got to Oregon and drop one more PR.

Well, that didn't happen. Clearly, it was in my plan but not in God's. I went to nationals and ran horribly! I was so confused and angry, and I refused to speak to anyone. At that point, I was so mad at God. I even called my pastor, crying and yelling. I asked why God would bring me that far to run the way I had. I felt like I should've been left at regionals with the time I'd run. I was ready to pack my bags and leave because I had no reason to try to compete with those girls.

That summer, I was at church having a conversation with someone about how I hated my job at the time. She said, "Well, you didn't tell God what kind of job you wanted. You just said you wanted a job, and that's what you got. So, be careful what you ask for." We laughed and moved on. Later, I was thinking about how my senior year had ended, and I thought about that conversation at church. I'd never asked God to allow me to score points and earn a medal in my race. I just had said I wanted to score points for my team and earn a medal, and I'd done just that. Technically, that's getting what I wanted. And, I did qualify for nationals and my last year, just like I'd wanted. God was good to me all along, but I just couldn't see it at first.

Do all things without grumbling or disputing, that you may be blameless and innocent, children of God without blemish in the midst of a crooked and twisted generation, among whom you shine as lights in the world, holding fast to the word of life, so that in the day of Christ I may be proud that I did not run in vain or labor in vain. Even if I am to be poured out as a drink offering upon the sacrificial offering of your faith, I am glad and rejoice with you all. Likewise you also should be glad and rejoice with me.
–Philippians 2:14–18

Jonathan Hood

Hometown: Mississauga, Ontario
Sport: Football
Age at time of story: 23

There is no victory without sacrifice. The question is, what are you willing to give?
–Jonathan Hood

I was a top pro prospect coming out of my senior year in 2008. I'd had some NFL workouts, and many Canadian Football League (CFL) teams were interested in me. I was drafted twenty-sixth overall to the Edmonton Eskimos. After they drafted me, they called and told me they were very excited and that I'd be playing free safety and would have a chance to compete for a starting spot. I went there pretty confidant and showed up well. I had an interception on a really good quarterback during rookie camp, and I was fast, strong, and dominating.

By the end of camp, they'd put me on the practice roster. It was between me and another guy they'd drafted before me, who wasn't very fast and was constantly getting chewed up during film sessions.

I stayed on the practice roster for half of the season until they nudged me to go back to school to play out my fifth year, and they would re-sign me afterward. I decided to go to the University of Western Ontario to begin my master's degree. I had a lot of fun and a great year there, in which we ended up losing in the national finals. After that season, Edmonton re-signed me.

They constantly called and told me how excited they were to have me the next year. They told me they were bringing in a veteran free safety who'd retire soon. I was to come in, back him up, and start when he left. A week before my flight, I met with one of the national scouts. He really liked me and shared the high hopes he had for me. The next day, I received my plane ticket; two days later, I got cut from the team before I'd even gotten there.

My agent called and told me he was working on it. A few weeks passed, and I still wasn't on a team, so I fired him. I made calls to some teams myself and had a bit of luck with the Argos. They gave me tickets to games and implored me to watch practice. I watched and hung out with my friends who were playing. I trained extra hard and worked as a personal trainer. I called many resources and prayed they'd come through. I got a call back from a football analyst for The Sports Network (TSN) whom I know. He told me about a combine that wasn't for guys like me, but he'd let me participate. I did it and tore it up. I got interest from a bunch of teams once again.

I was invited to a private workout with the Hamilton Tiger-Cats and did very well. I went to another private workout and did fairly well. It came down to Hamilton and Saskatchewan. I got an offer from Hamilton, went to training camp, tore it up, and played three years with them. I signed with Toronto last year and just finished my first season with the Double Blue.

Most of my support has come from my mother, little sister, and my friends. I have a very good core support group that gives me prayers, words of encouragement, etc. My mom always says, "The best is yet to come." My boy and I push ourselves when we train like we're pros.

I have a pretty good pastor and remember sitting in services in which she spoke about victory. I felt she was speaking directly to me. She said, "Your victory is near." But, it didn't come that month. Again in another sermon, she said, "Just as

Jesus rose in three days, you shall receive your breakthrough in three days." This time, I brushed it off, but in three days I got a call from Hamilton. They were going to sign me! I also went to a church retreat in April, and the youth pastor whom I'm now pretty close with prophesied over me, saying I'd play for the Ticats. We are very close now!

I stuck to the verse "God works for the good of those who love him and are called according to his purpose." (Romans 8:28)

I knew there was something special inside me that had to be let out on the football field. I knew I'd play. I even traveled to Orlando with no money to participate in a tryout for the United Football League (UFL), a new football league that was opening up in the United States. I've always been a firm believer that you can do and have whatever you want as long as you work for it. It was instilled in me at a young age; my dad would make me do work around the house or clean his car whenever I wanted a new toy.

Don't focus on your obstacle, know what you want, and focus on the plan you'll carry out to get there. Never be idle, always produce, and know your victory is around the corner. But, it'll take hard work, dedication, and persistence to take hold of it. Persist until you succeed!

When we have a buffet in front of us, it may be difficult to have the hunger, passion, and desire of a starving person. You have to want something so badly that you feel you'll die if you don't get it. You have to do this knowing you'll live and knowing everything you need is around you. Take hold!

Therefore, since we are surrounded by such a great cloud of witnesses, let us throw off everything that hinders and the sin that so easily entangles. And let us run with perseverance the race marked out for us.
– Hebrews 12:1

Eseroghene Omene

Hometown: White City, Saskatchewan
Sport: Track and Field
Age at time of story: 12

Do not pray for an easy life, pray for the strength to endure a difficult one.
–Bruce Lee

At this stage in my life, it's hard to pinpoint the hardest things I've had to go through as an athlete. I say this because, even though I've had many life-changing and altering experiences, I'm at a point that allows me to see and understand why I went through what I went through and how it's helped me become who I am now.

I've wanted to go to the Olympics since my earliest days that I can remember. I grew up a black girl living in a place called "White City," which consisted predominantly of white people. Let's just say I dominated any sport I played. I had no reason to think I wouldn't make the Olympics when I was young. In my eyes, and in my family's eyes, I was the best around. There was really no full understanding of what was needed to make it to the big stage.

I could say losing my father when I was twelve was one of the hardest thing I went through as an athlete. Coming from a family with five children, it could've been easy to get lost in the trauma of losing a parent. As a young female, losing your father can shape the type of person you grow up and become. Commonly, the example is a woman who grows up with no father, spends her whole life trying to please men, and craves the attention of males to fill that void. That could've easily been me. I was definitely sad and devastated when my dad passed away.

When you're young, you believe your dad is the strongest person out there, and nothing can bring you or him down. So, when this thing called "cancer" took him from me, I was shaken. I think what made me different is how I handled that experience. When my dad passed away, I didn't feel as though I'd lost him. From that day, at the age of twelve, until today, I've always felt my dad has been watching me — watching and protecting me, making sure I'm making good decisions and making sure I'm working hard. I've always felt he's watching me and smiling.

I've had a handful of people in my life pass away from cancer. Up until their last breath, they fought. Seeing and experiencing that gave me the idea that, if these people I love so much can fight so hard to live, who am I to give up when times get hard?

Losing a parent when I was such a young age definitely helped shape me as an athlete. I've had many ups and downs in trying to become the best athlete I can be. During the ups, I know I got there because of the support of my father, and through the downs, his voice echoes in my head, telling me never to give up. My family has been my solid brick wall of support, with most of it coming from my mom. Watching her raise five children, who've all become very successful adults, was an amazing example to grow up around.

His grace is sufficient for me, for His power is made perfect in weakness. For when I am weak, I am strong.
–2 Corinthians 12:9–10

George Chomakov

Hometown: Plovdiv, Bulgaria, and Madison Heights, Michigan
Sport: Soccer
Age at time of story: 18

If you fall, fall on your back. If you can look up, you can get up.
–Les Brown

The hardest thing I ever had to go through was during my push to become a professional soccer player. I was invited to a combine in California, at the end of which they'd select a team of twenty-five players to go overseas and play against professional teams, with a chance of being signed. There were over 500 people at the combine. It was three days full of scrimmages and workouts.

I was really nervous weeks before I even got there, but I knew in order to achieve my dream, I had to get out of my comfort zone. Once I got there, I realized I was one of the youngest people at the combine. I knew it would be a big test for me, but I felt confident. After the first two days, the coaches spoke to me, were really pleased, and basically told me if I performed one more day the way I had been I'd be on the team. They liked the way I played, my attitude, and my presence as a leader, even at such a young age. I was really happy and confident. The last day, they started making cuts. From 500 people, it was now down to the last 50, and I was pleased to have made it that far, but I knew it was far from over. There were two more cuts I'd have to survive before I could be on the team traveling to Europe.

They brought us all in together and named people who hadn't made it. I wasn't on that list, so I'd survived the first round, but there was one more. At that point, there were thirty of us left, and five of us wouldn't make it. We played a final scrimmage, and they brought us in again. As I was listening, I prayed to God for my name not to get called, but it did. I was the fourth person they called.

I was really disappointed. As I was on my way to the hotel, I kept thinking, "It's over. I've let down my family, my friends, and myself." On the flight back to Michigan, I cried and wondered why this had happened to me. Why had I not made it? What else could I do? Self-doubt kicked in, and everything seemed depressing to me. For two weeks, I didn't leave my room. I stayed there disappointed, overthinking and listening to music. I thought, "I spent so much money to do all this, and now I've failed. Now what do I do?" It was one of the toughest moments of my life because I didn't think I'd get more chances, and I wasn't used to failure.

For those two weeks, it was really hard to communicate with me, but family and friends were always there, giving off positive energy, sending me texts, and checking up on me. Most of the time, as I said, I was in my room, watching YouTube videos. Those videos helped me realize it wasn't over yet. Many people have failed, everybody fails, but we must never give up if we really want something.

I didn't give up because I truly believe we should follow our dreams, no matter how crazy they sound or how unrealistic they are. I knew if I trained harder and got my confidence back, I could do anything. We're here in this world to make it a better place. To do that, we need to experience happiness and have dreams, some bigger and some smaller. However, the sad part is not many of us try to pursue them. I'd rather be fifty years old thinking, "At least I gave it all I had and didn't make it," rather than thinking, "I wish I had tried." I never would be able to forgive myself. Trust God because, with him, we can achieve anything.

I still deal with self-confidence issues at times—we all do—but, I've learned I'm not perfect because nobody is. I'll work as hard as I can to make sure I improve as an athlete and human being every day, every second. Being mentally strong is a very important part of our everyday lives. I'm mentally stronger now. It's a lot harder for me to feel down and to get down on myself because of what life has thrown at me, such as injuries, rejections, and people trying to put me down. Through everything, though, I'm still here chasing my dream. I know one day it will come true.

We live by faith, not by sight.
–2 Corinthians 5:7

Christabel Nettey

Hometown: Surrey, British Columbia
Sport: Track and field, long jump
Age at time of story: 22

It was the summer of my senior year of college. I'd just received my diploma two weeks prior, and the last thing I had left to accomplish as a student athlete at Arizona State University was to claim an NCAA title in the long jump. It was in Oregon, a place that hadn't brought me many blessings in the past, but I figured this time would be different. My entire athletic year had been a complete fairy tale, and heading into the championship, I was ranked first. The next competitor was six inches behind me. I was the only female that year to have jumped over twenty-two feet, so in my mind and everyone else's, I'm sure, my first place was secured, and everyone else would be fighting for the last seven All-American spots.

I was competing on the first day of the three-day weekend. So, I was anxious but so ready to claim my title and then to relax and cheer on my teammates. Additionally, since it was my senior year, I was expecting to sign with an agent and end up with a decent shoe deal by the end of that weekend. I had it all planned out.

I remember that day I woke up thinking, "Wow, today is really the day." I got to the track two hours before the competition, as usual, and took the time to just reflect on my year and focus on the task at hand. I was in the second flight, so I watched in anticipation for the first flight to finish, so I could finally head out onto the field. During my warm-up run though, I felt faster than I'd ever felt, so my coach kept telling me to move my mark back. By the time our thirty-minute runway time had ended, I was over half a meter back from my original mark, but I was ready to go.

The actual competition is a blur to me. I'm sure that has a lot to do with my body's way of coping with the disappointing results. All I can recall is struggling down the runway and fighting to find the board. I kept thinking, "You have to stay calm. It only takes one jump." I even remembering thinking God wouldn't have brought me here and given me this opportunity to be so close to something amazing just to punk me.

As I took the runway for my final attempt, I wasn't even nervous. For some reason, I assumed everything would come together and I'd qualify for the finals, giving me an additional three jumps. I got the clap going, headed down the runway, took off, and landed. I didn't know immediately if it was a good enough jump, but I did know I hadn't touched the board. Instantly, I looked over to my coach, and the look on his face was not reassuring at all. I started to panic as I waited for them to put my mark up. And when they did, it felt like the world slowed down.

I almost didn't believe it was really happening. I'd never been in a situation like that in my life. I was so confused. I started crying as I collected my things and changed my shoes to be escorted off the infield. That night, I barely slept. I kept waking up thinking, "There's no way this is real life." I kept thinking that maybe tomorrow I would wake up and that would be the real day I was competing. But, of course, that wasn't the case.

It took time, but I knew there was more to come, and whatever it was or whenever it came, it'd be greater than what I could ever have asked for. I still had world championships to look forward to, and despite the fact that at the time it felt like my world was crashing down, I still hoped God would bring me through it all. It really tested my faith. All year, everything had seemed to be going as planned; I hadn't faced any setbacks. Because of that, it was easy for me to praise God. But, after this incident, I almost felt betrayed and hurt, which made me feel negatively toward worship. It showed me I have to be able to praise him at all times, not just the times when I'm getting what I want.

If we endure, we will also reign with him; if we deny him he also will deny us.
-2 Timothy 2:12

Andre Hamilton

Hometown: Toronto, Ontario
Sport: Track and field
Age at time of story: 14–21

I began running track during my early elementary school days from grades three to eight. I competed mainly at the elementary school city championships. During sixth grade, I was introduced to Bill Stevens, who'd be my coach throughout the rest of my elementary school and my high school days. Fast-forward to high school. That was a time when I feel track taught me the most. I started off high school thinking I'd be a champion. Lost and confused, I didn't have a main event. I was too slow for the 100-meter dash, too weak for the 400 meters, and not quick or strong enough for the 200 meters.

During that year, I was surrounded by greatness. The older kids in my training group were recent provincial champions, and my best friends were the number one–ranked grade nines in Toronto. I felt I was in their shadow, like I was just another runner on the team. "Little man" is what the seniors called me. I placed ninth at provincials in the 400 meters, missing the finals and running a very average time. Again, I felt like just another runner on the track filling a lane.

That summer, I temporarily quit track to be just a normal student in high school. I ended up feeling completely bored and useless. It was about mid-August when somehow, some way, I was back on the track training with my coach, Bill Stevens. I distinctly remember running 100-meter strides on the field, goalpost to goalpost. Bill came up to me and said, "You grew!" At that point, I couldn't even tell.

I went from being an undersized grade-nine student to a tall lanky grade ten. I put in a lot of work during my grade-ten base training. This base-training phase is when a beast was made. I grew this fire inside me that burned untamed. I was canny with my words and would clown around with any and everybody. My two very close friends, who were my main competition both off and on the track, would sit with me at lunchtime and crack jokes on one another. I was known to be the most aggressive one when it came to clowning on others. We put so much pressure on each other not to be the victim of the jokes. It got so far we'd clown each other for showing teeth while we run. During every race, I'd be saying to myself, "Don't show teeth," meaning I couldn't be caught in a picture showing strain. The goal was actually to make each race look easy. The pressure we put on one another pushed us to greatness. I won provincials that year in the 400 meters and 4x100 meters and placed in both the 4x400 meters and the 200 meters.

The following year, which was my grade-eleven year, was an up-and-down season. I knew from the start of the season the competition was going to be tougher because I'd be competing against much older athletes. The main highlight of that season was beating a high school teammate who'd had my number my entire life. It was the 200-meter metro final; I placed second in the finals, but all I cared about was beating my rival. My high school season that year was a bit disappointing because I placed fifth in the 400 meters and didn't make the finals for the 200 meters. However, I anchored both the 4x100-meter and the 4x400-meter teams to victories. My season really flourished in the summertime. I had an opportunity to make the world youth team, although my family didn't have the funds to support my going. I became the legion 400-meter champion and the fastest youth in Canada.

Grade twelve I call my bittersweet year. I was nationally known as one of the best sprinters in Canada. I placed first in the 400 meters, sixth in the 200 meters, first in the 4x400, and first in a record-setting time for the 4x100. Now, that's when life really began to catch up with me.

My best friend had already signed to a Division I school. Meanwhile, I was still stuck in Toronto. I had prestigious Division I universities interested in offering me full scholarships. I was unable to pursue any of these opportunities because my situation with the clearinghouse held me back. I stayed an extra year to get myself eligible. I got eligible, and I had to take a different route. Rather than directly going to a Division I school, I went to Wayland Baptist, a National Association of Intercollegiate Athletics (NAIA) school in Texas. Now, at the time, I was young and unaware of exactly what I was getting myself into.

I left Toronto in January for Wayland Baptist. This was probably the biggest mistake I'd made to date. I was one of those high school athletes who'd never lifted a day in his life. I ran off nothing but talent and training on the track. However, when I got to Wayland, they had me doing Olympic lifts, plyometrics, and all these new forms of training. My base training had been done in Toronto, and I'd never lifted any weights during that time. I competed in about two races before I got injured. At the time, my best was 47.37, and I couldn't break 49 my whole season there.

All through my season, I ran hurt, and I felt depressed, confused, and embarrassed. Lost, I thought that was it. I thought, "I suck, I'm slow, and I'm not who I thought I was." I went home during that summer, and my coach from home told me to give him two months to get me back to normal. I competed in three track meets that summer. First meet, I ran 48.3. I then ran a 300 meters in 33.31. I ended my season running a 47.54. It was refreshing to know what great coaching can do. I'm not going to sit here and rant about how bad the coaching was at my school. I just believe I was unprepared for the workload my body was going to endure. I went back to Wayland for another year, but things just didn't work out. I wanted to transfer. This is where my story takes a serious U-turn.

When I informed the coach at Wayland, he promised me I'd "never go to another American institution ever again." I'm hardheaded, so I thought nothing of it. I went home and was unable to sign with a new school for the fall semester. Again, I felt like a failure. I watched my friends, my family, and my loved ones move on with life; meanwhile, I was stuck. I felt like an underachiever, someone who'd had the opportunity but couldn't follow through. But, that didn't stop me from trying.

One thing I can say about myself is I never give up. I trained extremely hard that year, I took online courses, and I worked full time. I'd never thought I'd be where I was. Many nights, I sat, just staring at the walls, living in the past, and struggling to see the light. It was hard to wake up every morning, look into my mothers' eyes, and feel like I let her down. I felt like track was cheating on me, like I loved it so much, yet it was showing love to everyone but me. When I tried to go right, track would go left. I had no idea where to go. I put in the work, but clearly it wasn't enough because I wasn't where I needed to be. Looking back, that was a great point in my life that I needed. I was such a boy, so immature and confused. It was a great learning experience for me, to take the initiative to make something of myself. I watched my friends and loved ones move on and used it as motivation to better myself.

Middle Tennessee State University (MTSU) was trying to recruit me, Andre Hamilton. Coach Dean Hayes was going to me a chance to make my dream true. I signed to MTSU in August. There I was as comfortable as can be when, the night before my flight, I got a call from Hayes; he let me know the Wayland coach wouldn't sign a paper saying I was eligible. I was eligible; otherwise, I wouldn't have been able to sign with MTSU. He toyed around for a couple of days until I got my mother and the athletic director involved, and things quickly changed. So, there I was finally enrolled in university, doing what I loved the most.

I learned a lot throughout my track career about people, the sport, and myself. Here are some of the most important lessons I've learned.

People will love you when you're doing great. You'll feel invincible, but as quickly as you came up, you can fall just as quickly. You have to remain humble and always remember what it feels like to be at the bottom.

You're a lot stronger mentally and physically than you think. When you're put into an uncomfortable, foreign situation, you'll be amazed at what you can accomplish. You'll learn a lot about your capabilities and work ethic throughout.

You can be the fastest person in your country and yet still be nothing. Making world teams or competing internationally is a great wake-up call. Through all the fame and the glory, it's important to save face. Don't change your character when you begin to think you're becoming somebody. People always remember when you didn't have anything. It's so easy to get caught up in the hype, to forget the individuals who were always there for you, the individuals who went through hell and high water to see you succeed. People will always remember who you were.

The NCAA is a business. In business, there are no friends. Your success is their paycheck. If you don't meet what they need to maintain that paycheck, guess who they're getting rid of first? Not themselves, I can promise you that. It's kind of like a relationship with a girl. There are so many replacements, so you should never get too comfortable. Put in that extra work to make sure they won't have to search anywhere else. Make them proud of their decision to choose you.

Finally, if you want it, you should be doing whatever it takes to succeed. What works for one person might not work for you. Trial and error is very important in track and field. Eat, sleep, take your vitamins, recover properly, and try to remain stress free, as hard as that may be. Find some release therapy, no matter what it is, something to take your mind off of your sport. You spend far too much time practicing, prepping, etc. It takes a toll on your mind. Just find a hobby and learn to relax.

A man's steps are from the Lord; how then can a man understand his way?
–Proverbs 20:24

Sam Bluske

Hometown: Chaseburg, Wisconsin
Sport: Track and field
Age at time of story: 22

Faith keeps you going when fear tells you to stop. Have faith that no matter how difficult a situation is, you can do anything with God. Faith over fear.
-Unknown

As a Division I runner training at a high level, you're bound to have setbacks throughout your career and stumbles along the way. I've learned (possibly the hard way) that they're all meant to make you mentally tougher and to help you appreciate the gift you've been given. I've had an interesting but exciting college career that's helped me grow as an athlete but, more importantly, as a young woman.

I transferred universities the summer going into my junior year of college. When people ask me why I transferred, it doesn't always make sense to them. I never had an awful experience at my previous university, but my body was begging me to make the change—my heart wasn't in it. I went through the motions of being part of a team and put countless hours into training; however, something was missing.

I transferred to Iowa State University two weeks before classes started, but I immediately knew it was where I was meant to finish my running career. Because I hadn't been released from my previous university, I was forced to redshirt my entire junior year. My optimistic self kept reminding me everything happens for a reason and sitting out my junior year would be a blessing in disguise. I put in a solid year of training and had an average fourth year. I got back to racing and competing, but my training wasn't necessarily showing in my races. The summer going into my fifth year was crazy; our coach, who was the primary reason I'd transferred to ISU, took a new coaching position, and the entire coaching staff was let go.

We'd won two conference championships in a row prior to that cross-country season, and we'd just graduated the NCAA champion and two other All-Americans. We knew every person was going to have to step up and buy into the new coach in order to be successful. I was on my third college coach in five years, which can be frustrating in itself, and then a week into the school year, I was in the middle of a long run and stepped funny, causing me to fracture my foot. The doctors told me I had to take off a minimum of six full weeks from running and then three weeks of a slow return to running. After looking at a calendar, I quickly realized that would put me right on the Big 12 championships if everything went perfectly.

My fifth-year cross-country season, which was supposed to be the "blessing in disguise," seemed like a curse that would never get better, and it practically seemed like it was over. There were countless tears and many nights when I prayed God would send me a sign that it was time to just give up and throw in the towel. I kept going back to Romans 8:31: "If God is for us, who can be against us?" This verse constantly gave me hope and faith that God had a plan because he always has my best interest in mind, even when it doesn't necessarily make sense to me.

The next six weeks were rough. I spent two to three hours a day cross-training like a maniac, but I was blessed to have amazing coaches who were literally by my side every session. I never had a second to think about giving up. I was surrounded by my teammates who were the main reason I never wanted to give up; I was determined to be on the line with my teammates to represent Iowa State University at the end of the season, no matter what sacrifices it took. I refused to be on the sidelines. I was cleared to go on a run six days before the Big 12 Cross-Country (XC) Championships. My third run off of my stress fracture was the Big 12 Championships, which I never thought was going to be possible. I helped our team to its third consecutive conference title, and we jumped to number seven in the NCAA polls. On November 23, I found myself on the line of the NCAA championship meet, which my doctors and trainers (and sometimes I) had believed would be impossible. Our team ran to a thirteenth-place finish. (There are nearly 400 women's NCAA Division I teams.)

Running has taught me to be thankful not only when training is going great but also when I've hit rock bottom, because in the end, things can always be worse. So many athletes would dream to be in the position that many Division I athletes are in, and remembering your talent was given to you as a gift is one of the humblest realizations you can come to as an athlete. I've realized God has made my path rough so that I can draw nearer to him and remember all glory needs to be given to him. Constantly putting my faith and trust in God gives me hope every day that he has a plan grander than any I could ever imagine.

"For I know the plans I have for you" – this is the Lord's declaration – "plans for your welfare, not for disaster, to give you a future and a hope. You will call to me and come and pray to me, and I will listen to you. You will seek me and find me when you search for me with all your heart."
–Jeremiah 29:11–13

Clint Martin

Hometown: Boone, Iowa
Sport: Football
Age at time of story: 21

This story starts a lot earlier than when I was twenty-one, but that's really when I realized I was going through something and when the hard decisions came. Coming out of high school, I was an All-State athlete in track and football and decided to continue my career in track at Iowa State University. My freshman year, I'd had a pretty successful campaign until I tore my hamstring during the second outdoor meet of the year. I was crushed, but I eventually got 100 percent healthy again.

During the time I didn't race, I really got hit with the football bug again. I asked my coach if I could play football again, and the answer was a firm no. I let it go for the moment, but the itch only grew stronger. I played football every chance I got. I'd go after track practice to flag tournaments, not even considering what it would mean to my track career if I got hurt.

My sophomore and junior seasons, I really came into my own on the track, but I just didn't have the drive I'd once had. Having some bargaining power because I was running well, I approached my coach about playing football again. He said I could try out. I was excited! I had talked to the football coaches at other times, but nothing had panned out. This time was different because I was going to train the whole summer and get out of track mode into football form. I had my tryout, and I killed it. Right after the workout, a coach told me I'd put up scholarship numbers. I couldn't have been happier. That night, I got an e-mail saying I didn't make the team. I knew a couple of other guys who'd tried out and made it. I realized that, as long as I was running track, I wouldn't get my shot to play football.

I talked to my teammates, and they supported my decision to leave the team going into my senior season. Quitting track was the hardest decision I've had to make when it comes to athletics. I'd experienced success, but more than anything, I hated leaving my brothers on the team, but it was something I knew I had to do if I was ever going to play football again.

So, there I was with a year and a half left in school. I had no team and no coach. People thought I was crazy to quit track to try to play football because I was clearly "a track guy." My strength coaches said they'd continue to coach me because they knew my situation and saw the potential. I took the entire next year and just trained. I could've transferred, but I was already into my curriculum, and I had other things holding me to Iowa State.

I set my eyes on an arena team. A full year went by, and I was gearing up for a workout with the arena team. A week and a half before the workout, I hurt my knee. It was one of those moments that made me sit back and wonder if that was a sign I wasn't supposed to play football. Although I was not at 100 percent, I went to the tryout. You can imagine the results weren't what I'd hoped they'd be.

I found myself contemplating giving up on the dream. Little did I know, there was a semipro coach at the workout, and he liked what he'd seen from me. That season, I played football again for the first time since high school. Every week, I could feel my confidence coming back. I was truly returning to being a football player. Our team went undefeated and won the 2013 Semipro National Championship. I couldn't have been happier with how the season ended, but I knew that wasn't the end for me. I felt I was ready to take my game to the next level. I talked to a few influential people in my life and decided to step my training up and pursue a professional career in either the CFL or NFL.

So, here I am now, two months out from draft day. For the first time in my life, I'm being taken seriously as a football player. I have an agent, and I've begun to work out with teams. I have no idea how everything will turn out, but I'm fine with that. I'm fine knowing that, no matter what happens, I followed my dream and the talent and passion God gave me.

My primary support has come from a small circle composed of my close friends, family, and girlfriend. During this journey, my relationship with Christ has blossomed in a way I would never have imagined. The feeling that you have God's blessing is the best support.

Every time I had the feeling of "I want to quit," something extremely unlikely would happen. Something would stare me in the face saying, "Don't give up. I've got your back." I always saw these as signs to endure and press forward.

Plenty of things have happened to me up to this point that I used to think weren't fair. I've had to grow spiritually, mentally, and physically to overcome obstacles, but I wouldn't change the process for anything.

You will never be crowned if you always back down.
–Unknown

I will not set my eyes before anything that is worthless.
–Psalms 101:3

Django Lovett

Hometown: Langley, British Columbia
Sport: Track and field
Age at time of story: 21

Stand up to your obstacles and do something about them. You will find that they haven't half the strength you think they have.
–Norman Vincent Peale

In 2012, my sophomore year of base training, I was suffering from severe tendinitis in both knees. I was forced to take a month off from training and focus on rehab. Every morning, I went to work with my trainer, doing everything possible to get better. Instead of being out with the team preparing for the upcoming indoor season, I was stuck running on an underwater treadmill.

On January 31, 2012, I was finally cleared to practice. It was looking like I'd be ready to high jump for the indoor season after all. Things were looking up. Around one thirty in the afternoon, I got out of class and started heading toward my first indoor practice of the year. I had a grin on my face like nothing could hold me back. I was a presence of determination. I told myself I was going to come back even stronger; I was still going to claim the conference title. Nothing was going to hold me back. I had faith God would find a way.

I didn't have a car at the time, so instead of four wheels, I had two. My roommate had lent me his bike. It was an old beat-up ten speed, with a rusty chain and a torn-up seat. But, at least I had wheels to get me around, and I was running late for practice. I was in the bike lane, stopped at a red light and waiting for the walk signal; I was totally unaware of what was to come. After a few minutes, the light changed, and the walking man appeared. I had the right-of-way. Out of the corner of my eye, I saw a car behind me, signaling right. Aware that I had the right-of-way, I didn't think much of it and proceeded.

As I worked my way into the intersection, so did the lady in the right-turn lane. Without any time to react, I was knocked off my bike. Lying there in the intersection, I was conscious enough to know I had to get up and get myself out of the road. I gathered my composure and tried to lift to my feet. That was when I noticed my ankle. It sure as hell felt broken. However, knowing I had to get out of the intersection, I stumbled over and picked up the borrowed bike, which now had bent rims and a damaged frame, and I struggled to get to the sidewalk.

In a state of shock, I sat there with a blank stare. The lady who'd hit me ran over to see if I was all right. She had tears running down her face; it almost seemed like she was more terrified than I was. Before I even thought of dialing 911, I called my trainer to see if she'd come to my rescue.

The final diagnosis was a severe ankle sprain—on my jumping leg, the worst place for a high jumper to be injured. All I could think was "So much for my comeback." I was forced to sit out the entire indoor season.

That was by far the most difficult time in my track career. It was a setback that crushed me. For the second time in a row, I was put out of training for an extended period of time. I hadn't even set foot on a track, yet I was back to rehabbing and walking in crutches and a boot. However, I remembered hearing this quote by Willie Jolley: "A setback is a setup for a comeback." Once again, I was determined to get back to work, even though the indoor season was out of the question. It was Olympic year; I had my heart set on doing everything I could to qualify.

Monday through Friday, I had rehab from eight to nine o'clock in the morning and then again from one to three o'clock in the afternoon. I felt as though I were living in the training room. As this was going on, I knew that, if I was going to come out of this and still have a successful outdoor season, I'd have to keep my faith, so I kept telling myself God would find a way. I knew he wouldn't let me fail if I trusted in his plan, kept my faith, and kept working toward my goals.

That outdoor season, I was able to come back and place second at my conference championships and qualify for the NCAA finals. Later that year, I came in third at the 2012 Canadian Olympic Trials, just short of qualifying for the Olympics. Furthermore, I was blessed to qualify for my fifth national team and compete for my country at the 2012 National Association for College Admission Counseling (NACAC) Championships in Mexico. All in all, I would interpret my 2012 outdoor season as a successful comeback.

The biggest reason I didn't give up was that, deep down, I knew I had bigger and better things in store. I knew it was just one of many setbacks I'd encounter along my path to success. I knew God rewards those who persevere in hard times. I knew my friends and family all believed in me, which kept my spirits high and the fire burning. I've been blessed with an amazing support system that has always been there to encourage me along this path, making it impossible to quit.

Although 2012 might not have been my most glorious season, I learned more from that season than from any other in my career as a high jumper. I'd place that time as the start of my beginning to mature as a high jumper and an athlete. I've learned just how much hard work and dedication it really takes to become successful and to overcome the unexpected challenges that may block the path to achieving your dreams.

Furthermore, I've learned to accept the hardships as an opportunity to grow.

At every point of failure, there's a critical point of choice: a choice to sit down, sulk, and be defeated or a choice to get up, learn from the experience, and grow as an individual, both mentally and physically. I believe this has been an essential lesson for me. There are lots of twist and turns, and things will stand in the way of you and your dreams. Learning how to deal with the barriers along the way will make the journey that much more rewarding. Finally, that experience has helped to solidify my relationship with God and has helped me establish myself as a true Christian athlete.

God's glory gave me the strength, the will, and the mindset to put forth the hard work to overcome all of the obstacles that had been thrown before my path. I know my comeback was only possible through God's grace. I also couldn't have done it without the support from my trainers and the countless hours they committed to get me back into shape and good health, and, of course, the constant support from my teammates, coaches, friends, and family. I can't give enough gratitude to all those who helped to clear my path.

It is God who arms me with strength and makes my way perfect. He makes my feet like the feet of a deer; he enables me to stand on the heights. He trains my hands for battle; my arms can bend a bow of bronze. You give me your shield of victory, and your right hand sustains me; you stoop down to make me great. You broaden the path beneath me, so that my ankles do not turn.
–Psalm 18:32–36

David Sims

Hometown: Gainesville, Florida
Sport: Football
Age at time of story: 18–19

This point of my life is important because it's when I had to face the first piece of many adversities, the point that's one of my biggest downfalls and biggest uprisings at the same time. I really had to figure out what I wanted to do with my life because I had no clue. I'd messed up so badly at the end of my senior year of high school that I didn't graduate. I had no direction, no support group, and no anything. No one wants to be bothered with you if you don't have your things together.

So at that point, I was lost in the shuffle. I played video games all day, being a bum. I lived with my girlfriend's mother. I worked to put money in my pockets, but I quit every job I'd had because I'd realized I'm not a nine-to-five type of guy. I had lots of different jobs too. I'd worked at a Nordstrom warehouse, unloading boxes from trucks and sorting them by the post office box number; at the University of Florida's laundromat, which was a three-hour thing because I quit on my lunch break; and at Sam's Club, doing overnight stocking.

But, the job I still think about to this day is the one I had in waste management. I was a garbage man—at 19! Some days, while I rode on the back of the truck, I wondered if that was it, if I was going to ever step on the field again. I constantly thought about how I was going to change the situation I was in. After working there for a while, I finally decided I needed a change, so I left Florida and went to California to live with my grandmother. While I was there, my grandmother had me take classes to get my General Educational Development (GED) certificate, but that didn't work out very well. After two months of staying with her, I decided to go back to Florida, where I picked up from where I'd left off before I'd gone to California.

That's when I got the Sam's Club job doing overnight stocking. I wasn't there for very long either. At age nineteen, doing overnight stocking, I felt I had no life and no direction. That was the breaking point for me. It's when I decided to finally take control of my life instead of waiting for something to happen. That was the beginning of my junior college search that lead me to Butte College and a grind I feel can't be matched by anyone. I endured, and through that (and more) adversity, I found myself in the NFL.

Robin Bone

Hometown: London, Ontario
Sport: Track and field, various
Age at time of story: 16–20

Dream big, win big.
–Bobby Minor

Ever since I can remember, I've always been a dreamer. My whole life, I've dreamed about waving to a crowd and standing up on a podium for the whole world to see. I've dreamed about being a pop star and performing for millions of screaming fans. I am a dreamer. That's me, a full-time dreamer.

I've always aspired to be the best, no matter what I do. I'm not sure if that's something I learned from my parents or picked up along the way, but for some reason, I've always wanted to be number one — in everything. If you're sitting there thinking, "Wow, she is extremely competitive!" you're right. Whether I'm competing with my brother over who can put his or her seatbelt on the quickest or competing against some of the best athletes in the world, there's always one common thing: I want to win.

Here's the thing: Everyone wants to win, but not everyone understands what it means to be a winner. It's more than just winning. It's about the self-fulfillment. It's about conquering a goal and striving to be the best you can be. Once you've achieved your goal, it's the best feeling in the world. When I look back on something, it always amazes me how many times I've been knocked down. What makes me different is I always get back up.

Growing up, I did every sport you can imagine: gymnastics, football, lacrosse, basketball, softball, and the list goes on. Gymnastics was my true passion, and, in fact, it still is. In 2010, after being a competitive gymnast for almost thirteen years and earning over fifteen state championship gold medals, I had to give up my passion. For those of you who don't know, I am a "go big or go home" type of person. Unfortunately, this mentality caused me to endure five concussions over the course of my gymnastics career.

My last concussion was in the fall of 2009. I over rotated while rebounding from a simple gymnastics move I'd been doing since the age of five. I don't remember much of the incident, but I do remember thinking, "I'll be okay." By doctor's orders, I wasn't allowed to go back to school until my cognitive tests were clear. I was ordered to stay in a dark room without any stimulation, which would allow me to heal from trauma to the brain. That meant no computer, no cell phone, no TV, no seeing friends, and worst of all, no gymnastics. That was an incredibly hard time in my life.

Those of you who know what it's like to be so deeply passionate about something but not be able to engage in it know it's gut-wrenching. Time passed, and friends would bring me coloring books to color and make me cards. Eventually, they were allowed to come by for brief visits, but something was missing. That something was the way I felt when I was doing gymnastics. Think about how you'd feel if you'd done something you loved five or more hours a day, six days a week, but then had to sit in a dark room, not allowed to do anything. I was falling behind in school, missing out on the whole beginning of grade nine, and most of all, I was missing training for the upcoming competitive season.

After about a month, I was gradually allowed to start engaging in certain activities again, such as watching TV for small amounts of time, talking to people, and even planning with the school how I was going to get back into the swing of things. At around two months, I started going back to school part time, one period at a time, and worked with my teachers on how I could catch up in classes and still be able to receive credit without having to repeat the year or do summer school. Fortunately, all of the teachers at Darien High School in Darien, Connecticut, were extremely understanding and accommodating. I'm still so thankful today for all of their help.

I finally was able to get through a full day of school, still suffering from side effects, such as memory loss and severe headaches. People still would tell me, "You look so out of it." The truth is, I was out of it. I wasn't myself. I wasn't the normal, bubbly, and happy-go-lucky Robin. I was lost. It'd been over three months since I'd first gotten injured, and I still hadn't been cleared by the doctor to get back into gymnastics. I just kept waiting and waiting, hoping that the test results would get better and the doctor would give me the green light to proceed with my training. Unfortunately, that green light never came.

I will always remember this day. I walked into the doctor's office that time sure I finally was going to be cleared to get back into the gym and make up for the time I'd lost. I'd been tested, and I was sure I'd done much better than the last time. I was convinced. The doctor came in to talk to my family and me, and I knew it was going to be different than all the other times he'd come into the office. I'd always been told, "No, it's not safe to return yet to gymnastics." But, for some reason I knew this time was going to be different. I just knew this time was going to be better. I mean, after all, I was feeling much better and was now completely back in school. I was wrong.

The doctor came in just like all the other times. He explained my test results to my family and said he wasn't satisfied with the progress I'd been making. By this point, I'd started to really feel down. People always say, "Do what you love, and you'll always be happy." I wasn't happy. I wasn't able to do what I love. Tears started to well up in my eyes, just like every other time I'd visited the doctor. I was just so overwhelmed with frustration. This was out of my control, I couldn't help myself, and that was so frustrating. At that moment, I knew this doctor's visit wasn't going to go the way I'd hoped. He explained the still-existing problems and just kept saying how it was going to take time and that it was important to obey the orders if I ever wanted to get back to normal.

I told the doctor I wasn't ever going to get back to normal if I wasn't allowed to do anything fun. He looked at me and said, "Well, what is fun?" I told him in one word: gymnastics. The look on his face after I'd answered his question will always be in my head. It was a look I can't really describe. He softly said, "Robin, I don't think it is safe for you to return to gymnastics." Disappointed, I decided to ask when I was going to be allowed to return to the gym. Once again, he said with a look of shame on his face, "Robin, I don't think it is safe for you to return to gymnastics." It hit me; he wasn't talking about an amount of time it would take me to return. He was telling me it was over—just like that. He was telling me to end what I loved, the only thing in my life other than my family I was so truly passionate about.

At first I was angry. I couldn't believe he was telling me it wouldn't be safe for me to do gymnastics again. But still, how could this be happening? I kept asking myself why. I was in absolute shock. At that moment, my world was ending. How could I just stop and give up? How could I throw away everything I'd worked hours upon hours and years upon years on? I'd done everything right. I'd stayed in the dark room, I hadn't used my computer, and I hadn't seen my friends. I'd done everything right. Why wasn't I healed? Why wasn't I allowed to go back to doing what I love? It didn't make any sense to me at the time. I just cried. I cried and cried. I cried for days. I even cried to sleep many times.

To this day, whenever I talk about it, I still get very emotional. With time, I eventually understood that, if I'd gone back to gymnastics and had gotten another concussion, it wouldn't have ended so well. I could've ended up with very serious, lifelong cognitive issues and severe post concussion syndrome, which are not things I wanted to deal with my entire life. At age fifteen, though, that was really hard to take in and understand. Although extremely upset and in disbelief, I accepted what had to be done in order to pursue future aspirations. I'd known this doctor's visit was going to be different. I hadn't known "different" meant my dreams were going to be crushed and I was going to leave heartbroken.

Just like that, I'd learned the most important lesson in life: "Don't take what you have for granted." At the time, I kept thinking, "Why me?" I wondered and thought about it over and over many, many times, and the only thing I could come up with was that everything happens for a reason. Everything always happens for a reason. With the amazing love and support from my parents, I realized that, just because I couldn't do gymnastics, it didn't mean I couldn't be involved. My amazing longtime coach and mentor, Laurie DeFrancesco, told me I was and would always be part of the Arena family.

At first, it was hard to for me to enter the gym without being overwhelmed with emotions. So, after a little time away, I started coaching young gymnasts a few times per week. Those who can't do, teach. Coaching was a ton of fun, but being the active person I was (training five to six days per week for more than five hours at a time), I needed to get back into training. Training for anything.

I'd always played numerous sports growing up, and people had always told me I was fast, so I figured, why not try out for the high school track team? The track team seemed like the perfect option for me because the doctor had said I should only do sports in which I wasn't going to get hit in the head in any way. I went to tryouts (along with another 150 girls from my school), and I put up the best testing results for my grade, which really surprised me. My high school track coach, Steve Norris, who'd been coaching track for 100 seasons at that time and really had a great knowledge of the sport, told me gymnasts make great pole-vaulters. Immediately, a light went on in my head, and for the first time in a long time, I felt like I hadn't felt in months — excited!

I knew neither my doctor nor my parents would want me to do pole vaulting, a sport in which you plant a pole into a hole in the ground and catapult yourself into the air; however, I knew that, if I could talk it over with them, we might be able to come up with a compromise. So with long, drawn-out conversations and a few tears here and there, we finally came to a compromise: Robin wants to pole vault? Then, Robin will wear a helmet. Yes, a helmet. As mortifying as that seemed to me at the time, I've always been the type of person who'll make the best of a situation. So, my new challenge? How to rock a helmet. I added my last name to the back of the helmet in Swarovski crystals, and I was ready to go. If I had confidence, I could become an icon. Sure enough, I became "helmet girl" to anybody who saw me at competitions.

My first meet, I jumped five feet. To give you a perspective of how low that is, people high jump over five feet. I knew I could get better, but it was going to be a long journey. Pole vault is such a technical event, and I was just getting started. My only rules when I started to vault were don't be timid, don't be scared, and don't give up. I'm not a quitter. A month went by, and I got a little better. I started to jump around seven feet high, which wasn't that bad, but it wasn't good enough. It was really tough for me to go from being state champion in gymnastics year after year to doing something that I took last place in at almost every single meet. I started to get discouraged, and I was getting convinced that maybe pole vault wasn't for me. Maybe I should just go run the 100-meter dash instead. That was the toughest point in my pole-vaulting career. I'd been used to winning in gymnastics, and now I was on the bottom. I sure felt it. I thought about packing it in until, one time, I was waiting in line at a concession stand and my entire attitude toward pole vaulting changed.

I'd just finished the meet, and I was hungry, so I headed over to the concession stand to get a PowerBar and a Gatorade. I was standing in line, and in front of me were some of the state's top vaulters. I could hear them giggling and laughing at someone, so I started to pay more attention to what they were saying. When I heard what they were saying I almost couldn't believe my ears. I was the person they were making fun of, "the girl with the helmet," "the girl whose so bad they would pay to watch." I was standing in line as just the girl with the ponytail, not the girl with the helmet. They were saying things like "Not only does she have to wear that helmet but she sucks." "I'm so embarrassed for her." One thing that will never escape my ears is one girl's laugh. And, here's what separates me from most people: I wasn't sad, and I didn't feel bad for myself. I got that fire back in me. I felt that competitive drive I hadn't felt in a very long time. I was ready. I was ready to prove every single one of those girls and whoever else had doubted me wrong. I was ready to fight. I was ready to jump higher than them all. They were going to see Robin Bone, not just the girl with the helmet. And this time, I'd be sure to make them remember me.

I started training harder and for longer hours in the off-season, I watched YouTube videos and watched the world record holder over and over again until I'd learned something new. I was starting to get better, six inches higher this week, the school record of ten feet the next meet. I had started a buzz in my state. Everyone kept saying, "Who is that?" not because of what I was wearing on my head, but because I was beating them. That just fueled me more to keep going, to keep improving, to keep surprising people, and most of all, to keep proving to myself I can do anything if I set my mind to it.

Our conference title was coming up, the Fairfield County Interscholastic Athletic Conference (FCIAC) East championships. I jumped six inches higher than I had the week before. This time, I wasn't last; I was first. I shocked myself, and I just kept going. The week after that was the FCIAC championships, and I won! I kept winning, and it felt so great. I finally was back to me, a competitor. Class L States was coming up, and I was more nervous than before, but I just kept going. I jumped well and ended up with a gold medal!

I'd accomplished all of my goals except for one: the Connecticut indoor state record. I had one more chance to jump twelve feet, and it was at the Armory in New York City. It was a feat I'd my eye on since I'd wanted to prove to everyone that a helmet, a setback, and doubters will never stop me. So, my meet at the Armory came, and I was filled with many different emotions; however, every single one was positive. My family was there, just like at every other meet, and it didn't matter where this meet was; I was going to break that record. So my turn came. I made my opening height and cleared each height in the progression until I'd won the meet and could set the next height to whatever I wanted it to be. I set it at twelve feet one inch, which would be just enough to claim that state record. I got pumped up beforehand, and just like that, I was the new Connecticut state record holder.

Having that title was nice, but it wasn't the title I was so excited about. I'd reached my goal at the time. There's nothing like the feeling you get when you've reached your personal goals. This fueled me more than I could've imagined. During that time, I'd created a buzz on the track scene in Connecticut, and it felt amazing to be the girl with the helmet. It was then that I decided I wanted to become serious with pole vaulting.

At the end of my tenth-grade year, my family was traveling to London, Ontario, for a Football Hall of Fame dinner. Vickie Croley, the head track coach at Western University, called my family and asked if I wanted to do a practice with the pole-vault coach at Western. Immediately, I was so excited to actually get to work with a high-level coach for two hours. Dave Collins, the pole-vault coach at Western, invited me to practice with a small group of athletes a few hours before the dinner I was attending with my family. That two-hour practice turned into four and a half hours, and I decided to stay and practice and miss the Hall of Fame dinner, which was the whole reason I'd come to London in the first place.

After that practice, I knew I'd found what I was looking for without even trying. I wanted someone who could take me to the next level in pole vault, and Dave Collins, without a doubt, was my answer. His knowledge, combined with his passion for the sport, truly amazed me. I knew I needed to be coached by him. My trip to London ended, and I headed back to Darien with a new pole-vault coach who was based in London, Ontario. Some of you may ask how someone in another country could coach me in pole vault—the answer: via Skype.

From April 15, 2010, all the way through the rest of the high school track season, I'd go to the pole-vault pit, set up my computer on a table nearby, and connect on Skype, so Dave could watch my practice and coach me through the computer. After one session practicing with Dave in London, I'd returned to Darien and jumped a personal best by over half a foot and broken the Connecticut outdoor state record. The coaching through Skype was great, and I'd try to get up to London once in a while for some sessions to train with Dave.

However, it was a lot of work just trying to be coached by the person I wanted.

After one session in July, I remember the car ride home as clear as a bell. I'd asked my dad to videotape the practice with Dave, so I could refer back to it and watch the corrections he'd made. In the car, I was watching the video and told my dad, "Dad, I want to move to London, Ontario." My parents had always said that, after I graduated from high school, they'd move back to Canada, most likely to Toronto, where I'd been born and had lived at the beginning of my life. After I told my dad I wanted to move, he looked shocked. His only reply was "I'll talk to your mother." I knew my dad was shocked, but deep down inside, he was also excited. If we were to move to London, Ontario, we'd be joining some of our greatest family friends and a university atmosphere both of my parents had been through at an earlier time in their lives.

My family had moved to London by August. Sometimes, when you're chasing a dream, you have to make sacrifices. This wasn't a sacrifice in my eyes; this was an opportunity, to train with some of the best athletes in the world, to train with coaches who were so passionate and full of knowledge, and to turn my dreams into goals and eventually into reality.

After training with the Western Track and Field team for almost two years, I'm undoubtedly committed to Western University to continue my education and training for the next four years, and most likely beyond. Since moving to London, I'm a three-time national team member, a youth and junior national champion, a two-time Ontario University Athletics (OUA) champion, and most recently, the 2014 Canadian Interuniversity Sport (CIS) national champion.

When one door closes, another door opens. Pole vaulting is definitely a door I'm really happy opened. So, what have I taken from this whirlwind of an experience? It's more than I'd ever be able to describe. It'd be easy to look back on what has happened and say, "poor me," but I don't feel sorry for myself at all. I consider myself lucky to have had these experiences because they contributed to the person I have grown into over the years.

There are days when it'd be easier to sit on a couch and watch endless television, but, fortunately, I always think, "What if I couldn't run tomorrow?" or "What if I couldn't pole vault anymore?" It's those types of questions that keep me motivated and driven toward my goals. Having something I loved taken away from me really changed my perspective on many different things. I'm thankful for that. Many people could go through the majority of their lives never having learned what I'd learned by the age of twenty.

When I reflect on what the past few years have brought me, I wouldn't change a thing. You must always keep going. Here are a few Bible verses that have always provided me a solid ground when I'm feeling lost.

I will not be afraid of many thousands of people who have themselves against me all around.
–Psalm 3:6

People will always doubt you, diss you, and want to see you fail. This means you're doing something right! Only you control you, so prove them wrong. People will try to put you down; it's your job not to let them. It's a tough world out there; have strength.

I can do all things through him, who strengthens me.
–Philippians 4:13

There'll be times when you'll feel you've been thrown to the ground, had dirt kicked in your face, and been left to lie there. That's when you must have the greatest strength. Have faith because you're not alone; there is a plan for you. Brush the dirt off and stand up, stronger, taller, and mightier than you've ever been before. Lastly, have courage.

All things are possible for one who believes.
-Mark 9:23

All of the bumps and setbacks along the way are what build your character. The overall message I've learned and want to share with you is that it isn't how many times you fall; it's how many times you get back up. It's easy to wave the white flag, throw in the towel, and say you've had enough. But, keep going because one day it will be worth it.

Troy Joseph

Hometown: Toronto, Ontario
Sport: Basketball
Age at time of story: 19

Count your blessings.
-Unknown

The hardest thing I've had to go through as an athlete was undergoing micro fracture surgery on my left knee. It was the summer of 2011, and I'd just finished my redshirt freshman season, during which my team had won our first Northeast Conference (NEC) championship in thirteen years. I'd spent that whole summer preparing myself for the upcoming 2011–2012 season. Two weeks before I headed back to school, I decided to play in a pickup basketball game at a local gym with my boys. Little did I know that would be the last pickup game I'd play for the summer.

I came down from a rebound, and one of the other players ran into my knee. I fell to the ground, immediately hoping it was only a hyperextension injury. I took the remainder of that summer off, as ordered by my head athletic trainer, and was scheduled to have an MRI once I landed in New York. September came, I took the MRI, and the results showed a loose piece of cartilage floating around in my left knee, which at first didn't sound like horrible news. The doctors felt the same way and decided to operate on my knee, remove the cartilage, and give me an estimated six weeks of recovery time. I was only going to miss preseason and was expected to finish the recovery process before our first game of the season. The surgery was set for September 15, 2011.

The day I'd thought I never would have to face arrived. I was dressed in a gown and was ready to get the surgery over and done with, so I could start the rehab process. The next thing I remember was waking up in the waiting area. My athletic trainer told me that, while I was in surgery, they'd discovered where the floating piece of cartilage had separated from and that it had created a pothole-like shape in my knee. They then had decided to do microfracture surgery, which is basically drilling holes into the affected area in an attempt to let my own blood produce new cartilage. I was informed the healing process for microfracture surgery was three months and that I should possibly consider not playing basketball.

The doctors mentioned a few National Basketball Association (NBA) players, such as Amar'e Stoudemire, Tracy McGrady, Allan Houston, and Jason Kidd, who'd all been through the same procedure. Each of those NBA players' careers hadn't been the same afterward. Not playing basketball was not option for me, so I immediately started rehab the following day and set a goal of playing on the court by December. After months of rehab, December came, and I was nowhere near ready to compete in any type of basketball game. Upon doing more research, I found out, depending on the size of your lesion, your recovery time varies. My family and friends provided the most support for me during this time. They were always picking me up whenever I was down, encouraging me, and making sure I stayed on track, focusing on the task at hand.

The decision was then made that I'd miss the remainder of the 2011–2012 season, making that back-to-back redshirt seasons. We went on to win the championship for the second straight year and had the opportunity to make history by becoming the first team in NEC history to ever win three titles in a row. With that on my mind, and having sat out the first two championships, I was determined to come back strong and play my first season of college basketball. That summer, I didn't play a single pickup game but still lifted weights and put up shots every day. I finally got my shot to play in my first Division I collegiate basketball game on November 9, 2012, at the Barclays Center, home of the NBA's Brooklyn Nets, only seconds away from Long Island University (LIU). That season, we went on to make history and became the first team in NEC history to win three consecutive titles and compete in the NCAA tournament all three years!

The last championship felt the best for me because, despite the adversity I'd had to face throughout my first two years, I'd still been able to stick it out and get back on the court where I belonged. Even when the doctors and many others thought I wouldn't make it past the first season post-surgery, here I am, currently a starter in my fourth year at LIU-Brooklyn and playing strong on that same left knee. I was granted a fifth year by the NCAA for missing the entire 2011–2012 season because of my injury, during which I will be pursuing a master's degree in accounting.

I didn't give up, because I was so determined to play basketball again and live the dream I'd been chasing since elementary school. I also wanted to prove a lot of people wrong who'd thought my basketball career would be over. It feels good not having that "what if" feeling and knowing I never gave up.

It made me realize your life can change at any given moment without your control and forced me to figure out what I wanted to do once I stop playing basketball. It made me mature and realize that tomorrow isn't promised, so I try to be the hardest worker every day in everything I do. I never thought I'd ever be the one to have a major injury. When I did, it made me look at life differently.

Thanks be to God for his inexpressible gift!
–2 Corinthians 9:15

Shamawd Chambers

Hometown: Toronto, Ontario
Sport: Football
Age at time of story: 17

My life-changing experience was when I was seventeen years old and my brother Jonathan Chambers was taken from us at the age of twenty-one. At the time, I asked God why that had happened to my family and me, but I had to keep moving forward. Jon was murdered in March 2007, six days after his twenty-first birthday, an hour outside of Toronto. He was shot five times, three in the head and two in the body.

I dealt with major depression for just over a year, spending a lot of time sitting in my room feeling sorry for myself. The changing point for me was playing football in my last year of high school. I remember telling myself to just graduate and get out of school. That week was our first game of the year. I ended up scoring five touchdowns in the first quarter. After that moment, I never looked back. I had great support from my coaches as well as from my mother, who drove me to play football. I switched my entire course load into classes that would make me eligible to go to university.

I prayed to God and told him if he let me reach the places I wanted I'd be a pillar in my community and tell my story to all who'd listen. My supporters are the same people who've been there from the beginning, but I could never ask them to believe in me if I didn't believe in myself. My love and thank you goes to all who prayed and believed I could be great. I never gave up because I knew there are people who've gone through so many worse things than I have and still endured. God has a plan for me, but it was my choice to walk that path or not. I truly believe my life is where my God wants it to be. Life will throw punches at you, and some punches you won't be able to see yourself getting up from, but with God, all things are possible. I'm now a professional football player with the Edmonton Eskimos in the Canadian Football League, and I also spent time at the Philadelphia Eagles mini-camp.

For a brief moment I deserted you, but with great compassion I will gather you.
–Isaiah 54:7

Karlene Hurrel

Hometown: Edmonton, Alberta
Sport: Track and field, sprints
Age at time of story: 21

In the fall of 2011, I was gearing up for a great indoor season. I'd taken the summer off from running the Canadian track circuit and had put in a lot of hard work in the off-season. I was hungry for the 2012 indoor season and ready to compete! However, I was about to receive the worst news an athlete could hear: I was forced to redshirt my year because of a season-ending injury. I was told by the orthopedic surgeon that I had a serious tibial stress fracture. I was to refrain from training indefinitely. I was immediately sent to get a cast and was put on crutches for the next six months.

The injury was devastating to me, but hearing how long the recovery process was going to take affected me more. I was so lost. How could this have happened to me? I thought, "I'm in the best shape I've ever been in, and I've been working so hard!" To make matters even worse, I didn't even know I was as injured as the x-ray showed I was. At first, I'd had a few aches and pains in the lower half of my tibia. I brushed them off because I'd dealt with more serious injuries than those. I thought it was a mild case of shin splints because I'd experienced those in the past.

This was far more serious. On my x-ray, I could see a thick, dark line going right through my tibia, which only left one small layer about .05 millimeters thick that hadn't been fractured. The doctor looked at me in amazement saying, "I honestly don't even know how you are walking around all day without pain, let alone training! Your leg could have snapped in half at any given moment!" To put things in perspective about how serious the fracture was, the doctor explained that, had I kept training or even walking with that injury, my leg would've broken the same way Kevin Ware's (the NCAA basketball athlete) leg broke in the 2013 NCAA tournament.

I'd put all my energy, time, emotions, heart, and just about everything I had into this sport, only to have it taken away from me. I questioned God a lot and asked him why he'd take away something that meant so much to me. I was so angry with him and often blamed him for causing this to happen. I was in denial, I was angry, and I was extremely frustrated with my situation.

After weeks of being so bitter, I realized that wasn't helping my situation. I had one goal: Heal and get back on the track. As an athlete, I know that, when something isn't working to make me a better competitor, I have to find a different avenue to better myself. Instead of pulling away from the one thing that's never given up on me, I decided to draw closer. I began to realize God wasn't punishing me; he was, in fact, teaching me a very important lesson that not only affected my athletic career but also my life off the track.

The Lord has opened my eyes to become a more humble person. He has shown me I need to appreciate the gifts he has given me. I mentioned that I thought I'd put in the hard work that was required in the off-season and that I was ready to run fast; however, I wasn't doing everything I could to be a better sprinter. I wasn't doing the proper injury prevention techniques (all of which could have prevented this injury in the first place!), such as drinking plenty of water; taking my calcium supplement, which is extremely important for me because I'm lactose intolerant; and cooling down properly at the end of my workouts, such as doing stretches and cold tubing and getting treatment from trainers. Unfortunately, the injury was bound to happen. I just hadn't taken care of myself outside of my workouts, and clearly, being a sprinter is about so much more than just running. It's about taking care of your body, so you can recover.

To be honest, I'm actually grateful I experienced that injury. It truly changed my outlook on a lot of things in my life. I now have a greater appreciation for my coaches and the time they take to construct the workouts I have as well as the injury prevention techniques they provide for me. But, most importantly, I realize that I am not my sport. What I mean is, most athletes identify themselves with their sport, and when something terrible happens to them, such as a career-ending injury, they feel as if they have nothing left in their lives. This is not true! God opened my eyes to see so much more that I have to offer this world and to see the things I want for myself in the future. I have a more sympathetic outlook on those who don't have the wonderful opportunities and experiences that I have, being an NCAA athlete on a full-ride scholarship. And, during the time I had off, I got to know a lot more people, which allowed me to make new friends.

When I first learned of my injury, I wanted to give up on track and field more than anything, but I didn't, and I couldn't. God wouldn't let me. Maybe you can relate to this: When I'm down on myself and want to give up on everything, there's something inside telling me not to give up and to get up and fight harder than I ever have. I have to push through difficult times because I know things will get better. I believe that voice inside is God. He's for us and wants to see us become successful.

How do I know this is true? Since my injury, I recovered, and I came back less than nine months later, better, stronger, and faster than I was before my injury! I'd never made a final at a conference championship meet before, but I've accomplished that not once but four times since the injury. It gets better: I even became a first-team finisher in the Western Athletic Conference (WAC) this indoor season! Everything in my life has continued to improve the closer I've become to God. All I can do is be thankful and continue to praise him each day—because he is good and he is for us.

My advice to you if you're going through trials in your sport is to never give up! There's a reason behind everything you experience in this life. God would never put you though anything you couldn't handle, and all things are possible through him because he gives you strength. If you have fears, doubts, worries, or anxiety, cast all that on him and let him carry the burden. Realize he's trying to teach you something and turn your negative situation into a positive one.

What I saw was that, yes, I did have a very hard injury to deal with, but I'm so glad I experienced it because it changed me and made me a better woman, not just for myself but for others. It even brought me closer to God, the one I love most.

Max Mayfield

Hometown: Davenport, Iowa
Sport: Wrestling
Age at time of story: 18

Defeat is not the worst of failures. Not to have tried is the true failure.
–George Edward Woodberry

I've always loved wrestling as much as anything else in my life. But, I've also had a deep hatred for the sport. This sport is one that brings you face to face with every emotion possible, from the highest of highs to the lowest of lows. Heading into the Iowa High School state tournament my senior year, I had a record of 40-0. In the semifinals, I lost to the other undefeated wrestler at my weight and ended the tournament in fifth place. After that senior season, I wanted to remove wrestling from my life forever. I told my coach I didn't want to talk to any college coaches who asked about me.

About a month later, my dad asked me what it would take for me to wrestle in college. My answer was simple. I told him the only way I'd wrestle was if Cael Sanderson personally called me and asked me to wrestle at Iowa State. Cael was arguably the greatest collegiate wrestler of all time and was the head coach of one the nation's most historic wrestling programs. I figured there was no way I would ever hear from him.

A couple of weeks later, I was hanging out in the gym after a baseball practice when my phone rang. It was Coach Cael. I told him I didn't want to wrestle because I wanted to focus on being a great student and becoming an engineer. He told me he believed I could be a great engineer and a great wrestler. After that, I committed everything I had to the sport of wrestling and never looked back.

I'd never believed I could wrestle at a high-enough level to compete against the best guys in college. Coach Cael showed he was willing to believe in me if I could believe in myself. That turned out to be the push I needed to move to the next step. After I made that decision, I received endless support from my coaches, teammates, and family.

When I became a part of the Iowa State wrestling program, I learned how to love the process of becoming the best. Although I still had tough days on the mat, I knew if I could push through them that I'd become a better wrestler, which made the sport fun for me again. This is a lesson I've applied to my academic career and all other areas of my life.

And let us not be weary in well doing: for in due season we shall reap, if we faint not.
–Galatians 6:9

Naz Long

Hometown: Mississauga, Ontario
Sport: Basketball
Age at time of story: 15.

Work like a slave to eat like a King!
–Papoose

When I was fifteen, my family, friends, and I made one of the hardest decisions of my life. We decided I should leave home and go to Montrose Christian School, a prep school located in Rockville, Maryland. I'd visited the school, and I was thrilled to get started and to have things like an all-access gym, Jordan basketball gear, and the chance to play against and with the best players in North America.

Settling in at Montrose was hard. I lived in a house with the team and two great roommates who were my friends; they were used to being away from home—I was not. Throughout my year at Montrose, I was in the gym every day, working hard to give myself the best shot at obtaining my goal at that time, obtaining a Division I scholarship. I started at the point guard position for a top-five-ranked school in the nation, playing with guys who went to Duke, Washington, Virginia, South Carolina, and so forth. Although it was a great time playing with these players, I was the only one who didn't have any scholarship offers and never consistently got mail from any school. On top of all of that, I fought homesickness every day.

These mental struggles definitely started to show in my game throughout the year. I simply wasn't mentally ready for some of the games, and it showed through turnovers. I'd consistently turn over the ball. I was afraid of making mistakes. I'd continuously reiterate that to myself, and one night, I called my mother. We stayed up all night talking about my situation and concluded that I wanted to come home. I no longer wanted to play basketball. She wouldn't allow me to come home, and to this day, I remember her saying, "You have worked too hard and come too far. If I let you come home, I will be letting you fail yourself, and I will never do that."

That night, I took it upon myself to do everything in my power to get through the year and to get better. I did that, but alongside that, my belief that God was with me also grew. Back home, I'd never known who God was. I hadn't believed in God; I'd just been living life day by day. I wasn't raised in a bad area, but within every community, choices are made, both good and bad. Those decisions were made by me, I thought, and God had no role in that.

Throughout my year at Montrose, we had to go to church every Tuesday for an hour and a half. I always left there refreshed; everyone was singing and so positive. I loved every second of it. Going through this process got me questioning many things, not against God but for God. I wanted to know more about him and other people's stories. That eventually led me to have my own.

I went on to transfer from Montrose Christian and to a school in Las Vegas. I finally got over my homesickness and continued to better myself, my game, and my knowledge of God. Although I didn't go to church consistently after I left Montrose, I truly believe I wouldn't be where I am today without God, and I would've given up. I went on to obtain several scholarship offers to great schools and eventually accepted one to Iowa State University. My journey here at Iowa State is halfway finished but has had many ups and downs of its own. Thankfully, I have hit the ground before and have been at the highest points, so I feel there's nothing I can't overcome. Many people don't get to know the story of athletes like me nor do they get to see the grind and passion behind the scenes of getting onto that court, field, ring, etc. God has helped me during this great journey, and I feel that, without him, there'd be no me. Who knows what or where I'd be today?

Most of my support has come from my family and friends, whom I consider family. Having the support group that I have is truly a blessing and is something not everyone gets to have or see in their lifetime. Through the hard times of wanting to give up, my mother always called. When I didn't want to run that extra mile, my father was on Skype, letting me know never to give up. My friends and I were always in touch through social media, because texting costs money from an international standpoint, which was something big to me as well. Whenever I had an accomplishment, there would be a Facebook or Twitter post about it, showing me love. These people are not friends; they're family.

I didn't give up because I knew there was a purpose for me. I knew that, if I did quit, I'd fail too many people and would fail myself. Not giving up is something I take pride in and forever will, no matter what it is. I knew that, this journey would be hard, but a sign would always show me I could do anything I put my mind to and believed I could. God definitely played an important role in this as well. When I look back on my childhood days, I was a goon. I know for a fact that, without God, I wouldn't even have had the opportunity to pass the border and go down south to showcase my talents and obtain this scholarship education. For that, I am thankful. The journey and the people I've encountered have helped mold me. My coaches, teammates, friends, God, and, most importantly, my parents are the reason I am the person I am today.

Let the thief no longer steal, but rather let him labor, doing honest work with his own hands, so that he may have something to share with anyone in need.
–Ephesians 4:28

Anonymous Woman #5

Hometown: Pickering, Ontario
Sport: Track and field
Age at time of story: 18–22

Train up a child in the way he should go: and when he is old, he will not depart from it.
–Proverbs 22:6

As a child of God, once a strong foundation is laid for you, even if you stray for a while, the Lord will always calls you back. This is my story.

As a high school athlete, I was a social butterfly. I found a way to balance being a student, track star, and party girl with going to church almost every weekend. I knew being a party girl and a church girl was an oxymoron, but I was seventeen and having the time of my life. During my first two years of college, being a party girl was the last thing on my mind. I knew being away for school was a business trip. All I wanted to do was run fast, graduate, and one day represent my country doing what I love most.

I studied hard and worked hard. But after two mediocre seasons, I felt defeated. Maybe my dreams of being an NCAA Division I conference champion and national qualifier were too farfetched for little ol' me. On top of not performing the way I'd wanted to on the track, I wasn't having much fun. Hey, they say college is about having fun anyway, right? I felt I was missing out on the "American college" experience, so I went back to my partying ways. The track team was already known for being a bunch of party girls; I just joined the club. We showed up to practice hung-over, and at track meets, we were concerned only about making it back in time to hit up a party. With my partying, drinking, drama, and dropping grades, there was no hiding that my scholarship was in jeopardy.

That indoor season, my junior season, was the first year I hadn't made a conference final. I sat in the stands and watched as one of my closet teammates, the same one who was at all the parties drinking with me, won the title I'd wanted so badly. At that moment, I knew something had to change. Outdoor season was a bit better. I made a few adjustments but still not the changes that needed to be made. I remember it vividly, having my end-of-the-year meeting with my coach at our stadium and his telling me in his thick Bajan accent how he was ready to "ship my ass back home." The disappointment in his voice cut deep. I knew I'd been blessed with an amazing coach. I've heard many stories of athletes who'd had the worst experiences with coaches. I was one of the lucky ones. I had a great open relationship with mine; he believed in my talents more than I did.

This was the first time I wasn't going home for summer vacation because I had to do summer school. I'd messed around and had fun all year. There was nothing left for me to do but exactly what my coach told me: "Put your head down and go to work!" I worked my butt off that summer, both in school and in perfecting my craft. I spent a lot of time at the stadium. If I wasn't working out, I was picking my coach's brain, asking questions about track and field. Physically, running is one thing, but you also have to learn and understand your sport. By the end of the summer, I was in the best shape of my life. I was ready to run—fast! This was my senior year, and I'd put in the work to ensure it would be good one. Yet, there was one thing I still needed to change— my relationship with God.

In August when school started, I felt like I was the "last man standing." All my party-girl teammates were gone. I felt a lot of mixed emotions, not having my girls with me anymore.

But, I believe everything happens for a reason. So, I had to stay positive and try to embrace the new faces on the team. Lord knows, it was hard. I didn't like these girls; I wanted my old team back. I trained like a beast and let it be known that the top spot was mine. If they wanted to beat me, they'd have to work ten times harder. I was so hungry for a conference medal. But, God has a funny way of humbling us when we get too ahead of ourselves.

In October, I found out I had a stress fracture in my right tibia and would be out until at least December. I thought, "This couldn't be happening, not when I'm getting ready for my senior season." My coach tried to be as positive as he could about the situation: "This isn't a bad thing. Your body needs rest." Those were his very words as I sat in his office crying. I had to wear a walking brace, and I was only allowed to do bike workouts. If you're a runner, you know how boring that is.

I had extra time on my hands, and all my girls were gone. I didn't know what to do with myself. I felt so alone. I wasn't just sad or unhappy; I was depressed, like real-life depressed. I needed to get out of the rut I was in. I needed to be reminded that God works everything out for the good of his children, and that, no matter what, I was still blessed. I wrote inspirational quotes and Bible verses on sticky notes and posted them around my room and on my mirrors as reminders. By the end of the semester, right before I went back home for Christmas break, I was cleared to take off my boot and do easy workouts. As happy as I was to get out of that awful walking brace, I was scared. Would I be ready to compete? Would I be in shape to win conference? I refused to go out like a sucker with not one conference medal. Nope, it wasn't happening, not to this girl!

After the holiday, I arrived back at school ready to train. I knew for sure I'd miss the first half of the indoor season. But, I was still hopeful I'd be ready to run in time for conference. We had another new face added to the team, but this time, she was a senior, like me. She was a transfer student from another Division I college and an international student, like me. We clicked from the first day we met. We were so much alike yet different. Sarah became my big sister; she saw something in me that, most times, I didn't see in myself.

I eventually started going to the church Sarah attended; I fell in love. I remember one service, when my heart was so heavy; it was as if the pastor were preaching right to me. He did an altar call, but I stayed in my seat. He kept saying he felt there was someone still in his or her seat who needed to come to the altar. Still, I refused. He kept praying and saying that there was someone else and he wouldn't stop until the person came. I couldn't resist any longer. I got the strength to get out of my seat and walk to that altar. I left church feeling renewed; it was amazing! Later, I found out that Sarah had been continually praying I would start attending church with her. She gave me a journal and engraved Psalms 51:10 on it: "Create in me a pure heart, O God, and renew a steadfast spirit within me." That journal, my newfound church home, and Sarah's support helped me finally get my relationship with God where it needed to be.

I was still struggling on the track. I was in pain, and the amount of training I could do was limited. So, that forced me to redshirt that indoor season. By outdoor season, I was in better shape. I was allowed to compete but still had to wear the walking brace when I wasn't running. Thankfully, the dark cloud that had lingered over me for so long was gone. My relationship with God was stronger than ever, I was part of an amazing church, I was surrounded by amazing people, and I was accomplishing my goals on the track. That outdoor season, I set a new personal best for the first time in years. At the conference meet, I placed second in three of my four events. I'd finally received the conference medals I'd longed for. I remember crossing the finish line and jumping into my coach's arms; the next person I hugged was Sarah. The happiness I felt was beyond words. A few days later, I found out I was going to Oregon; I'd qualified for the NCAA Regional Championships. Who would've thought that, after being so depressed just a few months before, I could be this happy?

A new school year began, and because of my injury, I had an indoor season left. I knew I wanted my last indoor season to be just as special as my outdoor season had been. But I didn't want to succeed just on my own; I wanted the team as a whole to succeed. My coach hadn't won an overall team conference title in years. He was overdue for one. Sarah and I made it our mission to bring the team closer together. We had team dinners and movie nights and even went to church as a team. We moved as a unit on and off the track.

On the track, I was still battling the nagging pain in my tibia, and I was still in and out of the walking brace. It was annoying, but I knew I'd put in the work. I was mentally and physically in the best shape of my life. Just like that, it was time for my very last meet as a collegiate athlete, conference championships. I was excited. I felt like I was ready, and my teammates all looked like they were ready. It was time for us to put our heads down and go to work—together. The meet went exceptionally well.

I finally achieved the title of conference champion in one of my events. It felt great, but that wasn't the ultimate goal Sarah and I had set at the beginning of the year. After all the events were complete, we calculated that we'd placed second overall. We sat down, held hands as a team, and said a prayer. Win or lose, we were all thankful; we'd managed to come together for once and actually be a team. But, our calculations were off. By God's grace, we'd won; we'd done it! We won the overall team championship title! Just a year before, I was depressed and disliked the girls on the team. Now, I was crying tears of joy and celebrating with that same group of girls. I'd reached the end of my collegiate career and had ended it better than I could have ever imagined. I was happy. I was finally complete.

At times, you may lose yourself and feel like things may never get better, but let me tell you, there is always hope! I'm able to appreciate my success and happiness that much more because I know what it's like to be at rock bottom and depressed. Everything happens for a reason. I lost people to make room for better people. I've cried tears of pain, so I could cry tears of joy.

Consider it pure joy, my brothers and sisters, whenever you face trials of many kinds, because you know that the testing of your faith produces perseverance. Let perseverance finish its work so that you may be mature and complete, not lacking anything.
–James 1:2–4

Author Story: The NCAA Journey

Hometown: Markham, Ontario,
Sport: Track and field
Age at time of story: 18–20

NCAA story: Part 1

Getting a Division I athletic scholarship can either be the best move you ever make or a disaster depending on the school you choose. Receiving a scholarship is a clear indicator that, when you were in high school, you were good or even great. The problem is most athletes expect that to easily carry over to the next level. You now step into a world in which you're surrounded by other athletes who were just as good, if not better, as you when they were in high school. The adjustment can be very tough on many athletes. When you add in the fact that you're probably away from home for the first time, it just makes it worse.

When I embarked on my journey at Iowa State, I was ready for greatness, or so I'd thought. My older brother was in his last year at Texas Christian University (TCU) at the time, so I knew what I was getting myself into from conversations with him. A week before I got on campus, I was hit with one of those awful calls. The coach who'd recruited me let me know he was moving on to another school. I was already facing adversity, and I hadn't even gotten there yet. The coach was actually a great thing for me, not only as an athlete but also as a person, but it took me a few years to figure it out.

I believed my scholarship was threatened because a new coach was coming in who hadn't recruited me. I knew I needed to perform, or my money would be cut. As an incoming freshman, I already had high expectations of myself, but when the new coach was hired, the weight on my shoulders only got heavier.

I trained every day like I had something to prove, but I was young and very naïve in my thinking. I didn't understand that things were done differently, and I was no longer a star in Toronto. My drive led to injuries before the season had even begun. I suffered horrible pains and spasms in my back. I'd take a practice off, but when I came back, I'd just get hurt again. The weight on my shoulders had officially broken me — it literally broke the L5 in my back. I was slowly beginning to get that title of being "injury prone," which is the worst. It means that, no matter how talented or promising you are, you probably will never get there because you're always hurt. That tag wasn't on me like the price on some clothes at the store. It hung beside me everywhere I went; the only way I could shake it off was to work relentlessly.

By the time outdoor track and field came around, I was healthy and ready to go. I started off my career with a bang by winning the meet, running a new best time, and quickly establishing that maybe I was worth the money I was being paid. The season had its ups and downs. Of course, to me at the time, the ups were because of my talent and hard work, while the downs were because of my coach. That's where my mind was at.

I was at my first Big 12 outdoor championship in Lubbock at Texas Tech's track. The weather was beautiful. Lubbock is slightly at altitude, so I knew I had a good chance to run fast. I heard "set," and I was ready to go. Bang, Bang! — two guns, meaning there'd been a false start in the race. It was a kid from Texas who'd run much faster than I had, so I'd definitely dodged a bullet. When I heard the gun again, I got off to an amazing start and won the race. I won my heat, which allowed me to advance to the final and score some points for my team. I was the only freshman to do that, so I was proud of myself.

As I was walking back to the warm-up area to cool down and prepare my body for the next day, an injury slowly started to creep up on me. In the time it took me to sit down, take off my spikes, and put on my tennis shoes, my back had seized up by the minute. I stood up to cool down, but I couldn't jog. I have a very high tolerance for pain, so I can play things off like it's cool; that's exactly what I did. My coach came over with a huge smile and hugged me, and all of my teammates showed me love. I had to put on the fakest smile because I knew it wasn't going to last. That was the same injury that had taken away my indoor season, but it was much worse.

I just remember sitting in the stands with my good friend Bryce Colston, watching the remaining events for the day. That was my biggest mistake of the day. In that time, my back naturally built a brace for itself by swelling. Without my realizing it, my back was screaming, "Stop moving, Ian!" Well eventually, the meet finished, and I stood up to walk out, but my back completely shut down, and I fell to the floor. I was in tears as I lay on the ground, but I could hear what was going on around me so vividly. I guess where I was lying perfectly lined up with where someone would be lying if he or she fell off the top of the stands because a bunch of people thought I was dying. My poor friend Bryce went into panic mode, screaming and trying to get help. Even during such pain, I remember lying on the ground in tears and just laughing because of how everyone was acting.

If you haven't figured it out yet, my season was over once again. That was the fourth time my back had flared up and caused me problems, and my patience was getting thin. At that time, I needed someone to show me this. I was supposed to be one of the best athletes on my team, but I was always on the sideline injured. It wasn't a case of my not being able to perform at that level; it was an issue of my staying healthy at that level. To work for months on end only to go back to square one was just rough. I did that four times in sixteen months. How do you push on knowing you have no idea how to get yourself better? How do you push on knowing there's no guarantee of ever getting what you want?

Not only that, but we rejoice in our sufferings, knowing that suffering produces endurance, and endurance produces character, and character produces hope.
–Romans 5:3–4

NCAA story: Part 2

Age at time of story: 19

Nothing can stop the man with the right mental attitude from achieving his goal; nothing on earth can help the man with the wrong mental attitude.
–Thomas Jefferson

I was now in my second year at Iowa State and finally making my mark through the indoor season. I was winning races and climbing to the top of my conference rankings. The Big 12 championships were upon us, and we were blessed to have the meet at home in Iowa. For indoor track season, I was a redshirt freshman ranked third in a very tough conference. I was excited to run. I knew there were a few big names coming to town. I was ready to run. The gun went off, and I got a quick start and was feeling great. However, at 30 meters, I felt a pain in my hamstring I'd never felt before. I tried to keep going, but my body said "No!" With each step I took, the pain increased in my leg and in my heart. Before I knew it, I was on the ground, rolling across the finish line with dashed dreams. I'd pulled my hammy. Once again, my season dreams had been taken away.

To make matters worse, my mom had come all the way from Toronto to watch me run. I felt like I'd disappointed her to the max. I got up from that line with my torn hamstring. I threw my headband somewhere because I was so pissed, and I stormed off. I was heartbroken because I'd legitimately felt like I'd put in all of the work. I'd worked hard, slept well, eaten better, and gotten stronger in the weight room, but it had all ended with the same disappointing result. I'd put every ounce of heart I had into making sure my body was better. I'd read books on mental training. I'd read nutrition books. I'd researched common injuries for sprinters. But, I'd ended with the same result.

I was officially labeled "injury prone," which is a tough title for an athlete to shake. It messes with you mentally because you begin to expect injuries. You begin to expect downfalls and setbacks, even when they're nowhere near. My season was once again over. If you ever want to talk about wanting to quit because of injury, come talk to me first. If you want to sit back and take it as sign that you weren't meant to be an athlete, talk to me first. Oh, and if you think my situation sucked enough as it was, it got worse.

For his anger is but for a moment, and his favor is for a lifetime. Weeping may tarry for the night, but joy comes with the morning. –Psalm 30:5

NCAA story: Part 3

Age at time of story: 19–20

Any change, even a change for the better is always accompanied by drawbacks and discomforts.
–Arnold Bennett

With all the injuries I'd had at Iowa State, I went on a blaming rampage after my latest injury. I was mad at my mom for even showing up. I felt like my coach didn't know what he was doing. My athletic trainers couldn't get me healthy. The list went on. If you knew me in any way, you managed to make that list. The only name not on the list was my own. At that time at Iowa State, I probably made a bunch of people in athletic administration hate me because I went on that rampage. I didn't care who; all I knew was I wanted someone to get into trouble for all of my pain.

Whoever is slow to anger has great understanding, but he who has a hasty temper exalts folly. A tranquil heart gives life to the flesh, but envy makes the bones rot.
–Proverbs 14:29–30

Everything that had happened was enough fuel for me to transfer to another school. I was fuming mad, and we all know we should never make big decisions when we're angry. I was too proud to allow myself to admit I was the problem, not those who were surrounding me. God found a way to show me my true colors regardless. With the times I had run up to that point, I should have been able to transfer to a better school without too many issues. Unfortunately, my plans didn't match what God had in store for me. He humbled my thinking. I went through the entire disastrous process of asking ISU administration for permission to talk to other schools. Once I'd battled it out with my coach in a few dicey arguments, I was finally able to talk to some schools.

Here's how that went:

- Ohio State: The coach laughed at me and told me not to transfer.
- Florida State: I wasn't worth a scholarship.
- LSU: I didn't get a response.
- Clemson: They were very interested and got my hopes up. I was sure I was going to transfer there. The coach said he'd call me a week later to finalize things. He left me hanging and never said another word to me.
- Kentucky: I didn't get a response.

I was so excited for this process and to finally leave, but all it did was slap me and kick me in the face. I was already down on my knees pleading to God for strength to get through every day. It's not easy being at school when the whole team knows you plan to transfer. Every day is miserable; it's a battle to do everything you need to get done. For the first time in my life, I was forced to look in the mirror and make some real changes to my life. I decided that, from that day forward, I'd be the one I'd blame for everything. I wasn't going to scream at God, my coaches, my mom, or anyone else for what happened in my life because it was up to me.

When I found success, I'd say thank you to those who helped me. When I found failure, it would be because of me. The blame game of life was now over! I'd never have reached this place in my life if I hadn't gone through what God put me through. I needed to be at Iowa State, and I needed to be hurt and have track and field taken away from me for a while. God had finally gotten my attention. He showed me the problem always had been the man in the mirror.

The eye is the lamp of the body. So if your eye is healthy, your whole body will be full of light, but if your eye is bad, your whole body will be full of darkness. If then the light in you is darkness, how great is the darkness!
–Matthew 6:22–23

No one can serve two masters, for either he will hate the one and love the other, or he will be devoted to the one and despise the other. You cannot serve God and money.
–Matthew 6:24

The verse above doesn't stop there. You can't serve God and anything else. When people say they don't believe in a God, they're wrong. They do believe in a God; it's just that their God is something they serve here on this earth, whether it be money, other people, a career, etc. Track needed to be taken from me because it was becoming my God. It was becoming the number one thing in my life. I wasn't serving God, but I was serving myself through my running endeavors. It was time to get God back into his rightful place.

For everything there is a season, and a time for every matter under heaven:
A time to be born, and a time to die;
A time to plant and a time to pluck up what is planted;
A time to kill, and a time to heal;
A time to break down, and a time to build up;
A time to weep, and a time to laugh;
A time to mourn, and a time to dance;
A time to cast away stones, and a time to gather stones together;
A time to embrace, and a time to refrain from embracing;
A time to seek, and a time to lose;
A time to keep, and a time to cast away;
A time to tear, and a time to sew;
A time to keep silence, and a time to speak;
A time to love, and a time to hate;
A time for war, and a time for peace.
–Ecclesiastes 3:1–8

Pride goes before destruction, and a haughty spirit before a fall.
–Proverbs 16:18

I'd love to do one more book and share the stories of people who want to help others by telling their experiences. E-mail me anytime if you're interested at ian@cover-ground.co

Made in the USA
Lexington, KY
27 September 2014